COMPLEMENTARY &
ALTERNATIVE MEDICINE

COMPLEMENTARY & ALTERNATIVE MEDICINE

Legal Boundaries and Regulatory Perspectives

MICHAEL H. COHEN

Associate Professor of Law
Chapman University School of Law
Orange, California

THE JOHNS HOPKINS UNIVERSITY PRESS
Baltimore & London

© 1998 The Johns Hopkins University Press
All rights reserved. Published 1998
Printed in the United States of America on acid-free paper
07 06 05 04 03 02 01 00 99 98   5 4 3 2 1

The Johns Hopkins University Press
2715 North Charles Street
Baltimore, Maryland 21218-4319
The Johns Hopkins Press Ltd., London

Library of Congress Cataloging-in-Publication Data will be found at
the end of this book.
A catalog record for this book is available from the British Library.

ISBN 0-8018-5687-6
ISBN 0-8018-5689-2 (pbk.)

For Louis Panush,
a lion of love and learning.

CONTENTS

Preface and Acknowledgments xi

1. BIOMEDICINE AND HOLISTIC HEALING 1
The Biomedical Paradigm 2
The Holistic Healing Paradigm 3
Holism and Mechanism 6
The Use of Holistic Therapies 8
Scientific Substantiation and Methodological Issues 10
An Integrated Health Care System 13

2. BIOMEDICAL REGULATION IN HISTORICAL CONTEXT 15
The Emergence of Licensing 15
The Development of the Biomedical Community 17
The Response of the Regulatory Paradigm 21

3. STATE LAW REGULATION OF MEDICINE 24
The Police Power Rationale 24
Legal Definitions of the Practice of Medicine 26
Diagnosis, Treatment, Prevention, and Cure 26
Holding Oneself Out to the Public 26
Intending to Receive a Fee, Gift, or Other Compensation 27
Attaching a Title to One's Name 27
Maintaining an Office 28
Performing Surgery 28
Using, Administering, or Prescribing Drugs 28
Miscellaneous Definitional Provisions 29
Unauthorized Professional Practice 29
The Nonlicensed Provider 29
Independent Holistic Practice 31
Occupational Licensure 33

vii

CONTENTS

4. SCOPE-OF-PRACTICE LIMITATIONS 39

Licensing of Complementary and Alternative Providers 39
Chiropractic 40
Massage Therapy 41
Naturopathy 41
Homeopathy 42
Acupuncture 43
Lay Practice 45
Legislatively Authorized Boundaries of Practice 46
Scope of Practice: The Case of Chiropractic 47
Nutritional Care 47
Colonic Irrigation 49
Acupuncture and Other Modalities 50
Physical Examination and Other Procedures 51
Addressing Scope-of-Practice Risks 54

5. MALPRACTICE AND VICARIOUS LIABILITY 56

Physicians' Malpractice Liability 56
The Case of Chelation Therapy 56
Informed Consent 60
Assumption of Risk 62
Malpractice by Complementary and Alternative Providers 64
Professional Standards of Care 64
Heightened Standard of Care 66
Duty to Refer and Misrepresentation 68
Malpractice Liability of Health Care Institutions 70

6. ACCESS TO TREATMENTS 73

Treatments Requiring New Drug Approval 73
Nutritional Therapies 77
Dietary Supplements and Health Claims 79
Health Care Freedom 81

7. DISCIPLINE AND SANCTION 87

The Disciplinary Process 87
Homeopathy 88
Chelation Therapy 90
Ozone Therapy 91
State Medical Freedom Acts 92

CONTENTS

8. THIRD-PARTY REIMBURSEMENT 96
    Voluntary and Mandated Coverage 96
    Selected Exclusions and Coverage Issues 101
        Experimental Treatments 101
        Medically Necessary Treatments 103
        Health Care Fraud and Insurance Fraud 104

9. THE EVOLUTION OF LEGAL AUTHORITY 109
    Professional Licensure and Scope of Practice 109
    Malpractice and Professional Discipline 111
    Fraud and Health Care Freedom 112
    Integral Health Care 114
    Conclusion 117

    Notes 121
    Index 177

Preface and Acknowledgments

Legal authority creates a language, a culture, and a coercive vision of professional health care. Since the late nineteenth century, biomedicine's dominance of the educational institutions, research, resources, and reimbursement structures for health care has underpinned provider licensing, malpractice liability, professional discipline, and related legal rules. Federal and state regulatory schemes embodied the paradigmatic split within the healing arts between biomedicine and alternative health care. The legal rules in turn supported biomedicine as the culture's dominant provider of health care.

Biomedicine's dominance in the healing arts and regulatory schemes persisted until recently. Increased consumer demand for, and provider interest in, complementary and alternative therapies have begun shifting regulatory attitudes toward nonbiomedical treatments and providers.[1] A *New England Journal of Medicine* article reported that in 1990, Americans spent $13.7 billion on alternative health care, three-quarters of which came out of their own pockets and was not reimbursed by insurance companies. U.S. patients made 425 million visits to alternative providers, as compared to 388 million visits to family physicians and internists. Seventy-two percent did not tell their physicians about the alternative treatments.[2] The article concluded that physicians should ask their patients about the use of alternative therapies when obtaining a history. The authors further suggested that medical schools incorporate the study of alternative therapies in their curricula.

In 1992, Congress created an Office for the Study of Unconventional Medical Practices, later renamed the Office of Alternative Medicine (OAM) and then the Office of Complementary and Alternative Medicine (OCAM), at the National Institutes of Health. The congressional mandate was to "facilitate the evaluation of alternative medical treatment modalities, including acupuncture and Oriental medicine, homeopathic medicine, and physical manipulation therapies."[3]

Following the creation of the office, several states passed legislation conferring on physicians greater latitude to offer patients complementary and alternative therapies (see chap. 7). Federal lawmakers subsequently proposed legislation authorizing access, under certain circumstances, to treatments not approved by the Food and Drug Administration (FDA) (see chap. 6).[4] Concurrently, major medical schools began expanding course offerings on nonbiomedical therapies (see chap. 1). Academic and institutional health care centers began investigating, evaluating, and integrating therapies such as hypnosis and therapeutic touch.[5] In the state of Washington, the King County Council approved a natural medicine clinic as part of the King County Department of Health.[6] Other legislatures similarly have established mechanisms to explore the integration of complementary and alternative medicine into their health care systems.[7]

These legislative and institutional developments have been both significant and controversial.[8] They express a paradigm shift from strictly orthodox medicine (i.e., biomedicine) to more inclusive approaches to healing (see chap. 1). These approaches assert that biomedicine and technologically based healing modalities have limits and should interface with approaches such as chiropractic, acupuncture, naturopathy, homeopathy, nutritional treatments, and massage therapy. Such nonbiomedically based therapies view "healing" as broader than surgical and pharmaceutical intervention, and as addressing multifactored imbalances with contributory causes that include mental, emotional, nutritional, environmental, and spiritual elements.

Various terms have been proposed to describe the therapies as a whole; the semantic variations carry political and social implications. For example, the terms *unconventional, nontraditional,* and *nonconforming* connote deviance from generally accepted medical norms, permitting biomedical assumptions to judge the validity of healing. Moreover, these terms are ethnocentric, because therapies that vary from the conventions and traditions of biomedicine may be conventional or traditional in Chinese, Indian, Native American, and other medical cultures in which biomedicine is considered nontraditional.

The term *alternative* suggests use of the therapies as substitutes for biomedical care, while *complementary* suggests the use of such therapies in combination with biomedicine. Each term can be inaccurate: for example, nutritional therapies for cancer can be used either alongside chemotherapy or in efforts to stave off the treatment. The term *alternative/complementary* combines both concepts but is awkward, and in any event, the slash between the words implies a distinction that seems antithetical to a focus on wholeness.

The term *holistic* describes an orientation toward the whole being, encompassing different levels or aspects of health and imbalance. The term is useful, since it corresponds with personal wholeness and the theory of holism described in chapter 1. I generally favor the term *complementary and alternative medicine* for its relative neutrality. I view complementary and alternative medicine and biomedicine as historical rivals but future allies, contributing to an integrated health care system in which different modalities are used as necessary to maximize the patient's well-being. The process of integration will challenge providers and regulators to create new ways of thinking about health, disease, and the role of law in regulating health care and disease care.[9]

The articulation of legal rules appropriate to an integrated health care system should interest at least four interrelated audiences: (1) health care professionals who seek to minimize the legal risks of providing, or integrating into their biomedical practices, complementary and alternative treatments; (2) attorneys, judges, legislators, and agency officials who create the legal climate for complementary and alternative therapies; (3) patients interested in access to such treatments; and (4) institutional health care providers and insurers (including managed care organizations) pursuing the integration of complementary and alternative therapies in third-party reimbursement schemes and health plans. Ongoing efforts by all four groups to comprehend complementary and alternative medicine are creating the emerging moral and legal authority upon which the safe and effective practice of integrated health care can rest.

Legal authority, like medical authority, slowly is becoming more tolerant of patients' autonomy and more supportive of freedom of access to nonbiomedical providers and treatments. In this book, I describe that shift by analyzing the present legal status of complementary and alternative medicine. I also suggest ways in which regulatory structures might evolve further to support a comprehensive, holistic, and balanced approach to health, one that permits deeper integration of biomedicine and complementary and alternative medicine while continuing to protect patients from fraudulent and dangerous treatments.

Portions of this book appeared in different form as: "A Fixed Star in Health Care Reform: The Emerging Paradigm of Holistic Healing," 27

Arizona State Law Journal 79 (1995); "Toward a Bioethics of Compassion," 28 *Indiana Law Journal* 667 (1995); "Legal Ramifications of Homeopathy," 1:4 *Journal of Alternative and Complementary Medicine* 393 (1995); "Guaranteeing Freedom of Access to Healing: The Access to Medical Treatment Act of 1995," 1:6 *Alternative and Complementary Therapies* 408 (1995); "Scope of Practice Limitations on Unconventional Providers: The Case of Chiropractic," 2:2 *Alternative and Complementary Therapies* 110 (1996); "Holistic Health Care: Including Alternative and Complementary Medicine in Regulatory and Insurance Schemes," 38 *Arizona Law Review* 83 (1996); "Malpractice and Vicarious Liability for Providers of Complementary and Alternative Medicine," *Bender's Health Care Law Monthly,* June 1996, 3; "Complementary Medicine: Legal Status of the Nonlicensed Provider in the USA," 3:4 *Complementary Therapies in Nursing and Midwifery* (1997); and "Legal Authority and Holistic Health," in *Textbook of Complementary and Alternative Medicine,* ed. Wayne B. Jonas and Jefrey S. Levin (Baltimore: Williams & Wilkins, 1997).

I thank Professors Tom Baker, David Frankford, Hugh Hewitt, and Nancy Plant, as well as Jonathan Emord, Jerry Green, and the individuals noted in prior published articles, for insights and comments on the manuscript; Prudence Carter and Letoia Jenkins for research assistance; and my family, friends, students, teachers, and colleagues for their enthusiasm and support.

Complementary &
Alternative Medicine

I

BIOMEDICINE AND
HOLISTIC HEALING

When Sir William Herschel discovered Uranus in 1782, he announced that he had observed a new star. Later, when he noticed a measurement that was unusual for stars, he announced that he had discovered a comet. Months later, "after fruitless attempts to fit the observed motion to a cometary orbit," Herschel finally persuaded himself, and his community, that he had discovered a new planet. In other words, the discoverer and the scientific community recognized Uranus as a planet only when, "like an anomalous playing card, it could no longer be fitted to the perceptual categories (star or comet) provided by the paradigm that had previously prevailed."[1]

This is Thomas Kuhn's classic example of a paradigm shift. A paradigm is a shared set of assumptions about the world, by which individuals define the parameters of their reality and their investigation of this reality. Problems and methods outside the paradigm are deemed illegitimate. A paradigm gains acceptance when it solves problems more readily than competing paradigms. However, a paradigm can insulate a community from problems outside its boundaries, simply because these problems cannot be stated within the paradigm.

According to Kuhn, those who follow the paradigm find acceptance within the community, since they are committed to the consensus reality. Those who oppose the paradigm, or who define problems or articulate solutions outside the paradigm, are ostracized, since their method implicitly attacks the foundational order. The shift from one paradigm to another occurs by revolution rather than by accretion. Paradigm shifts exhibit the following steps: awareness of anomaly, observational and conceptual recognition, and finally, change of paradigm categories and procedures, often accompanied by resistance.[2]

The Biomedical Paradigm

Kuhn's analysis of paradigm shifting illuminates the historical conflict between biomedicine and holistic views of health and the disease process. The biomedical paradigm generally views disease as a biochemical phenomenon that can be classified into diagnostic categories through technological methods and treated, where possible, according to standardized, objectively validated mechanisms. The biomedical model gained ascendancy in the late nineteenth and early twentieth centuries, when Newtonian physics and Cartesian dualism dominated the intellectual world.

Newtonian physics views the universe as consisting of fundamental, irreducible building blocks made of matter. According to Newtonian theory, the motions and interactions of all material bodies obey a few simple laws. The universe is an immense, sophisticated clock, whose whirring objects follow predetermined courses. The interrelationship of parts is rational and follows basic laws.[3] Cartesian dualism asserts that bodies exist in space, subject to mechanical laws, while minds exist elsewhere, in an isolated, independent realm. It splits the "outer" world (objective and amenable to rigorous research) and the "inner" world (subjective, marginally accessible, and scientifically unreliable).[4]

In keeping with Newtonian physics and Cartesian dualism, the biomedical model views the body as a physical system, objectively analyzable in terms of its mechanical parts. Mechanism (the "body as machine" metaphor) and reductionism (the reduction of illness to a set of physical symptoms) dominate biomedical thinking. Disease is an outside invader that preys on a particular part of the body; treatment attacks the invader. Thus, some cancers are known as "malignant" tumors; chemotherapy aims to "attack," "fight," or "beat" the cancer.[5]

The biomedical model provides a clearly articulated scientific framework for understanding the disease process and mechanisms of remedy, and it excels at treating infectious diseases and acute or traumatic injuries. Biomedicine excels in emergency care: a patient who suddenly experiences heart failure needs a cardiac specialist, not an acupuncturist. The model also cures many conditions that have single, specific causes.

The model is less successful with chronic, multifaceted, and terminal illnesses, such as chronic fatigue, AIDS, and cancer.[6] Biomedicine rarely cures chronic, debilitating conditions such as arthritis, allergies, pain, hypertension, depression, and cardiovascular and digestive problems, which account for 70 percent of the health care budget in the United States and affect almost 33 million Americans.[7] The conditions exhaust current scientific knowledge, challenge the biomedical model's approach to diagnosis and treatment, or require treatments accompanied by toxic side effects.[8]

The biomedical model's orientation is frequently distant, detached, and deficient in empathy and warmth. The model alienates patients from their own being when their mental, emotional, and spiritual realities are seen as having little bearing on disease or healing. Feelings of depression, rage, social isolation, and bewilderment, and other subjective, but significant, experiences often are discounted, invalidated, or denied as hallucinatory.[9] Biomedicine creates feelings of dependence and personal estrangement as individuals "exchange the status of person for that of patient."[10] Hospitalization leaves patients surrounded by charts, tubes, and monitors, being spoken about rather than to, in incomprehensible debates among strangers. Eric Cassell gives the example of an attending physician and medical students standing outside the room of a dying patient whose suffering could not be controlled: "Did they speak about her suffering or what to tell her or do for her? No, they were reading her test results and X-ray films — irrelevant to her present problem but much simpler and more immediate."[11]

Biomedicine also is criticized for failing to recognize the limits of technologically oriented healing in the case of fragile or elderly patients. Despite their best intentions, physicians practice in an atmosphere of "cognitive dissonance . . . unsure of what to do for those who are neither curable nor dying."[12] Biomedicine imposes "technological violence" when a particular treatment — such as chemotherapy — either directly imposes the violence or "sets the stage for the advent of another [disease], perhaps even more cruel than the death one has just averted."[13] Thus, an individual cured of cancer at age seventy-five may be "set up" for Alzheimer disease at eighty.[14] Moreover, by orienting care toward biological preservation while denying the finality of death, biomedicine often distorts the dying process.[15]

The Holistic Healing Paradigm

The critique of biomedicine's medical and psychosocial limitations has led some caregivers to examine multifaceted approaches to health care, in an attempt to restore a broader role and meaning to the notion of healing.[16] Holistic modalities of healing adopt a wholeness or social paradigm of health care, which aims at a nonmechanistic, nonreductionistic understanding of the disease process. The holistic healing paradigm views diseases as having multiple causes amenable to multiple therapeutic interventions through a variety of systems of care, including biochemical, environmental, social, psychological, behavioral, and spiritual systems. It views conditions such as arthritis and chronic pain as having multiple, nonspecific causes (biological, environmental, psychological, social), and thus as amenable to intervention on multiple levels (pharmaceutical, individual or family counseling, support groups, nutrition, exercise, relaxation techniques). In holistic practice, the goal is balance, not only control of symptoms; subjective relief, not merely a favorable and scientifically measurable clinical outcome.[17]

To more clearly define holistic fields of practice, the National Institutes of Health convened a workshop in Chantilly, Virginia, with more than two hundred individuals who were leaders in their respective fields, to discuss the major areas of alternative health care and priority areas for research. The workshop produced a comprehensive survey of fields of practice and research obstacles and opportunities. The document, *Report to the National Institutes of Health on Alternative Medical Systems and Practices in the United States,* or, simply, the *Chantilly Report,* describes seven major fields of holistic practice: (1) mind-body interventions; (2) bioelectromagnetics applications in medicine; (3) alternative systems of medical practice; (4) manual healing methods; (5) pharmacological and biological treatments not yet accepted by mainstream medicine; (6) herbal medicine; and (7) treatments focusing on diet and nutrition in the prevention and treatment of chronic disease.[18] Relevant subfields include

1. *mind-body interventions:* psychotherapy; support groups; meditation; imagery; hypnosis; biofeedback; yoga; dance therapy; music therapy; art therapy; and prayer and mental healing
2. *bioelectromagnetics applications in medicine:* applications of nonthermal, nonionizing electromagnetic fields for bone repair, nerve stimulation, wound healing, treatment of osteoarthritis, electroacupuncture, tissue regeneration, immune system stimulation, and neuroendocrine modulations
3. *alternative systems of medical practice:* home health care; traditional oriental medicine; acupuncture; Ayurveda; homeopathic medicine; anthroposophically extended medicine; naturopathic medicine; environmental medicine; Native American medicine; Latin American community-based practices; and other community-based healing systems

4. *manual healing methods:* osteopathic medicine; chiropractic science; massage therapy; and biofield therapeutics
5. *pharmacological and biological treatments:* antineoplastons; cartilage products; EDTA chelation therapy; immunoaugmentative therapy; and other therapies
6. *herbal medicine:* European phytomedicines; Chinese herbal remedies; Ayurvedic herbal medicines; Native American herbal medicine; and others
7. *diet and nutrition:* vitamins and nutritional supplements; orthomolecular medicine (megavitamin therapy); Gerson therapy, the Kelley regimen; the macrobiotic diet; the Livingston/Wheeler regimen; the Wigmore treatment; the Ornish diet; the Pritikin diet; dietary management of food allergies; and the diets of other cultures

The common link is that most physical illness is viewed as connected to "an overload of emotional, psychological and spiritual crises."[19] For example, chiropractic deals with the relationship between the spine, the nervous system, and human health. Chiropractors aim to augment the body's innate self-healing primarily through spinal manipulation, "releasing pressure on nerves radiating from the spine to all parts of the body, and allowing the nerves to carry their full quota of health current (nerve energy) from the brain to all parts of the body."[20]

Massage therapy also aims to assist the body's self-healing by removing somatic blocks. Massage therapy involves sensitive touch and manipulation to affect the musculoskeletal system, the circulatory-lymphatic system, the nervous system, and other systems of the body. It views the musculoskeletal system as storing tension and stress, as well as toxins and traumas that serve as precursors to or companions of disease. Massage therapy aims to facilitate the release of painful emotional memories, stored in body tissue, that underlie or have accompanied the disease process.

Body-oriented psychotherapies (which add a massage component to counseling) and postural re-education therapies, involving awareness, movement, and breath (such as the Alexander technique and the Feldenkrais method), are related to massage therapy, in that they teach patients how to use their bodies to come into alignment, release destructive emotional patterns, and alleviate stress. Bioenergetic therapies similarly use touch, sometimes combined with movement and breath, and "noncontact touch" techniques (such as Mari-el, Reiki, polarity therapy, therapeutic touch, and touch for health, directed at biofields or human energy fields)[21] to aid self-healing. Bioenergetic therapies also view the body and chronic body postures as containing "body wisdom," clues to the etiology of disease and potential routes to healing.

Acupuncture views physical health as determined by a balanced flow of *chi* (vital energy) through the human organism. Chi circulates through twelve major energy pathways known as meridians, each linked to specific internal organs and organ systems. Acupuncturists insert special needles into points within the meridian system to rebalance the flow of chi and alleviate pain or promote health. Acupuncture includes manual, mechanical, thermal, electrical, and electromagnetic treatments based on concepts of traditional oriental medicine.

Naturopathy views disease in terms of bodily toxins and imbalances in the patient's "social, psychic, and spiritual environment."[22] Naturopaths emphasize preventive and lifestyle health measures, including nutrition, rest, and emotional well-being. They use herbal medicines, vitamin and mineral supplements, and adjunctive therapies such as counseling, colonic therapy, and physical therapy to support and strengthen weakened systems and restore balance.

While chiropractic, massage therapy, acupuncture, and naturopathy are four of the most commonly licensed modalities, holistic modalities in general view disease as reflecting health imbalances with systemic social and psychological, as well as physiological, implications. In the holistic healing paradigm, the patient's vulnerability is viewed not as a source of alienation and shame but as an opening toward deeper self-understanding. The emphasis on modification of lifestyle, nutritional support, and stress reduction aims to expand the patient's responsibility for the healing process and to provide tools to ameliorate many conditions for which biomedical cure is unavailable, inadequate, or incomplete.[23]

Holism and Mechanism

The philosophy underlying holistic practice was articulated earlier this century by Jan Smuts. In his 1926 book *Holism and Evolution*, Smuts described holism as the notion that "every organism, every plant or animal, is a whole, with a certain internal organization and a measure of self-direction, and an individual specific character of its own."[24] In wholes, "all the parts appear in a subtle indefinable way to subserve and carry out the main purpose or idea" (98). According to Smuts, nature expresses itself in wholes, ranging from atoms, molecules, and chemical compounds to "the creations of the human spirit in all its greatest and most significant activities" (98). Smuts expressed this "whole-making, holistic tendency, or Holism" as an organic, creative evolutionary force in the natural world and human affairs (99–102).

Smuts argued that a whole is more than the sum of its parts because the whole is not purely mechanical but has inner tendencies and interrelationships between the parts which give rise to something "more" (103). Evolution, or forward movement, consists in the development of "ever more complex and significant wholes"; the parts function in harmony, "either naturally or instinctively or consciously," toward a "definite inner end" such that together they form a distinctive character or identity (107). Smuts viewed the world and the human organism not as "a collection of accidents put together like an artificial patchwork, but [as] synthetic, structural, active, vital and creative" (107).

To understand the human organism as a whole, Smuts considered not only the physical body but also the "field," the organism's presence as "a historic event, a focus of happening, a gateway through which the infinite stream of change flows ceaselessly" (113–14). The organism in its field "contains its past and much of its future in its present" (115).

Smuts contrasted holism with mechanism, the view that wholes are merely and unalterably the sum of their parts. According to Smuts, mechanism views physical reality as a closed and complete system; holism values volition and consciousness and views life as "an active creative process [which] means the movement . . . towards ever more and deeper wholeness" (145–47, 154–55). The organism, as a whole, is a "synthesis or unity of parts," and thus possesses unity of action and a "balanced correlation of functions" (123–24). Whereas a mechanical system reacts to disturbance by adjusting to maintain equilibrium, a holistic system creates a new unity or synthesis, "the making of a new arrangement of old elements" (129). In this way, "wholeness, healing, holiness — [are] all expressions and ideas springing from the same root in language as in experience" (345).

Smuts's articulation of holism finds parallels in modern philosophical and bioethical systems,[25] and in general systems theory.[26] Holism is an approach to professional practice in which physicians, nurses, dentists, and even lawyers critique the treatment of clients as malfunctioning organs, degenerating gums, or detached legal abstractions.[27] Holistic health care views illness and wellness as expressions of an irreducible, unified whole, all parts of which interrelate "in a subtle indefinable way" to maintain health or create disease. The therapies consider the physical body within a field of social and biopsychic energy sensitive to emotional and environmental stimuli that contribute to pathology.[28]

The Use of Holistic Therapies

At least one of every three Americans uses nonbiomedical modalities of healing, including relaxation techniques (13%); chiropractic (10%); massage (7%); imagery, biofeedback, and hypnosis (6%); spiritual and energy healing (5%); homeopathy (1%); and acupuncture (less than 1%). Patients use these modalities most frequently for back problems, anxiety, headaches, chronic pain, and cancer or tumors, and less frequently for high blood pressure, diabetes, and pulmonary, dental, gynecological, urinary, and dermatological problems.[29] Children also frequently use holistic health care.[30] Worldwide, 70 to 90 percent of health care ranges from self-care based on folk practice to care based on an alternative tradition or practice; only 10 to 30 percent is based on biomedicine.[31]

One-quarter to one-third of major U.S. medical schools offer courses on complementary and alternative medicine. These schools and their course offerings include the Albert Einstein College of Medicine ("Complementary Medicine"), the Columbia University College of Physicians and Surgeons ("Survey in Alternative/Complementary Medicine"), the Harvard Medical School ("Alternative Medicine: Implications for Clinical Practice and Research"), the Johns Hopkins University School of Medicine ("The Philosophy and Practice of Healing"),[32] the Mount Sinai School of Medicine (whose courses include "The Power of Subtle Body: Innovative Qigong," "Hypnotherapy," and "Science of Yoga"), the Milton S. Hershey Medical Center at Pennsylvania State University ("Folk and Alternative Health Systems"), and the Yale School of Medicine ("Alternative Medicine in Historical Perspectives").[33]

A recent survey randomly sampled the use of unconventional medicine by U.S. physicians. Of 572 physicians responding, 92 percent encouraged at least one unconventional therapy, 83 percent at least two, 73 percent at least three, 63 percent at least four, and 51 percent five or more. In addition, 36 percent practiced at least one unconventional therapy, 19 percent practiced at least two, and 9 percent practiced three or more. Physicians were most likely to refer patients for relaxation techniques, biofeedback, therapeutic massage, hypnosis, and acupuncture. The physicians surveyed personally provided the following therapies to patients: relaxation techniques (22%); lifestyle diet (vegetarian, macrobiotic, etc.) (17%); imagery (7%); spiritual healing, biofeedback, and yoga (5% each); chiropractic, therapeutic massage, megavitamin therapy, energy healing, and herbal remedies (3% each); acupuncture (2%); and homeopathy, meditation, and Rolfing (1% each).[34] These statistics belie common myths about alternative health care — such as the assumption that only credulous, gullible, desperate, or ignorant patients use holistic therapies, or that providers of such services invariably engage in fraud and quackery. In fact, the prevalence of holistic therapies indicates not only that such therapies are in demand by patients but also that providers are interested in a broader understanding of healing and of the provider's role as healing professional.[35]

Physicians who have adopted some holistic practices criticize the biomedical model's disengagement from the emotional, nutritional, and social dimensions of illness.[36] Since medical education emphasizes the physician's authority, biomedicine tends to encourage patients' passivity and dependence.[37] While biomedicine recognizes the importance of good communication between physician and patient,[38] and good medical practice can, and should be, holistic, holism's view of persons and health as "synthetic, structural, active, vital and creative" suggests greater emphasis on emotional contact between patient and provider.[39] The patient's participation in healing is vital, not incidental. Holistic providers frequently take detailed histories and use multiple modalities, many of which are subjective and patient centered.[40] Holistic providers tend to spend less time practicing "defensively" and emphasize the inner healing process, as well as relationship, over external results and professional authority.[41] In other words, the provider-patient relationship aims at healing as well as curing.

Curing involves the eradication of disease at the physiological level. Healing involves a movement toward wholeness, growth, or greater balance on physical, mental, emotional, and social levels, "rather than just [a focus] on curing a given disease or disorder."[42] A patient may be healed without the disease being cured. A treatment that "cures" the patient often leaves room for healing — as occurs when a breast cancer patient leaves the operating room without cancer, but without a breast. By pointing patients toward creative resolution of their disease processes, holistic therapies aim to express the centrality of personal wholeness in health.[43]

Scientific Substantiation and Methodological Issues

The critique of holistic healing asserts that relying on emotional, psychological, environmental, nutritional, and spiritual elements to address disease is not only unscientific but also mystical and antiscientific. Holistic providers often are portrayed as dangerous magicians who lure patients with false promises of cure and steer them away from proper treatment. This viewpoint was expressed by an editor emeritus of the *New England Journal of Medicine,* who wrote that "the 'alternative'-medicine backlash reflects a strong element of antiscientism. Science is under attack from many quarters these days, and healing cults are yet another part of that attack."[44]

The characterization of holistic practice as a cult, backlash, or attack on science is overbroad. Holistic modalities by and large do not purport to diagnose and treat pathology as it is defined within the biomedical paradigm, and thus do not rely wholly for validation on the double-blind, randomized studies that are published in peer-reviewed journals following the scientific principles accepted within dominant medical circles. On the other hand, many holistic modalities do involve repeated observation, measurement, and comparison of results over multiple generations searching for unifying principles. Many providers advocate an expanded epistemology of science, which includes phenomenological and experiential data and thus addresses "the totality of human experience."[45]

Moreover, the attempt to portray biomedicine and holistic healing as representing valid scientific principles on one hand, and unprovable mysticism on the other, oversimplifies a number of complex methodological problems involved in properly investigating and understanding complementary and alternative therapies. Some holistic therapies are subject to "reasonable, responsible research and validation of safety and effectiveness."[46] Controlled studies have suggested that acupuncture is efficacious in treating osteoarthritis, chemotherapy-induced nausea, asthma, painful menstrual cycles, bladder instability, and migraine headaches, as well as in the management of chronic pain and drug addiction.[47] Similarly, studies of Ayurvedic herbal preparations and other therapies suggest that they have beneficial effects on breast, lung, and colon cancers and are useful in the treatment of mental health and infectious disease, in health promotion generally, and in the treatment of aging.[48] Recently, acting on the basis of extensive published research, the Agency for Health Care Policy and Research, a division of the U.S. Department of Health and Human Services, endorsed chiropractic care for low-back pain.[49]

Research efforts in complementary and alternative therapies, however, are challenged by the lack of dedicated facilities, the lack of training for researchers, and the lack of a central research database, and by inadequate funding, difficulty in designing protocols, and difficulty in obtaining appropriate peer review.[50] Moreover, randomized controlled clinical trials sometimes are impractical, unfeasible, or difficult to design. For example, the health benefits of tribal and folk practices such as the Native American sweat lodge are not easily amenable to scientific study, since they are performed within specific religious and cultural contexts.[51]

Further, some modalities, such as biofeedback, meditation, imagery, and dance therapy, require repetition and learning, rendering experimental results amenable to influence by the "thoughts, feelings, intentions, and attitudes" of the experimenter and the subject, and by the environment.[52] Other healing methods, such as chiropractic, vary by individual treatment, responding to subtle and continually shifting signals in the patient's body. Related therapies, such as biofield therapeutics, generate results for which no generally accepted scientific theory can account; most existing studies have measured only subjective changes such as levels of pain and anxiety.[53]

Moreover, physicians who integrate holistic therapies into their medical practices are threatened with loss of licensure, hospital privileges, and professional standing or are "forced to look outside the normal channels" for funding and publication.[54] The research gap also reflects biomedicine's rudimentary understanding of the role emotions play in the disease process. Although psychoneuroimmunology represents one attempt at scientific study of these effects, the biomedical model does not provide an adequate account of the biochemical basis for the patient's emotional and spiritual life and its effect on the disease process.[55]

It is also difficult to correlate some complementary and alternative modalities with Western technologies. When traditional Chinese doctors prescribe herbs, they are basing their prescriptions not on Western chemistry and pharmacology but on the effect that these herbs, which have multiple active ingredients, will have on the patient's chi. Similarly, acupuncturists' diagnostic and therapeutic roadmap, based on meridians (or lines of energy threaded through the body organ systems), does not correspond to Western anatomical systems.

Finally, because healing, as opposed to curing, includes growth or transformation, the relief of symptoms which is provided by biomedicine does not necessarily indicate a successful or complete treatment in holistic terms. Conversely, holistic treatments may result in temporary aggravation of symptoms but provide ultimate relief in ways that may not be immediately quantifiable. Furthermore, research on alternative medical systems "often is in effect, if not explicitly, cross-cultural," which means that "questions, concepts, diseases, treatments, and research protocols that 'make sense' in one setting may not make sense in another."[56] Studies within the paradigm may challenge conventional medical thinking.[57]

Institutions such as the Office of Complementary and Alternative Medicine are examining the methodological and research design issues raised by the attempt to systematically investigate complementary and alternative therapies and are compiling scientific bibliographies to facilitate the collection and evaluation of existing data.[58] For example, the Division of AIDS, in the National Institute of Allergy and Infectious Diseases, is creating a database of complementary and alternative AIDS therapies; the National Institute of Neurological Disorders and Strokes offers information on acupuncture; the National Institute of Mental Health provides biofeedback information; and the National Cancer Institute supplies information on medicinal herbs.[59] Academic institutions such as the Richard and Hinda Rosenthal Center for Alternative/Complementary Medicine at Columbia University also participate in collecting, disseminating, and evaluating information.

Although many biomedically trained professionals call for increased justification or validation of therapies such as acupuncture by Western, scientific methods, such research efforts may distort or devalue many nonmeasurable yet important aspects of these therapies. For example, it may be impossible or impractical to measure what is exchanged between provider and patient when a practitioner of oriental or Tibetan medicine uses pulse diagnosis, if the provider is evaluating subtle energies that have no counterpart in Western science.

Validation satisfactory to the biomedical community may make holistic practice conform to biomedical standards and force holistic therapies into a reductionistic or mechanistic mold (e.g., requiring a prescribed number of acupuncture treatments for a particular condition). Moreover, holistic providers may be just as inclined as biomedical providers to treat patients on an "assembly-line" basis or reduce a subtle exchange of chi to an insurable event. In short, bringing holistic therapies into a reductionistic, mechanistic model may come at the expense of the focus on wholeness and individuality which makes these therapies distinct.

An Integrated Health Care System

The movement from a strictly biomedical system of health care to an orientation that incorporates holism has generated controversy. As Kuhn's description suggests, the dominant segments of the health care community tend to condemn as illegitimate the problems and methods outside the paradigm (such as clinical judgments by chiropractors, naturopathic physicians, and acupuncturists). Health care innovators historically have attracted denunciation from the prevalent medical majority. Ambroise Paré, the "father of modern surgery," was denounced for using the ligature, which contemporaries characterized as hanging one's life on a string "when red-hot irons were always available," and for "blinding himself to the virtue of boiling oil as a surgical dressing." Andreas Vesalius, who published *De Fabria Humani Corporis* (1537), correcting contemporary dogma about anatomy, was denounced as a heretic and a fraud, and had to flee to Padua. Likewise, a sixteenth-century text on anatomy by Michael Servetus "was construed as an attack upon established order . . . [and] awakened a series of denunciations . . . so virulent that [Servetus] was forced to flee from Paris." He was apprehended and burnt at the stake, together with his book.[60]

In recent years, holistic providers have faced hostile medical boards and organized opposition from segments of the biomedical community. Physicians integrating homeopathy, ozone therapy, and chelation therapy into their professional practice have had their licenses revoked by state medical boards merely for using these therapies (see chap. 7). Licensed nonmedical providers offering nutritional guidance to support the healing process have been prosecuted for practicing medicine without a license, even when authorized by their licensing statutes to provide "dietary advice" (see chap. 4). Despite the inclusion of alternative therapies in medical curricula, providers face considerable professional risk.

The *Chantilly Report* explains resistance to complementary and alternative medicine in terms of "belief barriers," common misconceptions that prevent conventional physicians from "viewing anything labeled 'alternative' in a positive light." The barriers include overconfidence in high technology, safety in the status quo, a belief in the "'one true' medical profession," and stereotypes (e.g., the belief that complementary and alternative medicine "attracts people with 'weak' minds . . . who easily succumb to the 'sideshow' lures of 'snake oil' salespeople)."[61]

The shift to an integrated health care system requires deeper investigation of ways in which the two systems can function synergistically to maximize the person's wellness. For some patients, holistic and biomedical providers offer competing services with divergent philosophies: naturopaths, for example, function as primary caregivers in some states. For other patients, the two sets of providers are complementary: the holistic providers address deficiencies or imbalances of vital energy, aimed at facilitating the body's self-healing, while medical providers diagnose and treat biomedically defined pathology to eradicate symptoms and cure disease. Many patients turn to holistic health care professionals as "providers of last resort," when biomedical treatment fails or leaves chronic conditions unresolved.

The focus on social and psychological dimensions of illness and individual responsibility for the healing process makes holistic treatment particularly suited to complementing conventional care for chronic and terminal ailments. Moreover, because holistic health care emphasizes lifestyle, nutrition, self-care, and emotional well-being, it has an individualized, preventive orientation. But complementary and alternative medicine is no substitute for emergency care or necessary surgery.

In an integrated health care system, "physicians will preferentially employ means that aim at restoring the body to its natural state of balance rather than those that interfere with normal as well as abnormal biological processes, produce side effects, and reduce symptoms without addressing the causes of illness. . . . For example, we will insist on manipulation, acupuncture, massage, and baths for an injured back prior to even considering long-term use of anti-inflammatories or back surgery. Homeopathy, dietary changes, and herbal remedies — not antibiotics, antihistamines, or decongestants — will be the initial treatment for such common ailments as sinus and middle ear infections, diarrhea, hay fever, and other allergies."[62] More research and information-sharing will facilitate drawing on both systems in appropriate ways to maximize health.

Rather than mirror present biomedical resistance to complementary and alternative medicine, legal rules can enhance integration by protecting the best interest of the patient. The legal paradigm should provide a place of reconciliation and synthesis, recognizing the evolving process by which the various communities of professional healing practitioners are coming to terms.[63]

2

BIOMEDICAL REGULATION
IN HISTORICAL CONTEXT

As Thomas Kuhn suggested, new paradigms do not gain acceptance without revolution, because the debate is conducted in terms supplied by the old paradigm.[1] The existing paradigm finds expression in medical licensing statutes and in the way in which many courts have interpreted these statutes. Both preserve biomedicine's historical domination of professional healing practice.

The Emergence of Licensing

In the eighteenth and late nineteenth centuries, healers offered their services in an unregulated environment. The common law neither defined nor regulated the practice of medicine and did not make unlicensed medical practice a crime. New York was one of the earliest colonies to establish medical licensure.[2] The colonial assembly of the province of New York first met in 1683, and recorded legislation between 1691 and 1709. Only one section of the earliest legislation related to the medical profession: physicians and surgeons were exempt from military duty. In June 1760, the legislature passed an act "to regulate the practice of physick and surgery in the state of New York" (141). The rationale for this statute is expressed in terms of consumer protection: "Many ignorant and unskilful persons, in physic and surgery, in order to gain a subsistence, do take upon themselves to administer physick and practice surgery in the city of New York, to the endangering of the lives and limbs of their patients, and many poor and ignorant persons, who have been persuaded to become their patients, have been great sufferers thereby" (141).

The statute relied on certification by various government authorities and prohibited "practice as a physician or surgeon" in the city of New York by persons who had not been "examined . . . approved of and admitted" by certain government officials, "taking to their assistance, for such examination, such persons, as they in their discretion shall think fit" (142). If approved, the candidate received a license to practice "physic or surgery, or both," throughout the province (142). Any individual found practicing without the license would be fined five pounds.

In 1792, the legislature updated the statute. The nineteenth-century historian T. Romeyn Beck noted that the preamble furnished "the same melancholy picture of the state of medical practice." It stated: "Many ignorant and unskilful persons presume to practice physic and surgery within the city and county of New York to the detriment and hazard of the lives and limbs of the citizens thereof" (143). The bill essentially required that practitioners, in addition to being examined, approved, and admitted by a licensing board, have studied with a "reputable physician" for at least two years if the individual had graduated from college, and for three years otherwise (143).

In 1797, the legislature passed the first act applying to the entire state. The act required an applicant to show evidence of having studied or apprenticed with reputable physicians or surgeons for four years. Beck comments: "This law certainly reflects great honour on the framers of it. Its natural effect must have been to exclude many ignorant and presuming pretenders from the privilege of practicing in a licentious manner; and, at the same time, it laid the foundation for an improved race of junior physicians, who from the increased period of study, and the duties incident thereto, were calculated to exalt the standard of medical character" (145).

In 1806, the legislature passed a law to incorporate medical societies "for the purpose of regulating the practice of Physic and Surgery" (148). In 1807, the statute was amended to regulate the internal organization of the state medical society. The legislation contemplated that these medical societies would have the power to license medical practitioners, although a practitioner also could be licensed upon filing proof of graduation from a college of medicine.

Initially, the licensing laws were weakly enforced. From 1806 to 1844 (with the exception of seven years), the only penalty applied to unlicensed practitioners was a prohibition on suing patients for fees.[3] After 1825, the support for market competition which was championed by Jacksonian democracy led to the repeal of most state licensing statues.[4] By the 1870s, however, most states had reenacted their medical practice acts, returning responsibility for licensing to the legislature.

The Development of the Biomedical Community

The licensing of physicians originated in the drive to control lay practitioners and evolved into the consolidation of a medical establishment.[5] For a century and a half following the first settlements in North America, medical practitioners trained by undergoing apprenticeships. They were not highly regarded. The president of the New York State Medical Society remarked in 1818 that most were "ignorant, degraded and contemptible."[6] A contemporary historian likewise observed: "Few physicians among us are eminent for their skill. Quacks abound like locusts in Egypt."[7]

Groups of physicians promoted their own theories and therapies and condemned those of rivals. They also formed medical societies to consolidate prestige, power, and economic control over a patient population. In 1767, for example, thirty Connecticut physicians organized a society, petitioned the legislature for authority to examine and license practitioners, and condemned anyone who opposed their views as "an enemy of physic and all learning."[8]

By 1830, nearly every state in the union had a medical society. Most states acceded to lobbying by the medical societies and delegated licensing authority to them. Medical schools responded by demanding that graduates be licensed without further examination. The legislatures again acquiesced, which resulted in a dual system in which either the medical society or the medical school could grant a license to practice medicine. As the licenses granted by medical schools gained prestige, candidates flocked to the schools. Between 1800 and 1900, more than four hundred medical schools were founded.

Most were "proprietary schools," privately owned medical institutions with no affiliation to any university. Their graduates relied on bloodletting, purgatives and emetics, and blistering. A contemporary physician remarked: "Whoever sends for a physician of this sort expects to be bled, blistered or vomited, or submitted to some other painful or nauseous medication."[9] Physicians who did not employ such measures received their colleagues' condemnation. The paradigm was "heroic medicine," whose practitioners have been characterized as "ignorant, dogmatic, and committed to heroic therapy."[10]

Public rebellion against such practices gave rise to alternatives. The first major popular alternative was Thomsonism, a movement for healing which made use of botanical preparations. The founder, Samuel Thomson, attacked heroic medicine and advised patients to "depend more upon themselves, and less upon the doctors."[11] Thomson's discoveries grew out of an existing American botanical tradition that had already been practiced for two hundred years. Thomson encouraged citizens to follow the preparations indicated in his 1832 book *New Guide to Health*.

Although Thomson himself distrusted institutionalization, his followers organized local infirmaries and, mirroring the regular physicians (successors to heroic medicine), founded a Thomsonian society in an attempt to create a professional monopoly. Between 1827 and the start of the Civil War, at least twenty-two Thomsonian medical schools were founded.

The regular physicians attempted to discredit Thomsonians and sued Thomson and others for illegal practice. Over time, Thomsonism waned and "eclectic" physicians grew in favor. The eclectics drew from Thomsonians, Native American doctors, herb doctors, and others for their medical practice. Some eclectics were charlatans; others were reputable. Some eclectic therapies, such as various Native American drugs, later received scientific recognition and were incorporated into the Western pharmacopeia.

In time, the eclectic influence declined and homeopathy gained ascendancy. Homeopathy was founded by Samuel Hahnemann, a German physician with formal medical training. His theory of medicine held that what causes disease in a healthy person will cure the disease in a sick person. Hahnemann called this the "law of similars": "Like cures like." The law held that "instead of suppressing symptoms — which would inhibit the organism's inherent defensive reaction — a homeopathic medicine is prescribed for its ability to mimic those symptoms. The best way to heal ourselves of disease may be to steer our body's own defenses into, rather than away from or against, symptoms. By aiding the body's efforts to adapt to stress or infection, the organism is best able to heal itself."[12]

Hahnemann suggested that the patient be given whatever medicine would induce in a healthy person the same symptoms as would the disease. He believed that extremely small doses were necessary, and formulated a system of radical dilution. Hahnemann referred to regular medicine as "allopathic" because, unlike "homeopathic" medicine, regular medicine used remedies whose action was opposite to the symptoms caused by the illness.[13] Hahnemann also advocated fresh air, rest, diet, exposure to the sun, public hygiene, and other measures disregarded by contemporaries.

As homeopathy gained supporters in the United States, regular physicians took steps to purge homeopaths from their ranks. This included expulsion from medical societies, lawsuits, attacks in the medical literature, and attempts to turn public opinion against homeopathy. Allopaths stirred up public opinion against their competitors by means of public campaigns ostensibly promoting improved medical education, scientific rigor, and protection against charlatans. The American Medical Association (AMA) was founded in large part to limit the influence of the homeopaths, and early on, it prohibited regular physicians from consulting with the "irregular" practitioners.[14]

In response, homeopaths founded the Homeopathic Medical College of Pennsylvania. However, the AMA continued to seek ways to eliminate homeopaths from the practice of medicine and instituted a ban on discussing or reviewing homeopathic works in allopathic periodicals. By the mid-1850s, homeopathic practitioners had been expelled from the medical society of every state except Massachusetts, which followed in 1871. In 1881, the AMA convention enacted a resolution prohibiting regular physicians from signing any diploma or certificate for any individual who intended to support and practice "irregular" medicine.[15]

By the end of the nineteenth century, the elimination of homeopaths as their major competitors and the use of medical licensing laws to restrict and control entry into the profession enabled the regular physicians to dominate the healing arts.[16] Three additional factors solidified the consolidation of regular physicians into a biomedical establishment. First was the rise of scientific medicine. Pivotal discoveries included the use of anesthesia in surgery (1842) and the introduction of successful methods for disinfection in surgery (1865–97).[17] Scientific discoveries enabled physicians to systematize diagnosis and quantify the patient's condition.[18]

Second was the growing power of the AMA as the sole voice of U.S. medicine. In 1900–1901, the AMA undertook a major reorganization, with the aim of becoming an institution "whose power to influence public sentiment will be almost unlimited, and whose requests for desirable legislation will everywhere be met with the respect which the politician always has for organized votes."[19] In 1903, the AMA invited homeopaths to join the organization, but only if the homeopaths renounced their connection with homeopathic institutions and practices. The invitation further divided homeopathic ranks.[20]

Third was a report issued by Abraham Flexner, of the Carnegie Foundation for the Advancement of Teaching, in conjunction with the AMA Council on Medical Education, in 1910.[21] The *Flexner Report* exposed the weaknesses of the proprietary schools and urged commitment to university medical schools engaged in research employing full-time faculties.[22] In keeping with the Newtonian-Cartesian model, Flexner urged that medical students be "trained to regard the body as an infinitely complex machine."[23] Flexner questioned whether "'in this era of scientific medicine, sectarian medicine is logically defensible,' and of course, decid[ed] in the negative."[24]

In response to Flexner's observation that state licensing boards had the power to eliminate weak medical schools through stricter examination, university medical schools and the AMA Council on Medical Education cooperated with state licensing boards to raise standards. State licensing boards began to rely on the AMA council's recommendation in determining whether to honor a graduate's diploma. The council established a three-tier rating system for schools. Most states denied recognition to institutions designated "class C"; schools unable to receive AMA approval were forced out of existence. Between 1904 and 1915, ninety-two schools merged or closed.[25]

The *Flexner Report* advocated denying philanthropic funds to homeopathic schools. After the report was published, foundations supported only AMA-approved schools. For example, in 1913 the Rockefeller General Education Board gave $1.5 million to Johns Hopkins University and $750,000 to Washington University, in St. Louis, for chairs in pediatrics, surgery, and medicine; in 1921, the total endowment of the Hahnemann Medical College, of Philadelphia, was $325,000.[26] The three established homeopathic schools in Boston, New York, and Philadelphia gradually converted into regular medical schools.

While homeopathy and other "irregular" practices declined, the growing reliance on technology and medication transformed patients' experience of care. As control of medical education moved from private practitioners to an academic elite, a system in which patients freely chose healers changed to one of biomedical dominance. The AMA ratified the notion of distance between physician and patient in its 1947 code of ethics: "A peculiar reserve must be maintained by physicians toward the public in regard to professional matters, and as there exist numerous points in medical ethics and etiquette through which the feelings of medical men may be painfully assailed in their intercourse with each other, and which can not be understood or appreciated by general society, neither the subject-matter of such differences nor the adjudication of the arbitrators should be made public."[27]

The AMA continued to denounce competing modalities. As late as 1955, it declared osteopathy to be "cultist healing."[28] The AMA's 1956 *Principles of Medical Ethics* stated, "All voluntarily associated activities with cultists are unethical." These principles pitted medicine against chiropractic:

"Either the theories and practices of scientific medicine are right and those of the cultists are wrong, or the theories and practices of the cultists are right and those of scientific medicine are wrong." The AMA admonished physicians to adhere to medical doctrine, warning: "The physician who maintains professional relations with cult practitioners would seem to exhibit a lack of faith in the correctness and efficacy of scientific medicine."[29]

The case of *Wilk v. American Medical Association* suggests the extent to which the AMA, and particularly its Committee on Quackery, focused on preserving a professional monopoly.[30] In *Wilk,* chiropractors brought an antitrust action against the AMA and other medical groups alleging combination and conspiracy to eliminate the chiropractic profession. The court held for the chiropractors. It found, among other things, that the AMA had failed to establish that its alleged concern for scientific methods in patient care was objectively reasonable or justified its "nationwide conspiracy to eliminate a licensed profession."[31] The court observed that the AMA's Committee on Quackery had evidence that chiropractic "was effective, indeed more effective than the medical profession, in treating certain kinds of problems, such as back injuries" (363). Following the *Wilk* decision, the AMA changed its position and held that it was ethical for a physician to associate professionally with a chiropractor, if the physician believed that this was in the patient's best interest. Despite this change in posture, references to chiropractic and other modalities as "sorcery" and "voodoo" have continued to find their way into biomedical and legal discourse.[32]

The preeminence of biomedicine revolutionized the way in which individuals "think, eat, sleep, work, play, procreate, even die."[33] While in the nineteenth century patients were suspicious of medical authority, in the twentieth century they permitted such authority to establish the social definitions of illness and health. The broader notion of healing — which encompasses all aspects of health and wholeness — was narrowed to biomedical diagnosis and treatment.[34] Medical innovation advanced care but also dehumanized and mechanized the experience of care. While technological methods of diagnosis and treatment provided accuracy, they tended to "move the evidence . . . away from the patient" and to reduce the whole patient to an organ or body part amenable to application of a specific technology (36).

The Response of the Regulatory Paradigm

The late nineteenth century's political and economic establishment of biomedical dominance drove the regulatory paradigm toward a monopolistic perspective on health care licensure. For example, in *Smith v. People*,[35] an individual who purported to cure diseases by laying on hands was convicted for practicing medicine without a license. Smith argued that he did not tell patients what was the matter with them, that he practiced out of living rooms, and that he used only his hands to employ a "gift from the Almighty."

The court found that Smith had in fact practiced medicine because the medical practice act, "as a protection to public health," should be construed liberally. The court stated: "One form of examination is required of all sorts of healers. All applicants must be examined in anatomy, physiology, chemistry, symptomatology, toxicology, pathology, surgery and obstetrics."[36]

The *Smith* court interpreted the practice of medicine broadly to include "the practice of the healing arts commercially, regardless of the curative agency employed."[37] *Smith*'s broad and inclusive interpretation of medical practice is typical of decisions in other jurisdictions holding faith healers and other providers guilty of unauthorized medical practice.[38] For instance, in states that do not license naturopaths, practitioners of naturopathy have been prosecuted for the unlicensed practice of medicine.[39] Similarly, prosecutions of practitioners of mental suggestion, massage, hypnotism, nutritional advice, and even ear piercing suggest "how far courts are willing to go in supporting the medical profession's desire to protect its domain."[40]

Such broad enforcement and interpretation of medical practice acts reflects a biomedically oriented perspective. This also finds expression in judicial interpretation of scope-of-practice rules, which blur the line between services appropriate to the holistic profession and unlicensed medical diagnosis and treatment (see chap. 4). That the regulatory structure unconsciously incorporates biomedicine's position toward complementary and alternative providers further finds reflection in the way in which some conceptualize holistic practices. For instance, a health law hornbook refers to specialists such as acupuncturists and chiropractors as "nontraditional, nonconforming or innovative"[41] — even though these labels merely reflect a biomedical view of such modalities. Some suggest that bias against other healers has deeper roots than nineteenth-century rivalries or twentieth-century scientific optimism. For example, some trace biomedicine's derogation of midwives, as alternative providers of childbirth services, to the medieval campaign by the Catholic Church to discredit women healers as witches.[42]

Whether determining the legal boundaries of midwifery, faith healing, herbal and nutritional treatments, chiropractic, or innovative medical therapies, courts still tend to treat complementary and alternative medicine as deviant, dangerous, and anti-intellectual. In *United States v. Rutherford,*[43] a group of terminally ill cancer patients sued to enjoin the federal government from interfering with a shipment for sale of laetrile, a drug not approved as "safe and effective" under the Federal Food, Drug, and Cosmetic Act. The U.S. Court of Appeals for the Tenth Circuit held that the act's requirement that drugs be "safe and effective" did not apply to terminally ill cancer patients who would "die of cancer regardless."[44] The U.S. Supreme Court, reversing and remanding the Tenth Circuit's decision, held that Congress "could reasonably have intended to shield terminal patients from ineffectual or unsafe drugs."[45] The Court stated: "Since the turn of the century, resourceful entrepreneurs have advertised a wide variety of purportedly simple and painless cures for cancer, including liniments of turpentine, mustard oil, eggs, and ammonia; peat moss; arrangements of colored floodlamps; pastes made from glycerin and limburger cheese; mineral tablets; and 'Fountain of Youth' mixtures of spices, oil, and suet."[46] The Court reframed the question of access to treatment within a constitutional right to privacy as a question of medical fraud, ostensibly to protect patients from their own ill-advised choices.

In cases involving reproductive rights, courts similarly devalue patients' perspectives, defer to biomedical opinion, and uphold forced biomedical treatment, such as Caesarean sections during dangerous pregnancies.[47] The biomedical perspective dominates interpretations of informed consent doctrine and malpractice rules (see chap. 5).[48] In cases involving failure to disclose potentially dangerous side-effects of prescription drugs, courts are similarly deferential to physicians.[49] Courts also follow biomedical authority in interpreting insurance contract coverage for "medically necessary" services and "experimental treatment" exclusions (see chap. 8). The legal paradigm to date thus mirrors biomedicine's historical view of holistic practice as deviant, suspect, or "on the fringe."

3

STATE LAW
REGULATION OF MEDICINE

The Police Power Rationale

When health care providers assert a right to practice, they face the state's regulatory authority under the police power. This power to protect citizens' health, safety, and welfare authorizes states to decide who may practice medicine and to establish licensing boards that admit or exclude persons from practice. Such regulation is held to prevent indiscriminate practice of the healing arts by "unskilled and unlicensed practitioners" and to protect the public from "the menace of the ignorant, the unprepared, the quacks and the fakers."[1] Yet, because licensure is a political process, the power to protect public health, safety, and welfare has been used to exclude or suppress from professional healing practice those persons and modalities outside the biomedical paradigm.

The U.S. Supreme Court has upheld the states' use of the police power to regulate health care providers against the assertion that the state cannot prohibit certain purveyors of medical services from practicing. In 1888, in *Dent v. West Virginia*,[2] a physician challenged a state statute requiring him to obtain a diploma from the state board of health to practice medicine. The state board had refused Dent a certificate, claiming that the medical college he had attended was not "reputable" under applicable board rules. Dent argued that practicing medicine was his only means of support and that the statute had unconstitutionally destroyed his vested rights, depriving him "of the estate he had acquired in his profession by years of study, practice, diligence, and attention" (123). The Supreme Court upheld Dent's conviction for practicing medicine unlawfully, stating that the police power includes "prescrib[ing] all such regulations as, in its judgment, will secure or tend to secure . . . [the public] against the consequences of ignorance and incapacity as well as deception and fraud" (122).

Courts also have upheld the states' police power in medical regulation against free exercise, due process, and privacy challenges by providers and patients. In *Jacobson v. Massachusetts*,[3] the U.S. Supreme Court upheld the state's right to order compulsory vaccination for public school children. The Court rejected the defendant's argument that vaccination violated the "inherent right to care for his own body and health in such way as to him seems best" (26).[4]

Courts have found some limits to the police power in the area of forced antipsychotic medication for mentally ill patients.[5] However, in *Washington v. Harper* the U.S. Supreme Court held that a state's interest in maintaining the safety and security of its prisons justified forced medication of inmates in reasonable furtherance of this goal.[6] Other courts have upheld, against constitutional challenges, ordinances permitting involuntary detention and examination, and forced treatment, of a person reasonably suspected of having a venereal disease.[7] Courts also have upheld detention, giving the detainee a choice between staying in jail while an examination is conducted, and submitting to an immediate injection of penicillin, without examination, and thus being eligible for immediate release (1381).

The courts have found that the police power outweighs not only privacy and liberty interests but also free speech interests in the provision of and access to health care. For instance, in *State v. Hinze*,[8] a licensed pharmacist, holding a degree in naturopathy from a Canadian college, gave seminars in which he was introduced as "Dr. Hinze" and in which he provided information regarding homeopathic and naturopathic remedies. The court permanently enjoined the pharmacist from engaging in the practice of medicine without a license, and thereafter held him in contempt for violating the injunction.

On appeal, the Nebraska Supreme Court upheld the judgment, finding that the pharmacist had solicited information on participants' ailments, suggested specific remedies, and used the title *doctor* without explaining his educational background. The court further rejected the pharmacist's claim that his First Amendment right to freedom of speech protected the enjoined conduct. According to the court, any infringement on Hinze's freedom of speech "is, at most, incidental and is outweighed by this State's compelling interest in regulating the health and welfare of the citizens of Nebraska."[9] Although the *Hinze* court may have relied on the fact that the defendant suggested specific remedies for particular ailments, the decision reveals the breadth of the police power as a basis for curtailing patients' access to complementary and alternative medicine.

Legal Definitions of the Practice of Medicine

Each state has enacted a medical licensing statute (or medical practice act) pursuant to its police power. Although definitions of the practice of medicine vary by state, all states include some of the following: (1) diagnosing, preventing, treating, and curing disease; (2) holding oneself out to the public as able to perform the above; (3) intending to receive a gift, fee, or compensation for the above; (4) attaching such titles as *M.D.* to one's name; (5) maintaining an office for reception, examination, and treatment; (6) performing surgery; and (7) using, administering, or prescribing drugs or medicinal preparations.[10] Some of the permutations of the definition are briefly described below.

Diagnosis, Treatment, Prevention, and Cure

All states define the practice of medicine, in part, by using such words as *diagnosis, treatment, prevention, cure, advise,* and *prescribe.* These words are usually used in conjunction with *disease, injury, deformity,* and *mental or physical condition.* For example, New York defines the practice of medicine as "diagnosing, treating, operating, or prescribing for any human disease, pain, injury, deformity or physical condition."[11] Similarly, Michigan includes in its definition "diagnosis, treatment, prevention, cure, or relieving of a human disease, ailment, defect, complaint or other physical or mental condition, by attendance, advice, device, diagnostic test, or other means."[12] Some of the definitions are overly broad. If Michigan's statute is interpreted literally, "relieving . . . a . . . complaint . . . by . . . advice" constitutes practicing medicine. Similarly, under the Arkansas statute, "suggesting . . . any form of . . . healing for the intended palliation" constitutes the practice of medicine.[13]

Holding Oneself Out to the Public

Most states also include holding oneself out to the public as a medical practitioner in defining the practice of medicine. Some states describe this as "publicly professing" to assume duties incident to the practice of medicine, such as diagnosing, healing, and treating,[14] or "publicly professing" to be a physician or surgeon.[15] Other states, such as Hawaii, Minnesota, New Mexico, Oregon, Vermont, and Wyoming, also include "advertising" that one is a physician or otherwise authorized to practice medicine in the state.[16]

In Florida, New York, and North Carolina, the courts have included holding oneself out as a physician in the definition of the practice of medicine.[17] In Louisiana, an appellate court has interpreted the medical practice act to mean that the practice of medicine does not mean actually diagnosing and treating diseases, but rather, holding one's self out to the public as being engaged in the business of diagnosis and treatment.[18] By finding that "holding one's self out to the public" can suffice as practicing medicine, irrespective of actual diagnosis or treatment, legislatures and courts have further broadened the sweep of the definition.

Intending to Receive a Fee, Gift, or Other Compensation

A number of states define the practice of medicine as diagnosing and treating disease with the intention of receiving compensation, or a fee or gift. In some of these states, the courts have incorporated the requirement of a fee within the definition of the practice of medicine.[19] By way of comparison, the Hawaii, Louisiana, and Utah statutes specifically state that one can be held to practice medicine irrespective of compensation.[20]

Attaching a Title to One's Name

In about half the states, one has by legal definition practiced medicine if one attaches to one's name one or more of the following titles: *doctor, doctor of medicine, doctor of osteopathy, physician, surgeon, physician and surgeon, Dr., M.D., D.O.,* or other words or abbreviations intended to indicate or induce others to believe that one is licensed to practice medicine and engaged in the duties characteristic of the practice of medicine.

Delaware also includes using the word *healer* in connection with one's name.[21] In Nebraska, practicing Christian Science healing has been held to constitute the practice of medicine.[22] Ohio, Oklahoma, Oregon, and Vermont include using the word *professor* in connection with the person's name.[23] In Maine and Ohio, the use of any such words or letters is prima facie evidence of intent to represent one's self as engaged in the "practice of medicine or surgery."[24] For example, individuals are guilty of practicing medicine without a license if they use *M.D.* in a manner that induces a belief that they are engaged in medical practice.[25]

Maintaining an Office

In many states, maintaining an office in which to receive, examine, and treat patients constitutes practicing medicine. In Indiana, maintaining a "place of business for the reception . . . of persons suffering from . . . conditions of the body or mind" suffices.[26] In Texas, maintaining an office to treat people was held to constitute the practice of medicine, whether or not the defendant claimed to be a physician or medical practitioner.[27] In Utah, maintaining an office or other place of business for the purpose of attempting to "diagnose, treat, correct, advise . . . for any human . . . condition . . . real or imaginary" constitutes practicing medicine.[28]

Performing Surgery

Approximately half the states include performing surgical operations in the definition of the practice of medicine. Although the Massachusetts medical practice act does not mention surgery, the Supreme Judicial Court held that the "practice of medicine in any of its branches" includes the practice of surgery and the art of setting fractured bones.[29] Of the various statutory definitions, performing surgery is among the narrowest and most tailored criteria for prohibiting practitioners who lack appropriate education and training from engaging in medical practice.

Using, Administering, or Prescribing Drugs

More than half the states include the use, administration, or prescription of drugs or medicine in the definition of the practice of medicine. However, only a few define the term *drug*.[30] Indiana, for instance, adopts a broad and inclusive definition: "any medicine, compound, or chemical or biological preparation intended for internal or external use of humans, and all substances intended to be used for the diagnosis, cure, mitigation, or prevention of diseases or abnormalities of humans, which are recognized in the latest editions published of the United States pharmacopeia or national formulary, or otherwise established as a drug or medicine."[31] New Mexico's statute includes not only prescribing any drug or medicine but also "offering or undertaking to give or administer any dangerous drug or medicine for the use of any other person, except as directed by a licensed physician."[32] Such broad definitions of the word *drug* pose problems for nonmedical providers who offer herbal and nutritional therapies as part of professional practice.

28

Miscellaneous Definitional Provisions

Maryland includes ending a human pregnancy in its definition of the practice of medicine.[33] Delaware's medical practice act and New York's case law include the diagnosing of diseases of any person, including dead persons.[34] Treatments such as manipulation expressly constitute the practice of medicine in Arkansas, Maine, and South Carolina.[35] In Hawaii, the practice of medicine includes "hypnotism," as well as "the use of . . . any means or method . . . either tangible or intangible."[36] Although it is relatively unusual for medical practice acts to expressly include within the definition of medicine such modalities as manipulative therapy and hypnosis, such broad language reflects the late-nineteenth-century view of regular physicians that healing must come from legislatively authorized biomedical practice.[37]

Unauthorized Professional Practice

The breadth of medical practice acts puts at least three groups at risk of prosection for unlawfully practicing medicine. The first consists of providers who lack licensure. State prosecutors can argue that these nonlicensed practitioners are "diagnosing" and "treating" patients, as defined under the medical practice acts, and thus are practicing medicine unlawfully.

The second group consists of licensed providers (including physicians) who employ or refer patients to providers practicing medicine unlawfully, and therefore may be liable for "aiding and abetting" unlicensed medical practice.[38] The third group consists of licensed providers, such as chiropractors and, in many states, licensed naturopaths, massage therapists, and others, who are deemed to violate their legally authorized scope of practice by engaging in the diagnosis and treatment of disease (see chap. 4).

The Nonlicensed Provider

In some states, modalities such as naturopathy, massage therapy, hypnosis, and therapeutic touch are not specifically addressed by statute and thus may be viewed as encompassed by the prohibition on unlicensed medical practice. For example, *People v. Amber* involved an acupuncturist indicted for practicing medicine without a license.[39] At the time, New York had no acupuncture licensure. The defendant acupuncturist argued that the statutory prohibition on the unlicensed practice of medicine referred to "Western allopathic medicine" and did not encompass systems such as

Chinese acupuncture, which differs in its "philosophy, practice and technique" (611).

The court disagreed, holding that diagnosis constitutes any "'sizing up' or a comprehending of the physical or mental status of a patient" (612). The court added that whether certain actions constitute the practice of medicine depends on facts, and not on "the name of the procedure, its origins or the legislative lack of clairvoyance" (611–12). The court stated that "a statute intended to regulate, limit or control the diagnosis and treatment of ailments must necessarily be broad enough to include the gamut of those known, whether or not recognized and even those not yet conjured" (611).

The court emphasized that "the patient seeks treatment, not out of curiosity but only because he is suffering pain . . . [and] can expect the anticipated relief from the healing methodology" (612). In the court's view, even determining "the existence of a disharmony brought about by the disequilibrium of Yin and Yang" constituted a "diagnosis" under the statute (612). Such a determination required expertise — specifically, "palpating the twelve pulses to read the condition of the twelve organs and thus determine which of the twelve meridians must be used . . . to restore the vital essence of 'ch'i' or vital energy" (612). The court also noted that a practitioner need not use any particular language or mention a specific disease to make a "diagnosis" under the statute.[40]

Under the court's ruling, "every means and method . . . to relieve . . . infirmity" comes within the ambit of medicine (608). By defining diagnosis as any "sizing up" of a client's condition, including the relative balance of yin and yang, the court included nutritional, psychological, spiritual, and other nonmedical assessments of health under the statute's rubric.

Stetina v. State involved another nonmedical provider of health care lacking independent licensure.[41] The defendant, Stetina, was a nutritionist who practiced iridology. Stetina used questionnaires and examined the investor's eyes. She determined that the investigator had, among other things, "nutritional problems, abdominal problems, a slow electrical turnover, and poor circulation," and she recommended "a colonic irrigation (an enema), mineral water, kelp, amelade, progestine and more raw food" (1236).

Stetina argued that her conduct, which aimed at helping individuals follow proper nutritional advice, was outside the purview of the medical practice act, which aimed at "protect[ing] people from their own credulity" in medical matters (1237). Stetina further argued that medical doctors frequently give inadequate attention to the patient's diet and nutrition, making her practice a necessary and complementary modality. Stetina presented two witnesses who testified to their overall physical and mental improvement after a consultation.

The Indiana Court of Appeals upheld the lower court's permanent injunction, forbidding Stetina to practice medicine without a license. The court observed that the medical practice act was not solely designed to protect patients from their own gullibility and from fraudulent practitioners. Rather, the act intended to protect against "the well-intentioned but unskilled practices of health care professionals, as well as against those well-intentioned and skilled practices which simply exceed the scope of acceptable health care" (1238). The court concluded that whether Stetina's services had social and medical value was not susceptible to judicial determination, and required legislative determination. The appellate court agreed, however, that Stetina could "disseminate information concerning the value of good nutrition" and sell nutrition-related products to the public (1239). The line between merely disseminating information, on the one hand, and making a diagnosis, on the other, may be difficult to draw, particularly if, as in *State v. Hinze,* the provider suggests specific remedies for particular ailments.

Although providers such as acupuncturists now are licensed in many states, cases such as *Amber* and *Stetina* retain precedential value and express a judicial view of certain nonlicensed providers. In jurisdictions where acupuncture, naturopathy, massage therapy, hypnosis, energy healing, colon hydrotherapy, and other practices are neither specifically licensed nor specifically prohibited, their providers risk prosecution under state medical practice acts. In fact, courts have interpreted the medical practice acts broadly against providers in situations in which state legislatures have failed to create separate licensure. These providers include midwives, naturopaths, homeopaths, hypnotherapists, providers of colonic irrigation, nutritionists, and iridologists.[42] In addition, individuals offering ear piercing, tattooing, and massage have been indicted for unlawfully practicing medicine.[43] Courts have justified such broad interpretation of medical practice acts as facilitating the protection and preservation of public health.

Independent Holistic Practice

The broad reach and interpretation of medical practice acts expresses biomedical dominance and the conceptual narrowing of professional healing practice to biomedical diagnosis and treatment. Such narrowing is unnecessary. Lawmakers tend to view "diagnosis" and "treatment" as solely within the purview of biomedical physicians because biomedical physicians, until recently, succeeded in pushing alternative providers out of professional health care. Another view within the law acknowledges that such professional healing practice can coexist with biomedical practice. Massachusetts's medical practice act specifies that the prohibition on unlicensed medical practice does not apply to "clairvoyants or persons practicing hypnotism, magnetic healing, mind cure, massage, Christian science or cosmopathic method of healing."[44] Similarly, modern licensing statutes acknowledge that providers ranging from chiropractors to acupuncturists do engage in the "sizing up" of conditions (i.e., "diagnosis" and "treatment" within the limits of the providers' training [see chap. 4]).

While some medical practice acts are drafted more broadly than others, the case can be made for interpreting these statutes as prohibiting the nonlicensed provider only from engaging in the diagnosis and treatment of biomedically defined pathology.[45] In other words, the prohibition applies to furnishing or purporting to furnish "disease care" within the biomedical model, not "wellness care" within the holistic healing model. Thus, the statutes do not cover the entire spectrum of healing and do not prohibit independent holistic practice, which by and large aims at nourishing, balancing, or stimulating vital energy and may more properly be regulated through contract principles.[46]

For example, somatic (body awareness) practice provided by an instructor of the Alexander technique seeks not to repair the client's broken arm but to increase the flow of vital energy through the arm by teaching the client awareness of breath, posture, and movement.[47] Similarly, a client with asthma may see a nonlicensed hypnotherapist to increase his or her awareness of imbalance and tension associated with breathing.[48] Such services constitute "treatment" only in the sense that any healing intervention ultimately implicates cure. Lay naturopaths, homeopaths, iridologists, nutritionists, energy healers, and other providers should not be criminally liable under medical practice acts when they are not practicing biomedicine.[49]

This view is consistent with the maxim that courts should construe criminal statutes narrowly. It respects biomedical licensure within a larger universe of health care,[50] one that includes licensure of selected holistic providers.[51] Moreover, such interpretation accords with the policy goal of protecting patients from nonmedical providers who purport to cure a biomedically defined pathological condition using biomedical methodologies.[52]

Further, nutritionists, iridologists, energy healers (including non-nurse therapeutic touch practitioners), reflexologists, lay homeopaths, and others frequently practice in states that have no professional licensure for practitioners in these fields. Yoga and meditation teachers, Feldenkrais and Alexander instructors and other somatic practitioners, health food store proprietors, purveyors of nutritional supplements, and others routinely offer suggestions about client wellness that could, in the broad view of "diagnosis" and "treatment" articulated in *Amber,* be viewed as unlicensed medical practice. Such providers generally remain free from prosecutorial attention.[53]

Finally, interpreting medical practice narrowly is consistent with the exemption in *Stetina* for the dissemination of nutritional information. The exemption suggests a delineation between the furnishing of information, products, and/or services to encourage health (by nourishing, stimulating, and balancing vital energy) and purporting to cure disease as defined bio-medically. A Texas statute similarly protects dissemination of information by providing that the Texas medical practice act "shall [not] be construed to prohibit or discourage any person from providing or seeking advice or information pertaining to that person's own self-treatment or self-care, [or] . . . to prohibit the dissemination of information pertaining to self-care." The statute clarifies that it "confers no authority" to practice biomedical diagnosis and treatment.[54] Oklahoma's amended medical licensing statute likewise provides that the act applies "only to allopathic and surgical practices" and not to "any other healing practices . . . [including] homeopathy."[55]

Occupational Licensure

Occupational licensing provides standards that must be met by those entrusted with patients' health. Licensure also elevates the financial and social status of licensees in a "culture of professionalism."[56] This is a social view of occupation, initially popularized in the late nineteenth century, which inspired Americans' desire to be regarded as successful, middle-class professionals: plumbers "praised the dignity of . . . [their] work" as a "profession" rather than a "trade"; funeral directors seized upon the word *professional* to avoid being lumped together with makers of brooms, boxes, and baskets (34). The focus on "professional" practice spurred an increase in the number of institutions devoted to "professional" education. In health care, the number of "professional" medical schools rose from twelve in 1801 to eighty-six in 1899: "Specialists were consolidating their considerable status as they moved to monopolize the presidency of the AMA, control the faculties of medical colleges, pressure for the creation of specialty hospitals, dominate the staffs of general hospitals and dispensaries, and establish a clientele among persons with means and power" (85–86).

Licensure, creating specialization and professional monopoly, has allowed licensees to fend off nonlicensed competitors. According to Walter Gelhorn, the founding fathers would "have been aghast to learn that in many parts of the country today aspiring bee keepers, embalmers, lightning rod salesmen, septic tank cleaners, taxidermists, and tree surgeons must obtain official approval before seeking the public's patronage."[57] Licensing has been criticized for creating dubious distinctions between professionals and their "nonprofessional" competitors, and for providing an inefficient, ineffective means of excluding the untrained. As Gelhorn noted: "Only the credulous can conclude that licensure is in the main intended to protect the public rather than those who have been licensed, or, perhaps in some instances, those who do the licensing" (25). Many licensing restrictions use "irrelevancies as barriers to competition" — such as the requirement that commercial photographers "pass with flying colors a Wassermann test for syphilis" and the requirement that barbers receive instruction in "bacteriology; histology of the hair, skin, nails, muscles, and nerves; diseases of the skin, hair, glands, and nails; and other matters about which one may venture to guess few barbers are consulted" (13–14).[58]

Medical licensing has been criticized as protecting the licensed, not the patient, by insulating physicians from the economic threat of other providers. While medical licensure affords some level of consumer protection, it has proven ineffective in controlling incompetent or fraudulent practitioners.[59] Moreover, since medical licensing boards are staffed by individuals drawn from, and committed to promoting, the licensed profession, medical licensing accentuates the protection of the interests of parties other than patients.[60]

Medical licensing serves as the "key to effective control" over the profession: to practice medicine, one must obtain a license; to obtain a license, one must graduate from an approved school; and the list of approved schools maintained by licensing boards typically coincides with the list maintained by the AMA's Council on Medical Education.[61] Because the medical profession controls licensure and lobbies for broad interpretation of medical practice acts, even barbers, cosmeticians, and manicurists have sought separate licensing. Some of the resulting legislation has a ring of absurdity. For instance, a Nevada statute defines a "cosmetologist" as a person who engages, among other things, in the practice of "arranging, dressing, curling, waving, cleansing, singeing, bleaching, tinting, coloring or straightening the hair."[62] Some legislatures have "found it necessary to explicitly exempt shoe fitters from the requirements for a medical license."[63] Some courts have affirmed the medical profession's entitlement to insulation from competition: "The unlimited medical profession guards zealously their legal rights against the trespass and encroachment of others, and rightfully so, for they sacrificed many years of their lives in qualifying for this very highly skilled profession."[64] This is consistent with the court's view in *Amber* that the legal definition of "practicing medicine" embraces all healing arts, whether "known . . . or . . . not yet conjured."[65]

The biomedical establishment has used such jurisdictional control over the definition of professional healing to guard its professional monopoly even against competing allopathic providers. An example is litigation between podiatrists and orthopedic surgeons over whether treatment of the ankle is within the authorized scope of podiatric practice in Connecticut.[66] The late-nineteenth-century efforts to eliminate "irregular physicians" have continued in successive turf wars against osteopaths,[67] psychologists,[68] physician assistants, nurse practitioners, midwives, and others.[69]

Licensure offers nonlicensed holistic providers several benefits in addition to protection from medical practice acts. First, licensure creates a minimum level of professional competence, elevates the image of a profession, and assuages public and legislative concern over quality control. Licensure aims to "protect the uninformed against blatant incompetents, wily charlatans, and persons whose past delinquencies suggest the probability of future corrupt conduct."[70] Second, independent licensure prevents other professionals from gaining control over the licensed profession (for example, it prevents physicians and nurses from controlling acupuncture and massage therapy, respectively). Third, licensure furnishes a recognized basis for hospital privileges, insurance reimbursement, and other professional opportunities.

Some providers, such as some massage therapists and energy healers, oppose licensure. Licensure is not always politically feasible, and political mobilization for licensure may in fact be counterproductive (e.g., it may result in more restrictive massage ordinances). Further, some providers prefer to remain outside the regulatory system, finding regulation inappropriate or reductionistic and arguing that modalities such as skilled touch cannot be tested by uniform, written examinations. Finally, some fear that "the heart and art of the profession will be lost,"[71] as licensure increases bureaucratic control and brings subjective or intuitive modalities into the biomedical model.

Professional associations seeking to establish professional licensing regulation have at least three options. The first, mandatory licensure, prohibits unlicensed providers from providing the licensed services. The second, title licensure (or permissive certification), makes a demonstrable level of skill or training mandatory for those who would claim a particular occupational title. Uncertified providers may continue to offer services without risking prosecution for "unauthorized practice," provided they do not use the statutorily defined title. Psychology licensing statutes often use this approach: any individual may practice psychology, but only a licensed psychologist may use the title or describe his or her services by using the words "psychologist, psychology, or psychological."[72]

The third type of licensure is registration. Providers must register their name, address, training, and practice with the state to receive a registration certificate or license to practice. An appropriate state agency receives and investigates complaints against those registered and provides appropriate disciplinary measures. With mandatory registration, nonregistered providers are prohibited from practicing; however, registration typically imposes few, if any, requirements relating to training, knowledge, and skill. Registration offers a minimal level of consumer protection. It enables injured persons to locate and file complaints against offending professionals.

Because mandatory licensing often sets the highest requirements for training and skill, it offers holistic providers the greatest rigor, status, and prestige. Mandatory licensing may be most appropriate for a discipline such as acupuncture, which entails a fairly complex and sophisticated body of knowledge and whose practitioners have developed uniform requirements for examination and accreditation.[73] Registration may be more appropriate for modalities such as massage therapy, which require fewer hours of training and mastery of a more streamlined corpus of information and skills. The argument for mandatory licensure or registration is that only individuals meeting minimum standards of competence and conduct should be authorized to provide services to the public. Title licensure suggests that a broader class of professionals than those governmentally approved should be permitted to join the healing enterprise. In part, the choice depends on the extent to which practitioners who fail to meet the regulatory hurdle are perceived to present a public danger.

Many jurisdictions have chosen mandatory licensing schemes for complementary and alternative providers, along the lines of the medical practice acts. For example, Alaska's acupuncture licensing statute expressly provides that "a person may not practice acupuncture without a license."[74] Rhode Island and Washington provide that only licensed massage therapists may practice massage therapy.[75] Texas uses a mandatory registration scheme, which provides that an individual who practices massage therapy must register with the state. Registration requires the presentation before a regulatory board of satisfactory evidence of training.[76]

Holistic professions seeking licensure frequently create state-accredited educational institutions, professional organizations, and national professional accrediting bodies and examinations,[77] which then offer convenient and inexpensive bases for state licensure.[78] State legislatures look to professional organizations to accredit specific educational institutions within the profession or use these institutions or professionally developed examinations or certifying programs as bases for licensure.[79] Professional accreditation as a basis for licensure has developed significantly in professions such as acupuncture, naturopathy, massage therapy, and chiropractic. For example, Alaska's acupuncture licensing statute requires that the applicant have completed a course of study consistent with the core curriculum and guidelines of the National Council of Acupuncture Schools and Colleges at a state-approved school of acupuncture (or be licensed to practice acupuncture in another jurisdiction with equivalent licensing requirements) and be qualified for certification by the National Commission for the Certification of Acupuncturists as a diplomate in acupuncture.[80] Similarly, Alaska's naturopathic licensing statute requires that the applicant (1) have graduated from a four-year naturopathic school accredited (or being considered for accreditation) by the Council on Naturopathic Medical Education or a successor organization recognized by the federal Department of Education; and (2) have passed the Naturopathic Physicians Licensing Examination.[81]

Frequently the licensing statute will establish a professional board to approve professional educational institutions, clinical programs, and examinations as a basis for licensure.[82] One variation is the District of Columbia's naturopathic registration statute, which authorizes the mayor to establish standards of education and experience by which a person may qualify for registration as a naturopath, and permits the mayor in doing so to adopt the standards of a national professional association of naturopaths.[83]

Internal accreditation or certification can become the basis not only for initial licensure but also for upgrading professional status within an existing licensed profession. For instance, the National Commission for the Certification of Acupuncturists offers licensed acupuncturists additional certification in Chinese herbology.[84] Recently, the American Massage Therapy Association and other massage therapy organizations created the National Certification Board for Therapeutic Massage and Bodywork (NCBTMB). The NCBTMB created a national certification examination, consisting of 150 multiple-choice questions on the theory of massage and bodywork, assessment, and practice; human anatomy, physiology, and kinesiology; clinical pathology and recognition of various conditions; business practices and professionalism; and adjunct techniques and methods.

The NCBTMB examination was introduced to members of the massage therapy profession as an "optional" means to upgrade their professional status. However, thus far at least thirteen states and the District of Columbia have adopted the examination as a requirement for licensure. The examination has generated controversy among massage therapists and massage therapy organizations who resist the coercive effect of national certification. The examination's success among state legislatures suggests its double-edged nature. On the one hand, it provides the benefit of reciprocity—licensed providers who have passed the examination can practice in another state. On the other hand, the introduction of the examination as a means of national certification has increased the cost of, and the requirements for, entry to the profession. Moreover, once licensed, certified, or registered, providers must remain within scope-of-practice limitations, since, as described in the following chapter, practitioners who exceed their legislative authorization violate medical practice acts.

4

SCOPE-OF-PRACTICE
LIMITATIONS

Licensing of Complementary and Alternative Providers

In addition to defining the practice of medicine, states license specialists who practice within the parameters of biomedicine (e.g., dentists, veterinarians, pharmacists, physical therapists, and podiatrists), specialists who practice directly under physicians' supervision (e.g., physician assistants and respiratory therapists), and providers of complementary and alternative health care — specialists outside biomedicine (e.g., acupuncturists and chiropractors).[1]

State legislatures license the members of each of these three groups under their police power, and in the interest of public health. For instance, in Colorado "it is the intent of the general assembly that those citizens who wish to obtain acupuncture services be allowed to do so" and have information available to make informed choices when seeking acupuncture.[2] Arizona legislation asserts that, "since naturopathy is a health care system of diagnosing, treating and preventing disease, it has a direct relationship with the public health [and must] merit and receive the confidence of the public."[3] New Hampshire provides that naturopathic medicine "is a distinct health care profession that affects the public health, safety and welfare, and provides for freedom of choice in health care."[4] As Florida's hypnosis statute states, such modalities have "attained a significant place [in] the treatment of human injury, disease, and illness, both mental and physical."[5]

Allied practitioners are prohibited from practicing medicine. Frequently the prohibition is express. For example, California prohibits chiropractors from "the practice of medicine, surgery, osteopathy, dentistry or optometry."[6] Some statutes are more specific. Mississippi provides that a chiropractor "shall not prescribe or administer medicine to patients."[7] Similarly, in Michigan the practice of chiropractic "does not include the performance of incisive surgical procedures, the performance of an invasive procedure requiring instrumentation, or the dispensing or prescribing of drugs or medicine."[8]

Whereas physicians are granted unlimited ability to diagnose and treat disease, the scope of practice allocated to allied professionals is limited. The licensing statutes authorize nonmedical providers to offer services within a specifically designated scope of practice. Typically the statutes provide a general definition of professional practice, specify certain acts within the scope of practice, and/or delegate further definition of the scope of practice to appropriate professional regulatory boards.[9]

Chiropractic

At the turn of the century, chiropractors lacked licensure and were jailed for violating medical practice acts. Today chiropractors have licensure in every state in the United States, and in Washington, D.C.[10] Each state has its own statutory definition. The definitions vary in breadth and focus. Delaware defines chiropractic as the "science of locating and removing any interference with the transmission of nerve energy."[11] In Iowa, chiropractors "treat human ailments by adjustment of the neuromusculoskeletal structures, primarily, by hand or instrument, through spinal care."[12] In North Carolina, chiropractic means "the science of adjusting the cause of disease by realigning the spine, releasing pressure on nerves radiating from the spine to all parts of the body, and allowing the nerves to carry their full quota of health current (nerve energy) from the brain to all parts of the body."[13]

Some statutory definitions, such as Iowa's, emphasize the chiropractor's use of spinal manipulation and adjustment. Other statutes, such as Delaware's, make references to ambiguous concepts such as the location and removal of interference with "the transmission of nerve energy." The different kinds of authorizing language cause considerable confusion in interpreting the scope of chiropractic practice, particularly when providers move beyond spinal manipulation and into such areas as nutritional guidance, acupuncture, colonic irrigation, and energy healing, and the statute makes no provision for ancillary practices. Under Delaware's statute, for example, chiropractors can make the argument that although a particular practice does not entail spinal manipulation, it does facilitate the free flow of nerve energy, which is an integral part of chiropractic practice. Under a statute such as Iowa's, chiropractors can argue that language authorizing them to "treat human ailments" allows them to address a broad range of conditions and use a diverse range of healing modalities. Alternatively, courts may focus on statutory references to "adjustment" to limit chiropractors to spinal manipulation.

Massage Therapy

About half the states recognize massage therapy as a licensed profession.[14] In Colorado, massage means "a method of treating the body for remedial or hygienic purposes, including but not limited to rubbing, stroking, kneading or tapping with the hand or an instrument or both."[15] Connecticut provides that massage therapy is used, among other things, for the purpose of "maintaining good health and establishing and maintaining good physical and mental condition."[16] In the District of Columbia, massage includes "causing movement of an individual's body to positively affect the health and well-being of the individual."[17]

Idaho's massage therapy statute recognizes massage therapy as the "systematic manual or mechanical mobilization of the soft tissue of the body for the purpose of promoting circulation of the blood and lymph, relaxation of muscles, release from pain, restoration of metabolic balance, and other benefits both physical and mental."[18] Utah's refers to "rehabilitative procedures involving the muscles by nonintrusive means and without spinal manipulation."[19] New Mexico and Texas state that "massage therapy is a health care service."[20] Some states provide for the regulation of massage by local ordinance.[21] Massage therapists may not diagnose and treat pathology or practice medicine.[22]

Naturopathy

More than a dozen states license naturopaths.[23] Like the chiropractic and massage therapy licensing statutes, the naturopathy licensing statutes express state legislatures' decision to entrust patients to various approaches to health outside the biomedical model. For example, Alaska's naturopathic licensing statute defines naturopathy as "the use of hydrotherapy, dietetics, electrotherapy, sanitation, suggestion, mechanical and manual manipulation for the stimulation of physiological and psychological action to establish a normal condition of mind and body."[24] Connecticut includes counseling in its definition of naturopathy.[25] Similarly, Washington, D.C., provides that naturopaths "may counsel individuals and treat human conditions through the use of naturally occurring substances."[26]

Hawaii's statute describes naturopathy as "natural medicine, natural therapeutics, and natural procedures, for the purpose of removing toxic conditions from the body and improving the quality, quantity, harmony, balance, and flow of the vital fluids, vital tissues, and vital energy." Hawaii defines naturopathy as "natural medicine, natural therapeutics, and natural procedures, for the purpose of removing toxic conditions from the body and improving the quality, quantity, harmony, balance, and flow of the vital fluids, vital tissues."[27] It allows "diagnosing [and] treating" patients, "using a system of practice that bases its treatment of physiological functions and abnormal conditions on natural laws governing the human body."[28] New Hampshire refers to stimulation of the "individual's intrinsic self-healing processes," as does Montana.[29] Oregon also refers to stimulation or facilitation of "natural healing processes" and also authorizes minor surgery, aimed at "maintaining of the body in, or . . . restoring it to, a state of normal health."[30] The state of Washington authorizes naturopaths to engage in "diagnosis, prevention, and treatment of disorders of the body," as do Montana, New Hampshire, and Tennessee.[31]

To practice naturopathy, applicants generally must obtain a degree from a federally accredited school, complete a residency program, and pass the licensing examination. Currently, two recognized naturopathic colleges, the Natural College of Naturopathic Medicine, in Portland, Oregon, and Bastyr University, in Seattle, provide the requisite four-year training program. The curriculum includes the basic sciences and many standard medical school courses, such as anatomy, physiology, biochemistry, and pediatrics, as well as naturopathic courses such as massage, colon therapy, and nutrition.

Like chiropractic licensing statutes, the naturopathic licensing statutes of the various states provide differing scopes of practice. Arizona limits a naturopathic practitioner to dispensing a "natural substance or device."[32] Other states allow naturopaths to prescribe over-the-counter medications, nonprescription substances, and certain prescription drugs;[33] to perform minor surgery;[34] or, with appropriate training, to facilitate natural childbirth.[35] Licensing statutes tend to view naturopaths as primary caregivers.[36]

Homeopathy

Like definitions of chiropractic, massage therapy, and naturopathy, legislative definitions of homeopathy suggest a trend toward tolerance of a more varied view of health than biomedicine presently endorses. Homeopathy, in the state of Washington, means "a system of medicine based on the use of infinitesimal doses of medicines capable of producing symptoms similar to those of the disease treated, as listed in the homeopathic pharmacopeia of the United States."[37] Nevada and Arizona, each of which has a separate homeopathic licensing board, refer to the homeopathic principle "that a substance which produces symptoms in a healthy person can eliminate those symptoms in an ill person."[38] In Arizona, the practice of homeopathy includes "acupuncture, neuromuscular integration, orthomolecular therapy, nutrition, chelation therapy, pharmaceutical medicine and minor surgery."[39]

The training required to administer homeopathic medicines varies by state. For example, Nevada requires that the applicant have a medical degree from an accredited medical or osteopathic school and have received one year of postgraduate training in biomedicine or osteopathic medicine and six months of postgraduate training in homeopathy.[40] Other states allow nonphysician providers such as chiropractors, naturopaths, physical therapists, and veterinarians to use homeopathy as part of their legislatively authorized scope of practice.[41]

Acupuncture

Well over half the states license the practice of acupuncture or traditional oriental medicine.[42] Some states limit practice by requiring, for example, that "initial acupuncture treatment shall only be performed on presentation by the patient of a referral by or diagnosis from a licensed physician,"[43] or that the acupuncturist immediately request a consultation or recent written diagnosis from a licensed physician when the acupuncturist sees patients with "potentially serious disorders such as cardiac conditions, acute abdominal symptoms, and such other conditions."[44] Some states limit the practice of acupuncture to licensed physicians, osteopaths, and chiropractors, or permit nonphysician practice of acupuncture "in general collaboration" with physicians or osteopaths,[45] or require that the acupuncturist be "employed by and work under the physical direction, control, and supervision" of a physician.[46] Still others include acupuncture within the scope of practice of such professions as chiropractic (with appropriate training),[47] authorize acupuncture training as part of continuing physician education,[48] or authorize limited acupuncture practice for the specific purpose of treating drug and alcohol abuse in a clinical setting.[49]

Acupuncture reflects an approach to health based on manipulation of chi. The statutes describe acupuncture as the insertion of needles into the body or treatment of the body by mechanical, thermal, or electrical stimula-

43

tion, to regulate the "flow and balance of energy" in the body.[50] Maryland describes acupuncture as "a form of health care, based on a theory of energetic physiology."[51] Nevada states: "Traditional Oriental medicine means that system of the healing arts which places the chief emphasis on the flow and balance of energy in the body mechanism as being the most important single factor in maintaining the well-being of the organism in health and disease."[52]

Acupuncture statutes broadly refer to acupuncture "diagnosis" and "treatment." Colorado defines acupuncture as "a system of health care based upon traditional oriental medicine concepts that employs oriental methods of diagnosis, treatment, and adjunctive therapies for the promotion, maintenance, and restoration of health and the prevention of disease."[53] Maine provides that acupuncture, while "based on traditional oriental theories," "serves to normalize physiological function, treat certain diseases and dysfunctions of the body, prevent or modify the perception of pain and promote health and well-being."[54] New Mexico defines acupuncture as the use of needles to pierce the skin as well as "all allied techniques of oriental medicine, both traditional and modern," for the "diagnosis, prevention, cure or correction of any disease or pain."[55] Other states mention herbal medicine and specific techniques of oriental medicine.[56] Nutritional counseling, therapeutic massage, and lifestyle counseling also are included.[57]

The statutes sometimes include procedures such as "tonification," the "process of increasing the energy flowing along a particular acupuncture point's meridian," or energy channel; and "sedation," the "process of decreasing the energy flowing along a particular acupuncture point's meridian."[58] In New York and other states, acupuncture may be used for the treatment of alcoholism, substance dependency, or chemical dependency in a hospital or clinic program that has appropriate approval.[59] A drug intervention and case management program called S.T.O.P. (sanction, treatment, opportunity, progress), managed by the Multnomah County District Attorney and Public Defender Offices in Oregon, "sentences" drug use defendants to treatment, including counseling and acupuncture, instead of prison; successful completion of the program results in the indictment being dismissed.[60] Administrators report substantial cost savings in attorney and court time, a reduction in the property crimes used to fund drug use, and a reduction in chemical dependency among participants (7–14).

Legislative efforts to license modalities such as chiropractic, massage therapy, hypnosis, acupuncture, and naturopathy reflect a regulatory effort to bring complementary and alternative medicine into a health care system focused on pharmaceutical and surgical intervention.[61] By including diagnosis and treatment in many of the licensing definitions, and by incorporating such concepts as "energy flow" and "balance" into legislative authorization, licensing statutes erode the notion that healing can be recognized as valid only when scientifically legitimated by double-blind, controlled, randomized studies or otherwise accepted by biomedical orthodoxy.

Lay Practice

Because states license many varieties of complementary and alternative providers, the nonlicensed practitioner risks prosecution not only under medical practice acts but also under professional practice acts covering psychology, massage, chiropractic, and other fields; many of these statutes prohibit unlicensed practice.[62] For example, in *Feingold v. Commonwealth of Pennsylvania, State Board of Chiropractic,* an undercover state investigator visited an unlicensed provider. The defendant engaged in "crossing investigator's legs over the other, and further placing his knee behind the investigator's knee while his hands were on the investigator's arms and shoulders . . . pressing downward, [until] a 'pop' sounded from the investigator's back." The court upheld the defendant's conviction for the unlicensed practice of chiropractic.[63] Because states such as Pennsylvania neither license nor prohibit the unauthorized practice of massage, providers such as the defendant in *Feingold* must be careful not to cross the line into chiropractic. Similarly, in other jurisdictions, chiropractors, massage therapists, and other providers who engage emotional material underlying dysfunction must be careful not to cross the line into counseling or psychology.[64]

Providers' risk of prosecution for unauthorized practice is greatest where statutes are drafted in an exclusive or monopolistic fashion. An example is a Texas statute that includes "hypnosis for health purposes, hypnotherapy, and biofeedback" in its definition of the practice of psychology.[65] The state requires those practicing hypnotherapy to obtain licensure in psychology, or risk prosecution for the unauthorized practice of psychology. Under the Texas statute, not only lay hypnotherapists but also licensed professionals (such as chiropractors) who practice hypnotherapy but whose legislatively defined scope of practice does not expressly include it risk prosecution for the unauthorized practice of psychology. By contrast, some statutes include, within the alternative provider's scope of practice, an ancillary modality on a nonexclusive basis. In this case, authorizing the licensed provider to offer the modality (such as hypnotherapy) does not prohibit either unlicensed providers or other types of licensed providers from offering that healing modality. For instance, several states expressly authorize acupuncturists, chiropractors, or naturopaths to offer homeopathy.[66] In Montana, homeopathy is "not the exclusive privilege of naturopathic physicians" but may be offered by non-naturopaths, including lay practitioners, without violating naturopathic licensing laws.[67]

Legislatively Authorized Boundaries of Practice

Scope-of-practice limitations aim to ensure that providers offer services according to their skill and training and do not induce overreliance by patients on nonmedical therapies for a cure. Chiropractic furnishes an example. Chiropractic training focuses on the impact of the nervous system and spinal health on overall well-being. Thus, chiropractic treatment may facilitate the individual's return to wholeness through manipulation, but a patient with a life-threatening illness should not rely on that treatment to cure the disease. Courts sometimes err on the side of finding scope-of-practice violations, in part because they have not — to date — embraced holistic notions of health, in which providers are viewed as using a particular set of skills to help heal whole persons. Because the prevailing legal paradigm describes the scope of practice in terms of function (e.g., the notion that only medical doctors "diagnose" and "treat" patients, whereas chiropractors deal solely with spinal alignment), judicial decisions create blurred boundaries between the professions. Exceeding the statutorily authorized scope of practice can lead to investigation and disciplinary action by both the relevant professional licensing board and the state medical board. Furthermore, providers who exceed their statutorily authorized scope of practice may be found to have unlawfully practiced another licensed healing modality, such as medicine.[68]

As noted, some providers of complementary and alternative medicine hold ideas about health and disease that fundamentally challenge those of biomedicine.[69] The relationship between these practitioners and the medical profession is "unstable, full of unresolved conflict and tension."[70] Further, unlike dependent practitioners, who practice under physician supervision or referral, chiropractors, naturopaths, and acupuncturists prefer to receive patients directly. Thus, legal limitations on the scope of practice also trace the political and economic relationship between biomedicine and its challengers. Scope-of-practice issues become particularly acute as providers explore new therapeutic techniques and as the health care industry places increasing emphasis on healing modalities outside conventional medical practice.

Scope of Practice: The Case of Chiropractic

Chiropractic provides an informative example of scope-of-practice issues because, although chiropractors have well-established licensure in every state, many incorporate into their practice a broad range of therapeutic techniques that test the scope of their licensure. With chiropractic, the conflict over scope of practice may be inevitable: chiropractors address spinal and nervous system issues in patients with a variety of conditions, whereas biomedicine claims the exclusive authority to diagnose and treat, and many physicians would either limit chiropractors to spinal problems or, ideally, eliminate them. While each profession has unique scope-of-practice issues, chiropractic scope of practice is paradigmatic of the legal system's ability to accommodate, define, or integrate holistic health care.

Nutritional Care

Chiropractors' attempts to incorporate nutritional care into professional practice have been controversial, and in many ways parallel consumers' efforts to obtain greater freedom of access to vitamins, minerals, and food supplements (see chap. 6). The legal controversy may seem surprising, since relatively few biomedical physicians presently utilize nutritional support as an integral part of ongoing treatment. However, to the extent that nutrition involves a nontechnological path to wellness, embracing the patient's attempt at self-nourishment, nutritional care demythologizes medical authority and returns responsibility for self-care to patients.[71]

Some statutes include nutritional care within chiropractic scope of practice. Even if the practice is included, however, providers must examine the authorizing statute for limitations or restrictions in the authorizing language. For instance, Iowa permits "rendering nutritional advice" but prohibits a chiropractor from "profit from the sale of nutritional products coinciding with the nutritional advice rendered."[72] West Virginia's chiropractic licensing statute does not expressly authorize nutritional guidance but provides that "patient care and management is conducted with due regard for environmental and nutritional factors."[73] Louisiana provides that a chiropractor "may also make recommendations relative to the personal hygiene and proper nutritional practices for the rehabilitation of the patient,"[74] while Massachusetts permits "dietary and nutritional advice, as treatment supplemental to a chiropractic adjustment."[75] In each case, the chiropractor's ability to provide clients with nutritional guidance is qualified. It must be closely related to the chiropractic service, and the nutritional advice cannot cross the line into medical "treatment," although where the line lies is unclear.

In *Stockwell v. Washington State Chiropractic Disciplinary Board*,[76] a chiropractor challenged the result of a disciplinary action sanctioning him for, among other things, selling and dispensing vitamins. The relevant licensing statute did in fact authorize chiropractors to give "dietary advice." The court, nonetheless, held that mere advice differed from prescribing vitamins to treat disease. The court did not clarify the difference between "advice" and "prescription." In fact, the court acknowledged that the recommended vitamins and food supplements were commonly available in retail stores (914).

Other courts similarly have found chiropractors who recommended vitamins and food supplements to their patients to have engaged in the unlicensed practice of medicine.[77] *Foster v. Board of Chiropractor Examiners* involved administrative proceedings to sanction a licensed chiropractor for dispensing nutritional substances to a patient.[78] Although the substances that the defendant recommended were sold without prescription and were commonly available in health food stores, the state claimed that the chiropractor had engaged in prescribing drugs and thus had exceeded the statutorily authorized scope of practice. Georgia's definition of chiropractic was silent on nutritional care but authorized "utiliz[ing] the inherent recuperative powers of the body, particularly of the spinal column and the nervous system, in the restoration and maintenance of health."[79] The statute also prohibited the use of "drugs or surgery" by chiropractors and provided that chiropractors could not "prescribe or administer medicine to patients" (882).

The court held that the legislature did not intend to extend chiropractic beyond "existing statutory authorization to adjust the articulation of the human body according to specific chiropractic methods."[80] It further held that Georgia law did not authorize chiropractors to prescribe or dispense vitamins, minerals, or nutritional substances, and that such acts constituted the unauthorized practice of medicine. The *Foster* court relied on the limiting statutory language relating to drugs or surgery, rather than the broader statutory language referring to chiropractors' role in the maintenance of health and flow of nerve energy. In neither *Stockwell* nor *Foster* did the court accept the defendant's argument that nutrition is an inherent part of supporting the body's recuperative powers, which is essential to chiropractic care, to the holistic view of health, and to the legislative definition of chiropractic as embracing a view of health geared to the whole being.[81] Neither decision clearly drew the line between nutritional advice and medical drug prescription.

Colonic Irrigation

As with nutritional care, statutes vary as to whether they expressly prohibit or permit chiropractors' use of colonic irrigation.[82] Some jurisdictions, such as Washington, D.C., require additional certification for chiropractors desiring to include "counseling about hygienic and other noninvasive ancillary procedures."[83] Many statutes are silent, and judicial interpretations vary.

For instance, in *Ohio State Board of Chiropractic Examiners v. Fulk*,[84] the court held that colonic irrigation was within the scope of chiropractic practice. The defendant chiropractor had referred patients to an individual for colonic irrigations.[85] The individual was not a licensed chiropractor, was not licensed to perform such irrigations, and was not supervised by the chiropractor.[86] The court held that the colonic irrigations were "sufficiently related to hygienic and nutritional procedures in conjunction with musculoskeletal treatment" that it was not an abuse of discretion for the chiropractic board to find that the procedure fell within chiropractic practice.[87] Moreover, the court observed that the relevant statute listed procedures that chiropractors were restricted from performing; colonic irrigations were not included.

Although *Fulk* dealt with referral to an unlicensed practitioner, the decision suggests that, contrary to the approach in *Stockwell* and *Foster*, a court can find a procedure within the scope of a licensed complementary and alternative practice precisely because it has not been expressly excluded. Rather than viewing chiropractic as a "limited" healing art in contradistinction to biomedicine, the court in *Fulk* viewed chiropractic expansively, as supporting well-being through nutritional and hygienic measures complementary to spinal adjustment.

Acupuncture and Other Modalities

Arizona and Colorado are two states that expressly permit chiropractors the practice of acupuncture, while Louisiana and Ohio prohibit the practice.[88] In many other states, legislative guidance is absent. In such cases, courts rely on their conception of chiropractic as limited to spinal problems, or read such a limitation into legislative intent. For example, in *Stockwell v. Washington State Chiropractic Disciplinary Board*,[89] the defendant chiropractor, who included "meridian therapy" in his practice, was charged with practicing acupuncture. The therapy involved using pressure on acupuncture points on the body to relieve pain. The chiropractor attempted to distinguish meridian therapy from acupuncture by arguing that acupuncture required the piercing of skin and thus was prohibited as a "surgical act."

The court agreed that the chiropractor had not practiced acupuncture, since he had not pierced the skin. Nonetheless, because the chiropractor had, among other things, prescribed and sold massive doses of vitamins and had used urinalysis to detect cancer, the court found that revocation of his license was not arbitrary and capricious.

In *Acupuncture Society v. Kansas State Board of Healing Arts*,[90] the Kansas Supreme Court analyzed whether the legislature had intended to grant chiropractors the right to use acupuncture. The trial court, denying chiropractors this right, had made a finding of fact that "acupuncture, being neither 'fish nor fowl,' is a separate modality of treatment and is not a natural part of any other modality of treatment" (1313). The Kansas Supreme Court, reversing this decision, observed that acupuncture "certainly was not a natural part of any other modality or treatment known to the branches of the healing arts because it was not known to the Western World until the early 1970's [but in fact] was adopted by all three branches of the healing arts [medicine and surgery, osteopathy, and chiropractic] in the early 1970's, and became a modality of their treatment" (1314). The court further criticized the lower court's conclusions of law, including a holding that because acupuncture involves "the piercing of skin for treatment, not diagnostic purposes," it constitutes the practice of surgery, which was legislatively forbidden to chiropractors (1313). According to the Kansas Supreme Court, "surgery is what surgeons do — sever the tissues of the body for the purpose of penetration for treatment, replacement or removal of afflicted parts" (1315). The court agreed with the conclusion in *Stockwell* that the piercing of skin by a solid wire or needle for the purpose of acupuncture was not surgery.

Other courts have held that acupuncture constitutes the practice of surgery and hence is forbidden to chiropractors under medical practice acts.[91] In *Commonwealth v. Schatzberg*,[92] the court upheld a regulation by the State Board of Chiropractic Examiners, promulgated pursuant to advice from the state attorney general, which stated that the acupuncture was not within chiropractors' scope of practice. Chiropractic, according to the court, is "limited . . . [to] . . . the relationship between the nervous system . . . [and] misaligned or displaced vertebrae and other articulations."[93] Acupuncture deals with the "vital essence of the human body [which] is a mixture of Yin and Yang [and] is conveyed through the body in ducts or meridians which emerge at the surface of the body at certain designated points, at which points vital energy can be influenced by manipulation" (546). Crucial to the court's decision was its reliance on testimony that "there is little but speculation on why or how acupuncture works"; the notion that acupuncture is "of ancient Chinese origin and is based on the Chinese medical concept"; the legislative reference to chiropractic as a "limited science"; and the exclusion of chiropractors from the practice of medicine (546).[94]

Physical Examination and Other Procedures

The view of chiropractic as limited to spinal manipulation has dominated judicial interpretations of licensing statutes even when the challenged act appears to be an integral part of responsible practice. In *State v. Beno*,[95] the Michigan Supreme Court held that the scope of chiropractic does not include a general physical examination of a patient complaining of low back pain and a sore elbow. The defendant chiropractor argued that chiropractors were authorized to "diagnose an elbow ailment to determine [whether the] cause is local (i.e., originates in the elbow area) or results from nerve interference created by spinal subluxations or misalignments" (549–50). The attorney general argued that "the treatment of or attempt to treat an extremity falls outside the statutory authority of a chiropractor and constitutes the practice of medicine" (550).[96] The opinions expressed at different levels of review suggest contrasting legal perspectives on holistic health care and chiropractic scope of practice.

The hearing officer concluded that "x-ray of an elbow is outside the scope of chiropractic," since the "statute is clear and it stretches logic as to how the x-ray of a right elbow is any way encompassed by" the statutory authorization (551). Although Michigan's Board of Chiropractic, disagreeing, maintained that "diagnosis may involve other parts of the body since the nerve network, efferent from the spinal column, affects other parts of the body," the trial court found that "it stretches credibility to conclude that the elbow is so related to the spine that spinal subluxations or misalignments may produce nerve interference in the elbow. The logic of this position would extend chiropractic through the entire body and even the brain!"[97]

The Michigan Court of Appeals accepted the chiropractor's view that "nerve interference efferent [from] the spinal column may produce symptoms in other parts of the body."[98] The Michigan Supreme Court, reversing this decision, acknowledged the "hazy line between the jurisdiction of the health care professions" but emphasized its duty to interpret the chiropractic licensing statute so as to secure "protection of the health, safety, and welfare of the people of this state."[99] The court adopted the view that the chiropractor was not authorized to "examine the elbow to determine if there is nerve interference," since "the existence of a spinal subluxation or misalignment cannot be observed by examin[ing] areas away from the spine that may be experiencing the pain of nerve interference" (552–53). The court reasoned that giving chiropractors such diagnostic authority could mislead the patient into believing that a definitive diagnosis as to nonspinal injuries has been made, particularly in light of the chiropractor's testimony that "we must look wholistically, at the entire body."[100]

Thus, the prosecution, hearing officer, trial judge, and state supreme court in *Beno* all viewed chiropractic and spinal and nervous system health as disconnected from the rest of the body (e.g., the elbow). They further interpreted the policy goal of protecting patients' health as a mandate to limit, rather than support, the complementary and alternative provider's practice authority.

This perspective is echoed in decisions such as *Zabrecky v. Connecticut Board of Chiropractors,* in which the court held that a statute authorizing chiropractors to "treat the human body . . . by the oral administration of foods, food concentrates, food extracts or vitamins" did not authorize the defendant chiropractor to inject a substance or inform the patient about injecting a substance into the body.[101] According to the court, the purpose of the injection was "to treat the patient's cancer rather than any condition legally treatable by the practice of chiropractic."[102] Again, the line between treating disease and "treat[ing] the human body by" nutrition is left unclear. Further, the reference to "any condition legally treatable" implies that chiropractors may provide chiropractic care to patients with some conditions but not others (such as cancer).

The argument that chiropractors are limited to spinal manipulation has arisen in a variety of contexts. In *State Board of Chiropractic Examiners v. Clark*,[103] a chiropractor was charged by his own professional regulatory board with exceeding his scope of practice, with engaging in the practice of medicine, physical therapy, and cosmetology, and with engaging in fraud, deception, or misrepresentation in advertising his activities to the public (621). The chiropractor had used and advertised a helium neon laser, in conjunction with manipulation, for a treatment known as biostimulation. The device in question directed a beam of light toward certain points along "twelve energy channels" on the human body, known as acupuncture points. According to the chiropractor's testimony, the use of the laser, in conjunction with manipulation, was a procedure taught and approved by Missouri chiropractic colleges.

The board's evidence against the chiropractor consisted of a deposition of the chiropractor, an FDA paper cautioning against the use of the neon laser, and a copy of the chiropractor's advertisement. The relevant statute defined chiropractic as "the science and art of examination, diagnosis, adjustment, manipulation and treatment of malpositioned articulations and structures of the human body."[104] The board urged a narrow interpretation of this definition, limiting chiropractic to the "science and art of palpating and adjusting by hand the movable articulations of the human spinal column" (626). The court disagreed, observing that the board supported the development and teaching of expanded techniques such as biostimulation in chiropractic schools, and that the board had failed to carry its burden of proof that the defendant had engaged in the practice of medicine, physical therapy, or cosmetology. Finally, the court found no fraud, since the defendant had advertised a technique that was taught in chiropractic schools and in which he was trained.

A similarly broad view of chiropractic is found in chiropractic statutes that authorize a range of ancillary methods. For example, Alaska includes among chiropractic techniques "counseling on dietary regimen, sanitary measures, physical and mental attitudes affecting health, personal hygiene, occupational safety, lifestyle habits, posture, rest, and work habits that enhance the effects of chiropractic adjustment."[105] In some states, chiropractors' scope of practice is broadened to include areas of practice within the biomedical model, such as the taking of x-rays,[106] urine analysis,[107] the taking or ordering of blood tests and other routine laboratory tests, and the performance of physical examinations.[108]

Addressing Scope-of-Practice Risks

The "straight" school of chiropractic focuses exclusively on analyzing the spinal column to detect and eliminate nervous system interferences known as "vertebral subluxations." The "mixing" school uses a variety of procedures, including the manipulation of the body and soft tissues, massage, physical therapy, nutrition, acupuncture, counseling, hypnotherapy, and minor surgery. The mixing chiropractor believes in "expanding his professional armamentarium" to increase his or her professional range.[109] Thus, the mixer is "legislatively active to further broaden the law to . . . expan[d] his services" (365). As mixers move more deeply into the biomedical model, their practices will become more palatable to some referring physicians and to insurance adjusters but also may lead to increased malpractice risk (see chap. 5) and diminish reliance on holism.

Complementary and alternative providers and health care institutions utilizing such providers must examine whether procedures and therapies such as nutritional support, colonic hydrotherapy, acupuncture, diagnostic tests, and physical examinations exceed express legislative authorization. Further, because the line between dietary advice and treatment is unclear, providers should check decisions under applicable medical practice acts and their own licensing statutes. Selling dietary substances directly may be prohibited, and recommending nutritional changes to patients may be viewed as crossing the line into "prescribing" or "treating" under the medical practice acts. Providers face less risk when they recommend nutritional products for conditions relating to their authorized practice, as when chiropractors recommend B-complex vitamins to strengthen the nervous system. Providers face greater risk if they make nutritional recommendations for acute, chronic, or life-threatening conditions such as diabetes or cancer.

Definitions of the scope of practice must remain broad enough to permit innovation and creativity, yet contain enough precision to keep providers within the bounds of professional knowledge and skill.[110] Providers need to clarify that they are providing services within their scope of practice, particularly with patients who have serious or life-threatening diseases. Providers of services such as chiropractic should consider having their patients acknowledge in writing that the provider does not have an M.D. degree and does not diagnose and treat disease. The form should advise the patient to consult a licensed physician for diagnosis and treatment of any medical condition. The form also should state what the provider is legally authorized to do — for instance, in Delaware, "locating and removing any interference with the transmission of nerve energy." Such written documentation can help providers be clear about the risks and benefits of particular therapies. Providers thus can minimize the risk that clients' inflated expectations may lead to misunderstandings.

Although providers may lobby legislatures to include specific therapies in the applicable licensing statutes, novel practices will emerge which elude or defy statutory definition. Moreover, expanding the scope of practice can create professional turf battles between nonmedical professions if one group lobbies for exclusive control of a particular practice — such as counseling or colonic irrigation. Ultimately, the blurring of the lines with regard to scope of practice may lead to the displacement of mandatory licensure by title licensure or basic registration for nonmedical complementary and alternative professionals.

MALPRACTICE AND VICARIOUS LIABILITY

Physicians' Malpractice Liability

Malpractice is defined as unskillful practice that fails to conform to a standard of care in the profession and results in injury to the patient. Since complementary and alternative medicine is presently defined in terms of treatments (such as chelation therapy, ozone therapy, homeopathy, and nutritional and herbal treatments) not commonly taught in medical education or used in U.S. hospitals,[1] physicians integrating these treatments into conventional care depart from biomedical norms of practice—almost by definition—and thus risk liability for malpractice. Moreover, legislatures and courts frequently look to a lack of general medical acceptance of specific procedures or a lack of FDA approval as indicative of failure to follow the standard of care.

The Case of Chelation Therapy

Chelation therapy involves the use of the compound ethylenediaminetetraacetic acid (EDTA), together with vitamins and minerals, purportedly to clean out the arteries by breaking down arterial plaque. Chelation treatments were widely used during World War II to treat sailors who had lead paint poisoning. Since then, studies have been published concerning the effect of chelation on various parts of the body. Chelation is said to remove calcium deposits from the interior walls of blood vessels. Proponents claim that EDTA chelation helps to prevent circulatory disease, angina, heart attacks, and strokes and thus is an alternative to bypass surgery.[2]

The American College for Advancement in Medicine, the American Board of Chelation Therapy, and the American Holistic Medical Association have trained more than one thousand physicians to treat occlusive arterial disease with EDTA. These organizations, and providers receiving their training, claim that chelation therapy is more effective and safer than bypass surgery, from which approximately twelve thousand patients die annually.[3] But other professional organizations, citing the insufficiency of proper studies, have declined to accept EDTA as a proven treatment for cardiac disease or declare the treatment dangerous.[4]

The Food and Drug Administration has approved chelation therapy for the treatment of lead poisoning but not for the treatment of cardiac conditions such as blocked carotid arteries. The use of chelation therapy for heart conditions thus falls within the category of "off-label use." Off-label use occurs when physicians dispense medical drugs or devices for purposes other than those originally authorized by the FDA.

The FDA does not prohibit off-label use and, in fact, has stated: "Once [an approved] new drug is in a local pharmacy after interstate shipment, the physician may, as part of the practice of medicine, lawfully . . . vary the conditions of use from those approved in the package insert, without informing or obtaining the approval of the Food and Drug Administration. . . . Congress did not intend . . . [to] regulate the practice of medicine as between the physician and the patient."[5] Off-label use is widespread in the medical profession, especially in cancer treatment.[6]

Although off-label use of chelation therapy is not prohibited by current FDA rules, physicians using the therapy risk liability under state malpractice rules. In a malpractice action, the patient will claim that bypass surgery is the standard procedure for the patient's condition and that chelation therapy falls below the accepted standard of care. Since chelation therapy is not generally accepted in the medical literature or approved by the FDA for the treatment of arteriosclerosis, the provider may be vulnerable to this kind of claim. The court may be tempted to equate nonstandard care, which involves the choice of a therapy other than the one generally used for the condition in question (e.g., chelation therapy rather than bypass surgery), with substandard care — care that falls below the standard in the community and constitutes malpractice. Even if significant scientific evidence exists to show that chelation therapy is efficacious or results in positive outcomes for patients, courts may view the very selection of a nonstandard therapy as a failure to provide the requisite level of professional care.[7] At least one state has provided by statute that using chelation therapy to treat arteriosclerosis or any other condition (except heavy metal poisoning) without FDA approval constitutes unprofessional conduct,[8] which subjects the provider to disciplinary action, and in turn can trigger a civil malpractice action.

One potential defense available to physicians offering such treatments as chelation therapy is the "respectable minority," or "two schools of thought," defense. This defense provides that a physician who undertakes a mode of treatment which a respectable minority within the profession would undertake under similar circumstances does not incur liability for malpractice. In other words, physicians may choose between alternative approaches to diagnosis and treatment, so long as the approach they eventually select is accepted by a respectable minority in the medical community.

However, courts differ as to what constitutes a respectable minority. Some courts permit the respectable minority defense where there is only one physician in the community following a particular approach, whereas other courts require that the minority's view be adopted by a certain number of physicians; still others require that the minority view be "reasonable and prudent."[9] The rather fluid and imprecise contours of the defense may be further exaggerated in the case of complementary and alternative medicine, given the controversial nature of some of the therapies, the methodological challenges raised in chapter 1, and shifting levels of acceptance within the biomedical community. At least in reviewing a disciplinary proceeding, one court has found that a physician failed to follow even a respectable minority in the medical profession when offering metabolic therapy, using laetrile, in conjunction with chemotherapy.[10]

The defense of clinical innovation also may offer limited protection to physicians providing complementary and alternative therapies. The doctrine shields from malpractice liability those physicians who choose innovative therapeutic procedures to help particular patients or alleviate desperate situations.[11] The defense is available so long as the physician has not violated applicable legal rules, such as those requiring institutional review board approval for experimental or research-oriented therapeutic procedures.[12] However, the courts limit the defense to the use of innovative therapeutic procedures to help particular patients or alleviate desperate situations. Courts thus may not extend the clinical innovation defense to treatments outside the biomedical model or treatments provided to general patient populations.

Physicians' best defense against malpractice claims in these situations is rigorous biomedical research and responsible medical education to establish the complementary and alternative treatment as an appropriate choice for the condition in question. As medical schools further incorporate complementary and alternative therapies into the curricula, and conventional physicians increase their use of complementary and alternative therapies or their referral of patients to providers for such therapies, standards of care in medical communities and in medical malpractice cases will begin to incorporate these modalities.

Physicians facing malpractice claims then will be able to introduce expert testimony to demonstrate that the complementary and alternative therapy has, in fact, come within the standard of care for the condition in question. For example, if chelation therapy becomes more generally accepted in the prevention or treatment of cardiac disease, then malpractice exposure for using chelation therapy itself will diminish. Similarly, if herbal or homeopathic remedies are found to be as or more safe and efficacious than prescription medication for certain conditions, then using such remedies will fall within the standard of care. In fact, to the extent biomedical education and practice lag behind data showing that complementary and alternative therapies improve patient outcomes, utilizing such treatments may be considered providing care above, rather than below, the standard of care.

Paradoxically, more data regarding efficacy could increase the liability of conventional health care professionals for failure to incorporate complementary and alternative modalities. For example, one can imagine, on the basis of present research, that future investigation could uncover and validate cancer therapies complementary or alternative to, and less toxic than, chemotherapy and radiation; or that specific herbal or homeopathic remedies might be proven safe and effective for certain chronic conditions; or that therapies such as chiropractic, massage, acupuncture, or nutritional treatment might be indicated for relief of conditions such as chronic pain and drug addiction. Similarly, the interesting suggestion has been raised that if prayer is shown to be efficacious in treating disease, a physician will be negligent for failing to pray for the patient (or meditate on the patient's health) as part of standard treatment.[13]

In such cases, physicians who dismiss complementary and alternative treatments as quackery and rely entirely on conventional care might be held liable in medical malpractice for providing professional healing below the standard of care. Further, patients might claim damages for emotional distress resulting from their physicians' failure to disclose adjunctive therapies that could have reduced the level of physical or emotional injury (such as using massage therapy and acupuncture to control certain side effects of chemotherapy).[14]

Informed Consent

The common law doctrine of informed consent provides that an individual has the right to determine what will be done with his or her own body.[15] The doctrine protects the patient's bodily integrity by requiring the physician to disclose all information pertinent to the patient's decision to submit to a particular medical procedure. Informed consent also is a fundamental principle in the regulation of research involving human subjects.[16] The principle first was articulated in the Nuremberg Code, which was promulgated after the disclosure of experiments conducted by Nazi physicians in the concentration camps.[17]

In assessing the adequacy of informed consent obtained from patients before procedures, courts generally require the provider to have described the diagnosis (including testing and test results), the nature and purpose of treatment, the material risks and possible outcomes, the prognosis with treatment, the prognosis if treatment is declined, conflicts of interest or other information relevant to assessing the provider's motivations, and alternative methods of diagnosis and treatment.[18] Most states require the kind of disclosure of alternative methods and treatments that a reasonable medical practitioner would make under the circumstances. This includes "feasible and available" conventional medical treatments but does not usually include alternative therapies.[19] For example, the Minnesota Supreme Court held that informed consent requirements do not mandate disclosure that in-home birth is a viable alternative to management of pregnancy in a hospital.[20] A Louisiana appellate court held that disclosure of alternatives to chemotherapy was not required, since "in conventional medical wisdom, the alternative to chemotherapy in this situation would be simply to not undergo chemotherapy." According to the court, "even with information concerning the relatively low documented positive response rate, a reasonable patient who feared the recurrence of cancer would not have foregone chemotherapy."[21]

The informed consent doctrine, as presently conceived, insufficiently protects patients' interest in therapies outside biomedicine. For one thing, as the above cases suggest, the doctrine evolved within the biomedical framework and has not yet expanded to embrace choices outside that paradigm. For example, patients may wish to forgo the toxicity of chemotherapy in favor of nutritional, lifestyle-related, or other approaches to recovery from cancer; yet oncologists probably have no duty, under current informed consent standards, to disclose and discuss such approaches.

Marjorie Shultz has argued that vindication of patients' autonomy by requiring disclosure of certain information should not depend on whether the information is the kind that physicians typically disclose.[22] Rather, informed consent requirements should seek to fill the patient's need for information, and thus incorporate the full spectrum of available health care treatments. Moreover, Shultz argues, informed consent as presently conceived inadequately protects patients' autonomy in at least three relevant respects. First, where courts tie informed consent to the law of battery, the doctrine fails to protect the patient from nondisclosure in cases that do not involve nonconsensual physical contact.[23] Second, courts often use informed consent to protect medical choice but not to protect patients' interest in balance and wholeness.[24] Third, under the informed consent doctrine, certain outcomes are not recognized as injuries. Shultz provides the example of the patient who, properly informed, would have chosen a lumpectomy rather than a radical mastectomy. A court probably would deem an operation that wiped out the cancer but removed the breast "successful." In other words, the court would recognize the biomedical notion of curing but not a patient-centered universe of healing. Biomedicine dominates informed consent, since the injury resulting from inadequate disclosure is defined within the medical model.

The doctrine of informed consent could, however, evolve to undergird a right of access to complementary and alternative medicine. Whereas the respectable minority and clinical innovation doctrines serve as shields to liability, expanded informed consent rules, like more inclusive standards of care, serve to stimulate greater physician use of complementary and alternative therapies. *Moore v. Baker* involved a malpractice claim based on a failure to offer chelation therapy.[25] In *Moore,* the patient had a blockage in her carotid artery, which impeded the flow of oxygen to her brain. After a brief recovery from surgery, a blood clot developed. The physician had to reopen the operative wound, but the clot already had caused the patient permanent brain damage.

The relevant statute required physicians, before performing surgery, to inform patients of the risks and of alternatives "generally recognized and accepted by reasonably prudent physicians."[26] The patient sued for malpractice, on the basis of the neurologist's failure to disclose the existence of chelation therapy as an alternative to a carotid endarterectomy. The complaint alleged that EDTA was as effective as a carotid endarterectomy and less risky, and that the physician had failed to inform the patient fully, as a result of which, the patient agreed to the surgery.

To determine whether such nondisclosure constituted malpractice, the court reviewed the evidence regarding the acceptance of chelation therapy. The court concluded that although some physicians approved of chelation therapy, the plaintiff did not show that reasonably prudent physicians generally recognized and accepted the treatment. Therefore, the plaintiff did not prove that the physician had violated Georgia's informed consent statute.[27] The court's decision presumably would have changed if the plaintiff had been able to show that there was a sufficient level of professional recognition of EDTA chelation therapy as an appropriate treatment for her condition.

In *Gemme v. Goldberg*,[28] a Connecticut appellate court upheld the patient's informed consent claim in a case in which the physician had failed to inform the patient that corrective surgery was elective and that a more conservative treatment plan (involving dental bridgework) was an option. The court held that the jury reasonably could have concluded that the physician had breached the duty to obtain informed consent "by failing to disclose a viable alternative that might have produced a less perfect result but may have represented a safer or less invasive procedure" (326). Such an expanded view of the informed consent doctrine could increase conventional physicians' use of complementary and alternative medicine by requiring the disclosure of safe, efficacious choices outside the biomedical model.[29]

Some view informed consent as a poor substitute for well-formed agreements between parties and argue that the doctrine should not be extended beyond biomedicine and biomedical choices. In this view, structuring relationships between provider and patient to clarify roles and expectations about healing methods and outcomes provides a clearer, contractual means by which parties can expand treatment choices to include complementary and alternative medicine. Such an approach encourages the use of holistic modalities in a nonreductionistic manner (i.e., to nourish, stimulate, and balance vital energy, rather than to treat biomedically defined pathology).[30] This position in turn suggests a larger debate over the appropriateness of applying legal rules tied to the medical model to nonbiomedical, vitalistic forms of healing developed outside the model.

Assumption of Risk

The doctrine of the assumption of risk, by recognizing the patient's responsibility for some treatment choices, also could serve as a shield to malpractice liability for use of complementary and alternative medicine. In

Schneider v. Revici,[31] Edith Schneider learned that a lump had been found in her breast, refused a biopsy, and told her physician that she would seek a practitioner who would treat her nonsurgically. The physician referred her to two general surgeons, each of whom advised her to undergo a biopsy and possibly a partial mastectomy. Schneider instead consulted Emanuel Revici for "non-toxic, non-invasive" methods of cancer treatment that were not generally accepted by the medical community (989).

Schneider signed a detailed consent form acknowledging that Revici's treatments lacked FDA approval and that no guarantees were being made as to treatment results, and releasing Revici from liability. Revici commenced treatment with selenium and with dietary restrictions. He also recommended that Schneider have the tumor surgically removed. After fourteen months, the tumor had increased in size, and cancer had spread to Schneider's lymphatic system and left breast. She finally underwent a bilateral mastectomy, followed by sixteen months of conventional chemotherapy. She sued Revici, alleging common law fraud, medical malpractice, and lack of informed consent.

The jury returned a verdict for Schneider solely on the medical malpractice claim but found that Schneider was 50 percent comparatively negligent, and halved the award. On appeal, the U.S. Court of Appeals for the Second Circuit reversed and remanded for a new trial, holding that, because express assumption of risk was available as an affirmative defense to medical malpractice and, if proved, would totally bar Schneider's claim, the lower court had erred in refusing to instruct the jury on the assumption of risk. The court noted: "We see no reason why a patient should not be allowed to make an informed decision to go outside currently approved medical methods in search of an unconventional treatment. While a patient should be encouraged to exercise care for his own safety, we believe that an informed decision to avoid surgery and conventional chemotherapy is within the patient's right to 'determine what shall be done with his own body.' "[32] The court concluded that the evidence that Schneider had assumed "the risk of refusing conventional treatment to undergo the Revici method" was sufficient to allow the jury to consider the assumption-of-risk defense.[33]

The court also held that evidence as to the effectiveness of Revici's treatment had been improperly excluded by the district judge. The court rejected the plaintiff's argument that the issue in medical malpractice is not the effectiveness of the treatment "but whether that treatment is a deviation from accepted medical practice in the community."[34] In a later case, *Boyle v. Revici*,[35] the U.S. Court of Appeals for the Second Circuit further held that another patient's failure to sign a consent form did not preclude the jury from considering the assumption-of-risk defense. Thus, the jury could consider evidence that the patient "consciously decided not to accept conventional cancer treatment and instead sought Dr. Revici's care, despite known risks of which she was aware" (1063).

The court in *Shorter v. Drury* similarly found assumption of risk a significant barrier to malpractice liability.[36] Shorter, a Jehovah's Witness, bled to death after refusing a blood transfusion when a medical procedure perforated her uterus. Shorter had signed a document releasing the hospital "from any responsibility whatsoever for unfavorable reactions or any untoward results due to my refusal to permit the use of blood or its derivatives" (119). The jury found the physician negligent but reduced damages by 75 percent because of Shorter's assumption of the risk that she would die from bleeding. The court upheld the release, reasoning that the form did not exculpate the physician from his own negligence but only from risks created by the patient's refusal to accept blood transfusions.

The decisions in the two Revici cases and in *Shorter* frame the patient's decision to pursue unconventional treatment in terms of assumption of risk. This shifts the focus from the physician's decision making to the patient's choice. In this way, the assumption-of-risk doctrine provides a basis for the patient's right to select treatment modalities outside biomedical orthodoxy in spite of the objections of a physician or prevailing medical norms. The doctrine can serve to shield from malpractice liability the physician who, in consultation with the patient, chooses complementary and alternative medicine as part of a treatment plan.

Malpractice by Complementary and Alternative Providers
Professional Standards of Care

Generally, a practitioner of complementary and alternative medicine is held to a standard of care appropriate to the profession. For instance, in a malpractice action against a licensed chiropractor, the plaintiff has the burden of proving "the degree of knowledge and skill possessed or the degree of care ordinarily exercised" by practicing chiropractors in similar communities and under similar circumstances.[37] Thus, in general, a chiropractor is held to a chiropractic standard of care, a naturopath to the standard of care of the naturopathic profession, an acupuncturist to the same standard as other acupuncturists, and so on.

Typically, evaluation of malpractice by reference to the individual profession's standard of care is a matter of common law. In some states, the legislature provides a statutory definition for the standard of care to be applied. Nevada, for instance, defines homeopathic malpractice as "failure on the part of a homeopathic physician to exercise the degree of care, diligence and skill ordinarily exercised by homeopathic physicians in good standing in the community in which he practices."[38]

It is often difficult to determine exactly what protocols or procedures are within the standard of care for complementary and alternative medicine. Outside of biomedicine, standards of care are more fluid, because treatments involve widely varying schools of thought and techniques, and highly individualized or nonstandardized methods. Many treatments, such as massage therapy, draw on the provider's intuitive or subjective faculties as much as on uniform, professionally prescribed practices.

Despite the less formalized agreement around standards of care, some professions have established guidelines for practice which could serve as the basis for standards of care in malpractice actions. For example, the American Association of Naturopathic Physicians has issued guidelines to provide general criteria for naturopathic medical practice.[39] The guidelines list a range of therapeutics from which a naturopathic physician may choose, consistent with the legislatively authorized scope of practice in the naturopath's particular state. The therapeutics include acupuncture, homeopathy, natural childbirth, and massage therapy. Among other things, the naturopathic physician is obligated to keep up with changes in professional practice, to make appropriate referrals, to conform with the professional code of ethics, to take thorough histories, to maintain clear records, and to perform appropriate physical and mental examinations. The guidelines establish criteria for making diagnoses using conventional and other diagnostic methods (such as those of Ayurvedic and oriental medicine).

Similar professional standards exist in the chiropractic profession.[40] Both chiropractic and naturopathy are less removed in theory and practice from the biomedical model than are therapies such as acupuncture, which has developed even less formalized consensus around standards of care. Because acupuncturists treat imbalance and chi, rather than biomedically defined conditions or diseases, they do not generally rely on standardized treatments for treating particular ailments. Individual acupuncturists may treat colitis or anxiety differently — for example, varying the number of sessions, the placement of acupuncture needles, and the way in which herbal or other oriental medicine treatments will be used. Standards of care may vary from school to school, from community to community, or even among acupuncturists within the same school or community.

Nonetheless, even in acupuncture, the National Commission for the Certification of Acupuncturists (NCCA), with assistance from the Centers for Disease Control, has developed procedures such as the "clean needle technique" (CNT) as part of its national certification program. The purpose of CNT is to ensure that patients are treated with safe and sterile needles. The NCCA National Board examination requires that applicants demonstrate a knowledge of CNT adequate to maintain safe clinical procedures. Thus, although the acupuncture community to date has not established written guidelines setting forth standards of care for the profession, most courts probably would view CNT as part of the standard of care because the community as a whole accepts it as a baseline for safe clinical practice. A patient injured through unsterilized or contaminated acupuncture needles will probably succeed in a malpractice claim if he or she proves that the acupuncturist violated CNT guidelines.

There is little case law on malpractice claims against complementary and alternative health care providers, not only because standards of care are so diffuse,[41] but also because patients have different expectations of complementary and alternative providers than they do of biomedical physicians. Naturopaths, chiropractors, acupuncturists, massage therapists, and other providers on the whole render individualized and personalized health services, leading to a lower incidence of malpractice litigation.[42] Holistic providers take detailed physical and emotional histories and thus tend to spend more personal time with patients and have more emotional contact with them.[43] These providers ideally have patients take responsibility for supporting the healing process through appropriate nutrition; exercise and movement; meditation, breathing, and stress reduction; lifestyle changes; counseling; and emotional nourishment. They thus reduce malpractice exposure by structuring the provider-patient relationship as a collaborative venture to health. They offer treatments, such as acupuncture, that carry risks that are low and can easily be managed — for example, by learning to maintain patients' safety through proper needling technique.[44]

Heightened Standard of Care

Whereas physicians ordinarily may not testify against a nonmedical provider regarding the provider's professional standard of care, such testimony is permitted where there is an overlap in an area of knowledge or treatment.[45] The complementary and alternative provider then may be held to a heightened, biomedical standard of care. Such a heightened standard is appropriate where the complementary and alternative provider exceeds professional boundaries and moves beyond the legislatively authorized scope of practice. For example, if a chiropractor purports to use spinal manipulation to cure a patient's diabetes, the chiropractor will be held to a biomedical standard of care: the jury will judge the chiropractor's conduct against that of a reasonable biomedical physician under similar circumstances.[46]

In other cases, application of a heightened standard care may simply reflect the jurisdictional allocation of a particular professional practice to biomedical standards. For example, in situations in which chiropractors, pursuant to their legislative authorization, ordinarily take x-rays, perform urine analysis, take or order blood tests and other routine laboratory tests, or perform physical examinations, failure to perform the enumerated procedure may be judged against a biomedical standard of care and may constitute malpractice.[47] In these situations, chiropractors are acting within their legislatively authorized scope of practice but are judged by standards applicable to physicians. Choosing a biomedical rather than chiropractic standard of care in any particular case grants deference to biomedical authority and judicially crystallizes the debate among the two professional communities as to what constitutes competence in any given area.

As complementary and alternative providers' legislatively authorized scope of practice expands to include additional areas within biomedical practice, these providers may face heightened malpractice liability in their professional practice as a whole. Recently, for example, Oregon permitted acupuncturists the right to use Western diagnostic tests.[48] Once authorized to take x-rays, the acupuncturist who fails to do so, instead preferring to rely on diagnostic techniques of oriental medicine (such as pulse and tongue diagnosis), may be deemed to have violated the standard of care. Acupuncturists who feel that Western tests "have no place in Oriental medicine" will be held liable for failing to order such tests and will be forced to order Western tests "defensively," which is "one of the very behaviors for which we criticize our western practitioner cousins."[49] The same applies to providers such as chiropractors, whose legislative authority includes taking x-rays, conducting physical examinations, and other functions within the biomedical model.

Duty to Refer and Misrepresentation

Complementary and alternative providers are vulnerable to malpractice liability as well when they assume too much responsibility for the patient's biomedical condition and fail to refer the patient to an appropriate conventional professional. The duty to refer is theoretically appropriate to prevent patients from relying too heavily on nonmedical providers when they need biomedical attention. It ideally facilitates the safe integration of holistic healing modalities with biomedicine, since, like scope-of-practice boundaries, it forces nonphysicians to recognize the limits of their skill and training.

For example, in chiropractic care, courts impose a duty of reasonable care in the analysis and treatment of patients, which includes the duties (1) to determine whether the patient presents a problem treatable through chiropractic; (2) to refrain from further chiropractic treatment when a reasonable chiropractor should be aware that the patient's condition will not be responsive to further treatment; and (3) if the problem is outside the chiropractor's skill, training, and expertise, to inform the patient that the condition is not treatable through chiropractic.[50] In some states, this entails a duty to refer the patient to biomedical care when the condition is not amenable to chiropractic treatment.[51]

A chiropractor who negligently fails to inform the patient that his or her condition is not amenable to chiropractic treatment (or, in some states, a chiropractor who fails to refer the patient in such cases to a medical doctor) has committed malpractice. For instance, a chiropractor's negligent failure to inform the patient of a possible herniated disk and refer the patient to a physician has been held to constitute malpractice. Likewise, a chiropractor who takes an x-ray pursuant to statutory authorization, finds a fracture, and fails to refer the patient to a medical doctor is liable for malpractice.[52]

In many states, the oath administered to chiropractors by the state licensing board requires referral to medical doctors where the patient's problem exceeds the limits of chiropractic care. Such an oath may be admitted into evidence to show the standard of chiropractic care and violation of the standard.[53] The duty to refer also has been codified for other providers such as acupuncturists.[54]

The benefits of a tort duty to refer are clear when providers such as chiropractors overreach and purport to cure a patient of a disease such as diabetes or cancer. In other cases, violation of the duty may become a conclusory label for provider liability. Like other legal rules, such as scope of practice and heightened malpractice liability, the existence of a duty to refer merely frames the unresolved issue of where to draw boundaries of practice among competing healing professionals.

The problem is particularly difficult in light of the historical tension between various communities and philosophies. Once again, legal solutions tend to be jurisdictional rather than rational, dividing the patient into various areas of professional "turf"—for instance, chiropractors get the spine, massage therapists get the muscles, naturopaths get nutrition, acupuncturists get to poke clients with needles, psychologists get the emotions, and medical doctors get the rest of the body. Legal doctrine may evolve more rationally as historical antagonisms dissolve, collaboration replaces rhetoric, and different professional communities begin to integrate their diverse approaches to health care.

Misrepresentation provides yet another source of potential liability for complementary and alternative providers, on the one hand, and potential protection for patients where providers overreach, on the other hand. The tort of misrepresentation is triggered when health care providers make claims exceeding the boundaries of professional training and skill. For example, in claiming that chiropractic adjustment can cure diabetes, a chiropractor is liable for misrepresentation as well as malpractice. To show misrepresentation, a plaintiff must introduce evidence of intent to defraud, deceive, and/or misrepresent; deception alone is insufficient.

The plaintiff may prove that the statements were fraudulent, deceptive, or misleading by introducing expert testimony. At least one court has allowed the complementary and alternative profession itself to determine the range of allowable representations. According to this court, if the statements made by the provider were "within a generally accepted view of the science" of the provider's profession, then there is no misrepresentation.[55] This view may be too broad. Misrepresentation rules again pose the same conflict over legal boundaries appropriate to the nonbiomedical profession in question. The complementary and alternative provider's professional community may deem the challenged practice to be within its accepted view of science, but the biomedical profession may disagree. The question remains as to whether the alleged misrepresentation will be judged by biomedical standards, by standards appropriate to the complementary and alternative professional, or by some other standard such as reasonable patient expectations. In any case, a complementary and alternative provider is well served by limiting claims about cure and efficacy, by referring patients to conventional care where appropriate, and by appreciating the many unresolved issues concerning overlapping professional boundaries.

Malpractice Liability of Health Care Institutions

Health care institutions, including hospitals, nursing homes, clinics, and managed care organizations,[56] face at least two kinds of malpractice exposure when utilizing health care professionals who provide alternative and complementary treatments: direct liability (for an act or omission of the institution, also known as corporate negligence) and vicarious liability (for an act or omission of the individual provider).

Under the doctrine of corporate negligence, courts have imposed direct liability on health care institutions for negligently failing to properly supervise health care professionals. In *Darling v. Charlston Community Memorial Hospital,*[57] the plaintiff broke his leg in a college football game. Negligent care resulted in amputation of the leg. The Supreme Court of Illinois held the hospital directly liable for failure to take due care in supervising the treatment offered by its medical staff.[58] Similarly, in *Thompson v. The Nason Hospital,*[59] the Pennsylvania Supreme Court held that a hospital owes the patient a nondelegable duty to ensure the patient's safety and well-being at the hospital, a duty the court classified into four general areas: (1) a duty to use reasonable care in the maintenance of safe and adequate facilities and equipment; (2) a duty to select and retain only competent physicians; (3) a duty to oversee all persons who practice medicine within its walls; and (4) a duty to formulate, adopt and enforce adequate rules and policies to ensure quality care (707).[60] The court also included the duty "to recognize and report abnormalities in the treatment and condition of its patients" (708).

Ideally, complementary and alternative providers linked to health care institutions should have levels of training, skill, and professionalism commensurate with that of peers practicing within the biomedical model. Professional organizations can mitigate health care institutions' liability concerns by developing programs and criteria to ensure high standards in provider credentialing and care. Conversely, health care institutions that have complementary and alternative providers on staff, contractually engaged, or within a referral network can mitigate the risk of direct liability by ensuring that such health care providers are properly licensed, certified, or registered and have achieved the highest level of professional certification available. Health care institutions further should keep accurate records of the selection and review process for such providers and should investigate whether the selected provider has a history of being sanctioned or liable for negligent practice.[61]

Further, health care institutions can attempt to meet their duty to non-negligently retain and supervise individual providers through periodic review and monitoring of complementary and alternative providers, and internal risk-management programs. The institutions also must ensure that providers are delivering services within their legally authorized scope of practice. For instance, massage therapists should not be engaged in spinal manipulation, and chiropractors (absent specific legislative authorization) should not be recommending homeopathic remedies. Institutions need to develop recognized protocols for collaborative practice between providers and to clarify providers' specific roles within such collaborative or integrated health care. Due care further requires peer review of services and practices and utilization review, to ensure that complementary and alternative services are appropriate, cost-effective, and beneficial to patients.[62]

Even if health care institutions manage to avoid direct liability, they must address the risk of vicarious liability for the negligent acts of complementary and alternative providers within their domain. The doctrine of vicarious liability (or *respondeat superior*) considers individual providers to be agents of the health care institution rather than independent contractors. In vicarious liability, negligent acts of the agent are attributable to, and considered to be acts of, the principal. Courts frequently support the imposition of vicarious liability by finding "ostensible agency" or "apparent authority," in which the organization's structure gives the appearance that the provider is an agent of the institution.[63] Ostensible agency purports to protect the patient's expectation that the organization is responsible for the injurious conduct.

The ostensible agency theory has eroded the defense that individual physicians are independent contractors, rather than agents of the health care institution. The independent contractor defense is most likely to succeed where the patient directly contracts with the health care provider for a specific treatment, and the provider arranges for admission to a particular hospital, if necessary.[64] Independent contractors usually are responsible for their own income tax and method of receiving payment from patients, own their instrumentalities of practice, make their own clinical judgments, and do not submit such judgments to the medical authority of supervisors in the clinic. Conversely, the independent contractor defense will likely fail, irrespective of any contractual provision between institution and health care provider disclaiming responsibility for the provider's negligence, when the institution, among other things, exercises control over providers through rules relating to staff privileges, requires providers to meet institutional quality of care standards, requires consultation with appropriate staff physicians where appropriate, has exclusive control of patient billing and fees, and provides clerical and medical support personnel, as well as instruments and supplies, to providers at no cost.[65]

However, if a health care institution loosens its supervisory control over its providers to reduce the risk of vicarious liability, the organization also increases the risk of direct liability for the negligent acts of its providers. Further, the institution may be liable to patients under additional theories such as breach of contract for failure to deliver the level of care promised in its agreement.[66] Institutions must balance the risks of direct and vicarious liability. Institutions probably will err on the side of greater control, supervision, and standards, as the legal rules governing malpractice liability for complementary and alternative providers and treatments unfold.

6

ACCESS TO TREATMENTS

In crafting and interpreting food and drug law, Congress, the Food and Drug Administration, and the courts have been guided primarily by medical paternalism: the notion that patients' access to treatments should be filtered through a federal agency to protect the patients from worthless or dangerous treatments. Thus, legal rules and decisions traditionally have emphasized the perils of access to untested treatments and have granted less weight to the principle of patient choice or health care freedom. Although a full discussion of FDA authority is beyond the scope of this book, this chapter briefly describes the process for approving new drugs, the rules surrounding dietary supplements, and the broader topic of litigation over health care freedom, in the context of access to nutritional and other unapproved or disfavored health care treatments.

Treatments Requiring New Drug Approval

Food and drug law ostensibly protects consumers from unsafe, ineffective, and fraudulent treatments by ensuring the integrity and safety of foods and products sold as drugs. A brief history of pertinent federal food and drug law suggests the dangers of overrelying on legislative and agency authority to regulate access to modalities outside the biomedical model. Legislative concern over adulterated foods reaches back to ancient societies such as ancient Greece and Rome. Hippocrates (the "father of medicine") advised, "Let your food be your medicine and your medicine be your food." Theophrastus (370–285 B.C.) warned against the use of artificial preservatives and flavors in foods; Cato (234–149 B.C.) provided a method to determine whether wine had been watered down; Pliny the Elder (23–79 A.D.) described methods of detecting the adulteration of bread with chalk, vegetable meals, and cattle feed; Galen (131–201 A.D.) described market adulteration of pepper and other common food products.[1]

In the mid nineteenth century, interest in public health and sanitation led the U.S. Congress to pass legislation protecting the public from adulteration. In 1906, Congress passed the Pure Food and Drug Act.[2] Among other things, the act made the manufacture of an adulterated or misbranded drug a misdemeanor. It defined "adulterated" as "differing from the standard of strength, quality or purity," and defined "misbranded" as displaying any statement on the package or label that was false or misleading.[3] The act did not make prior governmental approval of safety or effectiveness a criterion for the marketing of new drugs.

In 1937, a drug manufacturer's marketing of exilir sulfanilamide without prior toxicity testing led to more than one hundred deaths. Congress responded in 1938 by enacting the federal Food, Drug, and Cosmetic Act (FDCA).[4] Among other things, the FDCA expanded the definitions of "adulteration" and "misbranding," required informative labeling, expanded governmental powers of enforcement and seizure, and, most significantly, provided that no new drug could be distributed in interstate commerce without FDA approval of a new drug application (NDA), by which manufacturers demonstrated that the drug was safe for its intended use.

In the early 1960s, the drug thalidomide, prescribed in Europe for pregnant women with morning sickness, caused deformities. In response, the 1962 Kefauver-Harris Drug Amendments added the requirement that a new drug be proven effective as well as safe for its intended use, before FDA approval of an NDA.[5]

Under the FDCA, proof of effectiveness now requires "substantial evidence" of effectiveness, which means "evidence consisting of adequate and well-controlled investigations . . . by experts qualified by scientific training and expertise to evaluate the effectiveness of the drug involved, on the basis of which it could fairly and responsibly be concluded by such experts that the drug will have the effect it purports or is represented to have under the conditions of use prescribed, recommended, or suggested in the labeling or proposed labeling thereof."[6] Typically, this involves extensive laboratory and animal testing and human trials before the FDA will approve the NDA for the new drug.

Testing goes through several stages. After identifying a therapeutic compound, researchers perform in vitro and animal studies to determine a product's pharmacological effects. The manufacturer submits an investigational new drug (IND) application to the FDA.[7] The application must contain information about the sponsor, the clinical evaluation plan, and each phase of the proposed clinical investigation process. If the FDA presents no objection, the sponsor conducts Phase I studies, which typically last six months and involve a small number of patients. Studies begin with a low dose and increase the dose only if toxic reactions do not occur; researchers determine which dosages are "reasonably safe" in light of the severity of the illness being treated.

Phase II, which ranges in length from one year to three years, enrolls a larger patient population in clinical trials to determine efficacy. If the FDA accepts the results of Phase II as demonstrating probable efficacy, Phase III begins. This phase, which requires one to two years, involves a risk-benefit analysis based on studies involving hundreds and even thousands of patients, confirming efficacy of the drug, and seeking the correct dosage and frequency of administration. Following the completion of Phase III, the manufacturer submits the NDA, showing evidence that "adequate and well-controlled" studies exist which show the new drug's safety and efficacy.[8] After FDA approval, Phase IV involves postmarket surveillance and studies to fine-tune the dosage and compare the drug's efficacy with that of other relevant drugs for the disease in question.

The entire approval process is expensive, burdensome, and difficult to carry out. Getting NDA approval can take upwards of ten years and cost upwards of $100 million; the typical NDA requires more than one hundred thousand pages of supporting documentation.[9] Moreover, the process creates a significant lag time between innovation and marketing of pharmaceutical technology.

As new drugs have emerged with promising therapeutic potential for diseases for which no approved therapy provides satisfactory treatment, the FDA has provided mechanisms for expedited approval of and expanded access to such drugs. For example, the FDA began granting, on an ad hoc basis, emergency-use INDs to physicians for patients in life-threatening situations. Similarly, the FDA would grant "compassionate INDs" to approve protocols for treatment use of investigational drugs for patients meeting the specific protocol criteria. The FDA can now grant "Treatment IND" status to drugs intended to treat "immediately life-threatening" or "serious" diseases.[10] Similarly, "parallel track" studies allow patients with AIDS and other HIV-related diseases who have no therapeutic alternatives and do not qualify for clinical studies to receive, through their health care providers, investigational new drugs while controlled clinical trials essential to establish the safety and effectiveness of the new drugs are carried out.[11] The FDA also can grant expedited approval to new therapies "intended to treat persons with life-threatening and severely-debilitating illnesses, especially where no satisfactory alternative therapy exists,"[12] and accelerated approval to certain new drug products "that have been studied for their safety and effectiveness in treating serious or life-threatening illnesses and that provide meaningful therapeutic benefit to patients over existing treatments."[13]

Such efforts to relax regulatory controls have satisfied some, but not all, critics of the drug approval process. Even if patients have diseases such as cancer or AIDS, or face conventional treatments with debilitating side-effects, their initial and continued access to unapproved treatments is controlled and monitored by a federal agency. The FDA may delay or even deny approval of access to the therapy, or may condition approval on compliance with specified guidelines. Such guidelines may result in certain patients or treatments being ineligible for expanded or expedited access. Such FDA control also can intrude excessively on the practice of medicine, by micromanaging the provider's use of the unapproved therapy.

The dangers of excessive regulatory control are best expressed by patients and their families for whom generally accepted biomedical care has failed, who freely and without coercion or misrepresentation have chosen alternatives, and who have found improved health using complementary and alternative medicine. Patients recently testified in Congress regarding a non-FDA-approved treatment known as antineoplastons developed by Stanislaw Burzynski, M.D. Mariann Kunnari testified:

> My son, Dustin, was only 2½ years old at the time he was diagnosed with a brain tumor the size of a golf ball. . . . The doctors told us Dustin had only a few months to live. The first treatment they offered us was radiation, but the radiation doctor told us that at his young age, Dustin would become a vegetable. And it would extend his life for maybe a few months.
>
> The next doctor wanted us to enroll Dustin in an experimental chemotherapy which was highly toxic. . . . The side effects included hearing loss, kidney and liver damage . . . and a possible leukemia. . . . We weighed the harm . . . but our oncologist told us that their opinion took precedence over us as parents. . . .
>
> Dr. Burzynski made us no promises. . . . An MRI six weeks after we started Dr. Burzynski's treatment revealed no tumor. . . . There were still no harsh side effects at all. The next MRI in September of 1995 revealed that the tumor had almost disappeared again. To this day it has not reappeared.
>
> . . . Dustin . . . is a happy, healthy four-year-old who has outlived his prognosis—there is no [FDA-approved] treatment that would have kept him alive with such good quality of life.[14]

Another witness testified concerning the conventional care his four-year-old daughter received for treatment of a brain tumor: "The chemo and radiation . . . burned her skull so bad she had second-degree burns and her hair never came back. To change her diapers, we had to wear rubber gloves because her urine was so toxic and it burned her. . . . At the end of six months, miraculously, she survived the standard treatment although there was a high expectation she wouldn't. She still had cancer. We were told, sorry. We've done everything we can. Now she's going to die, probably within a couple of months." The witness testified that after nineteen months of antineoplaston treatment, his daughter was free from cancer. Shortly thereafter, she died "of neurological necrosis. Her brain fell apart from the radiation. The autopsy showed that she was completely cancer free."

Mary Jo Siegel testified that the only option she had been given after being diagnosed with non-Hodgkin lymphoma was high-dose radiation, massive chemotherapy, and autologous bone marrow transplant: "I would lose my hair and experience severe nausea and vomiting. I would spend six weeks in isolation. The chemotherapy would damage my heart, lungs, liver, kidneys, and bladder. And radiation would damage my eyes, salivary glands, thyroid and reproductive organs. If I did live ten years, I might develop leukemia." Siegel's tumor disappeared after three weeks of anti-neoplaston treatment. Siegel's physicians responded: "Yes, she is perfectly well clinically. We don't know why she's improved. There's a scoundrel and a charlatan treating her." Other physicians dismissed the cure as a "spontaneous remission."[15] The FDA convened several grand juries against Burzynski in attempts to indict him for criminal fraud and for interstate distribution of an unapproved drug.

Such patient testimony and the reactions elicited highlight the reliance on medical paternalism, and dismissal of patient perspectives as unscientific, anecdotal, or born of gullibility and desperation. The claim that denying access protects patient welfare seems cold, bureaucratic, and indefensible to patients and challenges legislators to reconsider the mandate to protect, preserve, and promote human health.

Nutritional Therapies

The FDCA and FDA regulations affect nutritional therapies as well as treatments typically considered to be drugs. Although foods are exempt from the extensive premarketing clearance requirements of the FDCA, the act's definition of "drugs" includes "articles intended for use in the diagnosis, cure, mitigation, treatment, or prevention of disease," and "articles (other than food) intended to affect the structure or any function of the body of man or other animals."[16] This broad definition resembles the sweeping definition of "medicine" in the medical practice acts. It is biomedically oriented and, like the medical practice acts, jurisdictionally monopolistic: the definition purports to bring a broad range of therapeutic modalities under FDA jurisdiction. For example, when a manufacturer intends to market a nutritional therapy to treat disease (e.g., psyllium husk to treat colon cancer), the manufacturer must submit an IND application and complete the FDA approval process. Because nutritional therapies cannot be patented, companies do not invest in the FDA approval process for such products, cannot make unapproved health claims for these products,[17] and cannot market the products as intended to cure or treat disease.[18]

Licensed health care professionals who recommend or prescribe an independently manufactured nutritional product to patients or other providers theoretically are not subject to FDA enforcement action.[19] However, the FDA has been known to read its jurisdiction broadly in cases against complementary and alternative providers. Perhaps the best-known example is the 1992 FDA raid on the office of Jonathan Wright, M.D., in which FDA agents seized files and injectable vitamins at gunpoint.[20] Even if the FDA does not proceed with any enforcement action or criminal penalties, FDA investigation and information sharing with other prosecutorial agents could become a basis for disciplinary action by the state medical board, and civil malpractice litigation by the patient.

The Access to Medical Treatment Act (AMTA) was introduced in Congress to increase patients' access to unapproved therapies, subject to certain safeguards, and to broaden providers' ability to offer non-FDA-approved treatments nondangerous. The legislation gives an individual "the right to be treated by a health care practitioner with any medical treatment (including a treatment that is not approved, certified, or licensed by the Secretary of Health and Human Services) that such individual desires or the legal representative of such individual desires," if the practitioner personally examines and agrees to treat the individual and the administration of the treatment is within the provider's authorized scope of practice.[21] Furthermore, the treatment may be provided only if (1) there is "no reasonable basis to conclude that the treatment itself, when used as directed, poses an unreasonable and significant danger to such individual"; (2) in the case of a treatment requiring and lacking FDA approval, the individual receives written notice that the FDA has not approved, certified, or licensed the treatment, and that the individual uses such treatment at his or her own risk; (3) the provider notifies the patient in writing of the nature of the treatment, including, among other things, "reasonably foreseeable side effects"; (4) no advertising claims are made as to efficacy; (5) the label of any drug, device, or food used in such treatment is not false or misleading; and (6) the individual signs a written statement indicating informed consent as to items 1 through 4 and acceptance of the treatment.[22] Providers must report to the secretary of health and human services if they discover that treatments used under the AMTA are in fact dangerous. The secretary then must "properly disseminate information" regarding the danger of the treatment.[23]

Congressional consideration of the AMTA signifies an important shift to permitting access when the patient has received sufficient information to make an informed choice about the treatment. Rather than "invok[ing] the political process to prevent those consumers who want . . . to take riskier drugs from doing so," this approach assumes that consumers can, with certain protections, "make their own cost-benefit analysis."[24]

Although the AMTA does not purport to preempt state law, a federal law authorizing access to complementary and alternative health care could signal state medical boards to grant physicians practicing complementary and alternative medicine greater flexibility. Such federal legislation would further broaden third-party reimbursement of complementary and alternative therapies and expand consumer access to a fuller range of treatments than authorized by biomedicine or accepted by the FDA.

Dietary Supplements and Health Claims

Legislation concerning nutrition, labeling, and health claims arose out of congressional recognition that the use of nutritional supplementation to increase health promotion and disease prevention is significant: 100 million Americans supplement their diets with vitamins, minerals, herbs, amino acids, or other nutritional substances.[25] In 1990, Congress enacted the Nutrition Labeling and Education Act (NLEA)[26] to ensure that the public would receive clear information about the relationship of nutrition to disease. The NLEA directed the FDA to approve disease-related health claims to be used on labeling for foods and nutrients (other than those consumed in the form of dietary supplements) if "significant scientific agreement" existed. The standard required "significant agreement among qualified scientists that the claimed link between a nutrient and disease is valid, taking into account the totality of publicly available scientific evidence." This was more flexible than the standard for new drug approval, which required proof of safety and effectiveness based on "adequate and well-controlled clinical investigations."[27]

The NLEA further directed the secretary of health and human services, and by delegation, the FDA, to establish a procedure and standard for health claims for dietary supplements.[28] The FDA, after completing a rule-making to implement this provision of the NLEA, declined to adopt a more lenient standard and decided to adopt the same standard established for foods, namely, permitting only health claims supported by "significant scientific agreement." The FDA further rejected all except one of the health claims submitted by manufacturers for dietary supplements. The FDA's interpretation of the NLEA and related matters has been controversial.[29]

In 1994, Congress enacted the Dietary Supplement Health and Education Act (DSHEA).[30] The DSHEA aimed to "protect the right of access of consumers to safe dietary supplements . . . in order to promote wellness."[31] In enacting the DSHEA, Congress found that the FDA had "pursued a regulatory agenda which discourages . . . citizens seeking to improve their health through dietary supplementation. In fact, the FDA has had a long history of bias against dietary supplements . . . [and] pursued a heavy-handed enforcement agenda against dietary supplements for over 30 years."[32]

The DSHEA reaffirms that dietary supplements are "foods," thus exempting dietary supplements from the requirement of new drug or food additive approval.[33] The statute defines "dietary supplements" to include products that contain, either individually or in combination, vitamins, minerals, herbs, or other botanicals, amino acids, or other products for use to supplement the diet by increasing total dietary intake.[34] The dietary supplement must be available for consumption as a tablet, capsule, powder, softgel, gelcap, or liquid, or, if not intended to be taken in such form, must not be represented as conventional food and must not be represented for use as the sole component of a meal or diet.[35] All dietary supplements must be so labeled.[36]

Among other provisions, the DSHEA authorizes the use of literature in connection with the sale of dietary supplements by modifying the definition of "labeling." Specifically, the DSHEA provides that the use of a publication in conjunction with sale is not "labeling" under the FDCA if the publication (1) is not false or misleading; (2) does not promote a particular manufacturer or brand of dietary supplement; (3) presents a balanced view of the available scientific information; (4) if displayed in a store also selling dietary supplements, is displayed separate and apart from the dietary supplements; and (5) does not have appended to it any information by sticker or any other method.[37] This means that dietary supplement retailers may sell books, reprints of articles, abstracts, bibliographies, and other publications as part of their business under the above conditions; the government bears the burden of proof to establish that a book or article is false or misleading.[38]

The DSHEA further allows manufacturers to include a statement of a supplement's nutritional value, provided that (1) the statement claims a benefit related to a classic nutrient deficiency disease and discloses the prevalence of such disease in the United States, describes the role of a nutrient or dietary ingredient intended to affect structure and function in humans, characterizes the documented mechanism by which a nutrient or dietary ingredient acts to maintain such structure or function, or describes general well-being resulting from consumption of a nutrient or dietary ingredient; (2) the manufacture of the dietary supplement has substantiation that such statement is truthful and not misleading; and (3) the statement contains a disclaimer that the statement has not been evaluated by the FDA.[39] The statement may not claim that the product will diagnose, mitigate, treat, cure, or prevent a specific disease or class of diseases.[40]

Under the DSHEA, the FDA may take enforcement action to remove misbranded dietary supplements from the market. Misbranding occurs, among other things, when the manufacturer fails to list the name of each dietary ingredient of the supplement, and the quantity of each such ingredient.[41] The DSHEA also provides for regulations prescribing good manufacturing practices for the production of dietary supplements.[42]

Lawmakers continue to seek a balance between agency control over nutritional supplements and health claims, and interest in a less tightly regulated market.[43] The DSHEA suggests a legislative decision to leave a significant portion of treatment choices with the consumer, rather than the physician or a governmental agency.[44]

Health Care Freedom

Alongside regulatory innovations concerning new drug approval and nutritional treatments, patients have brought litigation seeking to establish a right to experimental treatments irrespective of FDA approval or acceptance by biomedical orthodoxy. The courts have found constitutional protection for more specific medical matters such as contraception,[45] abortion,[46] and the right to be disconnected from artificial life support.[47] For example, in *Cruzan v. Director, Missouri Department of Health*,[48] the U.S. Supreme Court held that a competent person has a constitutionally protected liberty interest in refusing unwanted medical treatment, including lifesaving hydration and nutrition.[49]

Yet, paradoxically, most courts have denied the existence of a right to select the treatment of choice based on the constitutional right to privacy. As noted, in *United States v. Rutherford* the U.S. Supreme Court rejected terminally ill cancer patients' efforts to obtain laetrile and concluded that Congress reasonably could have intended to protect terminally ill patients from ineffective or unsafe drugs such as laetrile.[50] On remand, the U.S. Court of Appeals for the Tenth Circuit held that while a patient has a constitutionally protected right to decide whether or not to undergo treatment, the patient's "selection of a particular treatment, or at least a medication, is within the area of governmental interest in protecting public health" and is not encompassed by the constitutional right to privacy.[51]

People v. Privitera involved charges against physicians for supplying laetrile to patients in violation of a California statute.[52] The California Supreme Court followed the view, expressed in *Rutherford,* that the constitutional right of privacy does not grant patients a right of access to drugs of unproven efficacy, and upheld the statute as rationally related to protecting public health. Chief Justice Bird dissented, stating: "Cancer is a disease with potentially fatal consequences; this makes the choice of treatment one of the more important decisions a person may ever make, touching intimately on his being. For this reason, I believe the right of privacy, recognized under both the state and federal constitutions, prevents the state from interfering with a person's choice of treatment on the sole ground that the person has chosen a treatment which the state considers 'ineffective'" (927).[53]

Justice Bird's view finds expression in statutes and cases recognizing certain unconventional treatment choices. Oklahoma permits chelation therapy, by prohibiting the disciplining of physicians solely on the basis of their use of chelation therapy.[54] Massachusetts, in its Patient Rights Act, provides that every patient or resident of a licensed hospital or health or mental health facility has "the right to freedom of choice in his selection of a facility, or a physician or a health service mode."[55]

In *Andrews v. Ballard*,[56] a group of patients challenged rules established by the Texas Board of Medical Examiners proclaiming acupuncture to be the "practice of medicine." The plaintiffs argued that the rules effectively eliminated the practice of acupuncture in Texas, thereby depriving them of the constitutional right to obtain acupuncture treatment.

The U.S. District Court for the Southern District of Texas agreed that plaintiffs had a constitutional right, encompassed by the right of privacy, to obtain acupuncture treatment, and held that the challenged rules effectively deprived them of that right, were not necessary to serve the state's interest in protecting patients' health, and were unconstitutional. The court reached this holding by first describing the right to privacy as an expression of "the sanctity of individual free choice and self-determination as fundamental constituents of life."[57] The court found in prior Supreme Court privacy cases two criteria marking decisions protected by the constitutional right to privacy: first, they must be "personal decisions," and second, they must "profoundly affect one's development or one's life."[58] Medical decisions, like decisions relating to "marriage, procreation, contraception, family relationships, and child rearing and education," are "to an extraordinary degree, intrinsically personal."[59] Medical decisions, including the decision to obtain acupuncture, can "produce or eliminate physical, psychological, and emotional ruin," destroy one's economic stability, determine whether one will experience a life of pain or pleasure, and for some, make the difference between life and death.[60]

The court noted that many individuals, including one of the plaintiffs, seek acupuncture only when Western medicine fails them. Acupuncture is their "last hope"; denying them the treatment may mean condemning them to "endure without hope the misery that is theirs."[61] The court criticized the Tenth's Circuit's distinction in *Rutherford*, between refusing or choosing treatment and selecting a particular type of treatment, since, as with laetrile, denying patients the right to select a particular treatment may be equivalent to denying them the right to be treated. The court concluded that the decision to obtain acupuncture is protected by the constitutional right to privacy.

The court next asked whether the challenged rules effectively violated the right of privacy by significantly interfering with the decision in question. If not, the rules needed only be "rationally related" to a "constitutionally permissible" purpose; if, however, the rules did significantly interfere, they should be "narrowly drawn" to serve a "compelling interest."[62] The court found that the rules did impose a significant burden on the decision to obtain acupuncture treatment,[63] and that the rules were not narrowly drawn to serve the state's interest in protecting public health (1057).

The court observed that the rules' restriction of the practice of acupuncture to licensed physicians was based on a finding that acupuncture is an "experimental procedure, the safety [and effectiveness] of which have not been established." According to the court, this finding had been adopted by a board of medical examiners that lacked expertise in acupuncture and did not hear testimony or receive evidence from experts about it. Moreover, according to the court, "acupuncture has been practiced for 2000 to 5000 years. It is no more experimental as a mode of medical treatment than is the Chinese language as a mode of communication. What is experimental is not acupuncture, but Westerners' understanding of it and their ability to utilize it properly."[64]

In prohibiting the practice of acupuncture by nonphysicians, the medical board had cited three dangers of such practice: misdiagnosis, improper administration of acupuncture, and delayed remedy of complications arising during the acupuncture treatment. In response, the court observed that the danger of misdiagnosis could be remedied by requiring that patients consult with physicians prior to obtaining acupuncture treatment; that the danger of improper placement of needles was not remedied by restricting the practice of acupuncture to those least schooled in the art (i.e., physicians); and that the danger of delayed treatment of complications could have been remedied through less drastic means, such as requiring acupuncturists to take courses in emergency medical treatment, or requiring that acupuncturists have ready access to physicians.

The court noted that it was striking the challenged provisions not because they were "unwise, improvident, or out of harmony with a particular school of thought," but only because they were unconstitutional.[65] Finally, the court suggested a variety of constitutionally permissible alternatives: the legislature could grant acupuncturists full independent status; it could allow independent practice by acupuncturists but require diagnosis by or referral from physicians; it could establish minimum standards of skill and knowledge for acupuncture practitioners; or, if feasible, it could require acupuncturists to practice under the supervision and control of physicians.

The approach in *Andrews* is supported in cases such as *Suenram v. Society of the Valley Hospital*,[66] in which the New Jersey Superior Court held that a terminally ill cancer patient, having tried chemotherapy, had a fundamental right to choose laetrile as a last resort. According to the court, "where a person is terminally ill . . . and unresponsive to other treatments, the public harm is considerably reduced" (146).

Other courts have disagreed with the approach in *Andrews*. For example, in *New York State Ophthalmological Society v. Bowen,*[67] ophthalmologists, their patients, and professional associations brought a class action challenging the constitutionality of a provision of COBRA (the Consolidated Omnibus Budget Reconciliation Act of 1985) which prohibited Medicare billing for an assistant cataract surgeon unless pre-approved by an insurance carrier or designated state peer review organization. The U.S. Court of Appeals for the District of Columbia rejected the notion that the constitutional right to privacy protects all choices made by patients and their physicians or subjects to "strict scrutiny" all governmental interference with their choice of treatment (1389). The court noted the difficulty in determining what kinds of medical decisions should be accorded "the same high degree of solicitude now reserved for first trimester abortions" (1390).[68] The court stated that it did not rule out the possibility that a particular medical decision, such as a choice regarding eyesight, might be entitled to constitutional protection. In such a case, however, plaintiff would need to show "medical necessity" and the "unavailability of equally effective alternative therapy" (1390).

The concurring judge observed that the sole interest advanced in favor of the statutory provision restricting individuals' ability to have a second surgeon present in a cataract operation was the need to prevent individuals from "being harmed by making unwise expenditures of their own money."[69] Thus, the asserted state interest not only was paternalistic but was limited to protecting the pocketbook of the supposed beneficiaries. The concurring opinion criticized the majority's requirement of "medical necessity" as infringing on the patient's autonomy interest. While agreeing that such an interest might not rise to the level of constitutional protection, the opinion argued that the patient should not be prohibited from investing in a health measure merely because of differing views about its value.

Two recent cases have added to the jurisprudence of patient decision making. In *Compassion in Dying v. Washington,*[70] the U.S. Court of Appeals for the Ninth Circuit held that a person who is terminally ill has a constitutionally protected liberty interest in determining the time and manner of his or her death. The court observed that when such an individual "wishes, free of any coercion, to hasten his death because his remaining days are an unmitigated torture, that person's liberty interest is at its height. For such a person, being forced to live is indeed being subjected to '. . . suffering that is too intimate and personal for the State to insist on.' "[71] The court stated that "by permitting the *individual* to exercise the right to *choose* we are following the constitutional mandate to take such decisions out of the hands of the government, both state and federal, and to put them where they rightly belong, in the hands of the people . . . and precluding the state from intruding excessively into that critical realm" (839). The U.S. Court of Appeals for the Second Circuit, in *Quill v. Vacco,*[72] similarly authorized physician-assisted suicide, overturning a New York statute that defined the act as manslaughter.

These appellate court decisions, although reversed on appeal to the U.S. Supreme Court, suggest a different balance between the state's interest in controlling medical care, and individual authority and choice. Particularly when patients face serious or life-threatening disease and when conventional biomedical treatment has failed or presents unacceptable risks and side effects, filtering access to therapies through a federal agency undervalues patients' interest in care for their own bodies. The right to health care freedom continues to be raised in litigation, in administrative appeals to the FDA, and, as discussed in the next chapter, in the legislative process.

7

DISCIPLINE AND SANCTION

The Disciplinary Process

Licensure authorizes professional practice, as defined in relevant licensing laws, and subjects the licensee to specified procedures and penalties for misconduct.[1] Although biomedical physicians are said to have an unlimited scope of practice under state medical practice acts, their departure from conventionally accepted medical standards to provide complementary and alternative modalities creates the risk of medical board discipline for "unprofessional conduct." Unprofessional conduct (or "professional misconduct") includes such acts as obtaining the license fraudulently; practicing the profession fraudulently, beyond its authorized scope, with gross incompetence, or with gross negligence; practicing while impaired by alcohol or drugs or while convicted of a crime; permitting or aiding an unlicensed person to perform activities requiring a license; or failing to comply with relevant rules and regulations.[2] In some states, unprofessional conduct includes "any departure from, or the failure to conform to, the standards of acceptable and prevailing medical practice . . . irrespective of whether or not a patient is injured thereby."[3] The reference to "acceptable and prevailing medical practice" suggests that practitioners who integrate complementary and alternative therapies into their practice subject themselves to legislatively authorized sanction merely for deviating from conventional biomedical wisdom.

Disciplinary proceedings against licensees involve preliminary procedures (a complaint, an investigation, filing of charges, service of charges, and notice of hearing) and adversary proceedings before a hearing panel of the appropriate state board (resulting in a written report that includes findings of fact, a determination of guilt or nonguilt, and a recommendation of the penalty to be imposed).[4] The hearing panel's decision is reviewed by the licensing board, which makes a decision and issues an appropriate order.[5] The possible penalties include censure and reprimand, suspension, revocation or annulment of license or registration, a fine, further education, and public service.[6] Theoretically, suspension or revocation is designed not to punish the licensee but rather to protect the life, health, and welfare of the public by preventing the "evils which could result from ignorance or incompetency or lack of honesty and integrity."[7]

The complaint to a state medical board, triggering investigation, may be made by any person,[8] even anonymously. Once a complaint has been filed, the medical board need not limit its investigation to the specifics of the complaint.[9] This means that medical boards can use grounds unrelated to the allegations, such as inadequate record keeping, to sanction responsible physicians whose medical philosophy simply differs from that of board members. The medical board can open multiple investigations against the same practitioner. In such cases, physicians may be forced to enter into settlements with state medical boards to avoid further censure.[10]

State medical board records are confidential.[11] Although the licensee may appeal, a court will not reverse the medical board decision unless there is no rational basis for the exercise of discretion complained of, or unless the board's action is arbitrary and capricious.[12] Perhaps because the standard of review is so high, relatively few medical board decisions result in published judicial opinions. The existing cases primarily involve physicians' use of homeopathy, ozone therapy, and chelation therapy. These cases, discussed below, arose not because of demonstrated injury to patients or even complaints by patients, but because the treatments challenged medical boards' view of safety or effectiveness within the practice of medicine. Homeopathy historically has posed a political and philosophical challenge to biomedicine; ozone and chelation therapy link health and healing to ecological factors. Further, to the extent that such treatments divert patients from conventional biomedical practices, including surgery, they pose an economic challenge to biomedicine.[13]

Homeopathy

In re Guess involved a licensed physician practicing family medicine who administered homeopathic remedies to his patients when conventional treatment failed.[14] The Board of Medical Examiners of North Carolina charged Guess with "unprofessional conduct," alleging that his use of homeopathic medicines departed from "standards of acceptable and prevailing medical practice in North Carolina."[15]

At the hearing, there was no evidence that the homeopathic treatment offered by Guess ever had harmed a patient. The decision in *Guess* is similar to that seen in *Rutherford* and other cases: the regulatory authority claims to champion patient welfare, while the patients appear on the provider's behalf. Guess's patients testified that homeopathy had helped them after biomedicine had failed to provide relief. Nonetheless, following the hearing, the board revoked Guess's license to practice medicine but stayed the revocation so long as he refrained from practicing homeopathy.

Guess appealed to the superior court. Upon review, the court reversed and vacated the board's decision, finding that the board's findings, conclusions, and decisions were "not supported by competent, material and substantial evidence and [were] arbitrary and capricious."[16] The appellate court rejected the superior court's reasoning but affirmed the superior court's order reversing the board's decision.[17] According to the appellate court, the board "neither charged nor found that Dr. Guess's departures from approved and prevailing medical practice either endangered or harmed his patients or the public."[18] In the court's opinion, the revocation of a physician's license must be based on conduct detrimental to the public and not "upon conduct that is merely different from that of other practitioners" (835).

The North Carolina Supreme Court reversed the appellate court's decision and reinstated the medical board's decision, finding that the statute, which allowed the board to revoke a physician's license for "any departure from, or the failure to conform to, the standards of acceptable and prevailing medical practice . . . irrespective of whether or not a patient is injured thereby," did not require the board to find an actual threat of harm to patients.[19] The court also rejected the argument that the board had acted arbitrarily in selecting Guess for sanction on the basis of his use of homeopathy. Finally, the court rejected the argument that the board's decision invaded patients' constitutional privacy interests in choice of treatment.[20]

The broad language in the statute analyzed in *Guess,* permitting revocation of licensure for "any" departure, without requiring any showing of injury to a patient, and without providing a definition of "acceptable and prevailing medical practice,"[21] suggests that practitioners can become targets of bias on the part of state medical boards hostile to a particular therapy. In *Guess,* the defendant was a "highly qualified physician" who, according to the dissent, used homeopathic medicines "as a last resort when allopathic medicines . . . [were] not successful."[22] His was "not a case of a quack beguiling the public with snake oil and drums, but a dedicated physician seeking to find new ways to relieve human suffering" (841). The board lacked testimony proving harm to patients and chose Guess for termination of licensure because of his interest in homeopathic medicine.

Chelation Therapy

State medical boards have sanctioned physicians using EDTA chelation therapy without a showing of patient injury. *Rogers v. State Board of Medical Examiners* began with an order by a county medical association to discontinue the use of chelation therapy.[23] The physician refused and was expelled. The state medical board then issued an administrative complaint, followed by a hearing, at the conclusion of which the physician was reprimanded, ordered to cease using chelation therapy in the treatment of arteriosclerosis, and placed on probation for one year. The physician sought judicial review.

The court observed that neither the hearing officer nor the board had made any finding that chelation therapy was harmful or hazardous to the patient. Rather, the board's decision had been based on the hearing officer's determination that chelation therapy is "quackery under the guise of scientific medicine."[24] The court further observed that the physician had offered chelation therapy as a "treatment" rather than a "cure" for arteriosclerosis, and only after fully disclosing to the patient that chelation therapy had not been proven effective and was in fact disfavored by the medical mainstream (1040). According to the court, the record contained neither allegation nor proof of "fraud, misrepresentation, coercion or overreaching" (1041). In fact, the physician's patients desired to testify as to the beneficial effects of chelation therapy on their health. The medical board, however, specifically excluded these patients from the board hearing on the grounds that "patients themselves are not competent to make those judgments" (1041 n. 3).

The court held that, because of due process rights granted to patients by the Florida state constitution, the board could not, in the absence of a showing of harm, fraud, coercion, or misrepresentation, deprive the patients of their right to receive chelation therapy "simply because that mode of treatment has not received the endorsement of a majority of the medical profession."[25] The court pointed to innovators in medicine and science who were scorned by colleagues: "We can only wonder what would have been the condition of the world today and the field of medicine in particular had those in the midstream of their profession been permitted to prohibit continued treatment and thereby impede progress in those and other fields of science and the healing arts."[26]

The appellate court affirmed the lower court's decision, looking to the due process rights of physicians rather than patients. The appellate court held that the medical board's action restraining the physician from further use of chelation treatment was an arbitrary and unreasonable exercise of the police power and was unconstitutional under the Florida constitution's due process clause.[27]

The applicable Florida statute, like the statute in *Guess,* defined unprofessional conduct as "any departure from, or the failure to conform to, the standards of acceptable and prevailing medical practice in . . . [the physician's] area of expertise as determined by the [state medical board], in which proceeding actual injury to a patient need not be established."[28] Unlike the *Guess* court, however, the appellate court in *Rogers* concluded that absent evidence of fraud, deception, harm, or quackery, and because sanctions were imposed solely because the board did not accept chelation therapy, the board's limitation on chelation therapy lacked a reasonable relationship to the protection of public health and welfare.[29] The court thus interpreted the Florida constitution's due process clause to limit medical boards' ability to sanction physicians for "any departure" from prevailing and acceptable medical standards.

Ozone Therapy

Atkins v. Guest involved a New York physician whose use of ozone therapy, an alternative cancer therapy, made him the target of a medical board investigation.[30] Atkins's patient had been diagnosed with breast cancer, had undergone a left mastectomy, had six months of chemotherapy, and was cancer-free for four years until a blood test indicated the presence of cancer cells (235). She consulted Atkins, who commenced ozone therapy and a nutritional program. During the second week of treatment, the patient felt weak and was sent to a hospital. She then was transferred to another hospital's emergency room, treated in a hyperbaric chamber, and released with no apparent side effects or injuries.[31] The emergency room physician who treated the patient complained to the relevant professional authorities about Atkins's ozone therapy treatment.

The Board of Professional Medical Conduct issued a subpoena seeking production by Atkins of the patient's medical records. Atkins moved to quash the subpoena and to compel the board to produce the complaint against him. In evaluating Atkins's motion, the court observed that the patient willingly revealed her name in an affidavit in support of Atkins's petition to quash the subpoena,[32] and that the complaining physician publicized his complaint against Atkins in the media (237).

Despite these findings, however, the court rejected Atkins's assertion that he could not legally be found negligent or incompetent merely for practicing ozone therapy. The court held that this issue was "best left up to the Board." To issue a subpoena in such an investigation, the board needed only " 'some basis for inquisitorial action' . . . not a threshold substantiation of the charges made in the complaint."[33] The court declined to quash the subpoena, holding that the legislature intended that during the course of an investigation the board's subpoena powers would override the physician-patient privilege.[34] The court also declined to order the release of the complaint for Atkins's use in a defamation action, holding that this was prohibited by the relevant statute's requirement that the complaint be kept confidential.[35]

State Medical Freedom Acts

Cases involving homeopathy, chelation therapy, and ozone therapy suggest the disciplinary risks that physicians face when using alternative and complementary therapies. Physicians who offer their patients self-hypnosis and therapeutic touch,[36] intuitive diagnosis,[37] environmental medicine,[38] and other treatments described in the *Chantilly Report* or taught in medical school courses on alternative health care similarly risk discipline, including loss of licensure, for deviating from the current biomedical model.[39] The twin issues of physicians' vulnerability and medical boards' unfettered discretion in disciplining physicians challenge medical freedom and innovation and discourage a patient-centered approach that integrates nonbiomedical alternatives.

Physicians who come under investigation face damage to their reputation as well as possible loss of livelihood. They often have a limited right to discovery and face prosecutors who have "startling . . . combinations of functions."[40] These procedural hurdles make defense difficult and burdensome. Added to the emotional, financial, and professional costs is the fact that complaints are initiated anonymously, may be motivated by jealousy or competition or be emotionally charged, and are not screened for probable cause or personal animus.

A concern about abuse of medical boards' disciplinary authority is expressed in recent statutes curbing such authority in the case of physicians offering innovative, experimental, or complementary and alternative treatments. For instance, some legislatures have prohibited medical boards from basing a finding of unprofessional or dishonorable conduct solely on the fact that a licensee practices chelation therapy, so long as informed consent is obtained and other criteria are met.[41] The common thread running through these statutes is the legislative desire to protect patients from actual harm,[42] rather than ratify distrust of controversial therapies.

While some statutes limit their focus to chelation therapy, others address health care freedom more generally. Alaska enacted the first such statute in 1990 and was followed by Washington (1991), North Carolina (1993), Oklahoma (1994), New York (1994), and Oregon (1995).[43] The statutes vary according to the individual state's existing legislative framework and political temperament. For example, Alaska's legislation provides that the medical board "may not base a finding of professional incompetence solely on the basis that a licensee's practice is unconventional or experimental in the absence of demonstrably physical harm to a patient."[44] Unlike the statute in *Guess,* Alaska's statute requires a finding that "demonstrably physical harm" resulted from the unconventional or experimental therapy. The language places the burden of proof on the state medical board and specifies that there must be actual physical harm, and not merely the speculation of harm or the inference that the patient was harmed by using alternative therapies rather than, or in addition to, biomedicine.[45]

Washington's legislation provides that "the use of a nontraditional treatment by itself shall not constitute unprofessional conduct, provided that it does not result in injury to a patient or create an unreasonable risk that a patient may be harmed."[46] Unlike the statute in *Guess,* the Washington statute requires a showing of injury to a patient or unreasonable risk of injury. The specified level of harm is lower than in the Alaska provision; however, the statute clarifies that physicians should not be disciplined merely because they use therapies that are "nontraditional."

The North Carolina legislation enacted in response to *Guess* directly amends the disciplinary provisions of the state's medical licensing act. The statute provides that "the Board shall not revoke the license of or deny a license to a person solely because of that person's practice of a therapy that is experimental, nontraditional, or that departs from acceptable and prevailing medical practices unless, by competent evidence, the Board can establish that the treatment has a safety risk greater than the prevailing treatment or that the treatment is generally not effective."[47] North Carolina's law thus also requires proof that a patient was harmed, and places the burden on the state medical board to establish by competent evidence a safety risk or lack of effectiveness.

Oklahoma's legislation provides that the medical board "shall not revoke the license of a person otherwise qualified to practice allopathic medicine within the meaning of this act solely because the person's practice or a therapy is experimental or nontraditional."[48] The statute does not mention patient harm. Like North Carolina's statute, however, it frees physicians from the threat of discipline simply because of their use of an "experimental or nontraditional" practice or therapy such as homeopathy, chelation therapy, ozone therapy, or nutritional and herbal treatment.

Oregon's legislation provides that "the use of an alternative medical treatment shall not by itself constitute unprofessional conduct."[49] It defines "alternative medical treatment" as a treatment "that the treating physician, based on the physician's professional experience, has an objective basis to believe has a reasonable probability for effectiveness in its intended use even if the treatment is outside recognized scientific guidelines, is unproven, is no longer used as a generally recognized or standard treatment or lacks the approval of the United States Food and Drug Administration; [as long as that therapy] . . . is supported for specific usages or outcomes by at least one other physician licensed by the Board of Medical Examiners; and . . . poses no greater risk to a patient than the generally recognized or standard treatment."[50]

New York's legislation provides that nothing in the medical practice act shall be construed to prevent a licensed physician from using "whatever medical care, conventional or nonconventional, . . . effectively treats human disease, pain, injury, deformity, or physical condition."[51] The legislation also creates a board for professional medical conduct, to contain at least two physicians "who dedicate a significant portion of their practice to the use of non-conventional medical treatments."[52]

Supporting legislative history notes that one in three Americans uses complementary and alternative therapies, that the federal government has recognized these therapies by creating the Office of Complementary and Alternative Medicine, that Columbia University and the Albert Einstein Medical College both have departments of alternative medicine, and that Albany Medical College offers classes in alternative medicine.[53] The legislative history also notes that the statute addresses "concerns regarding the treatment of non-conventional physicians in the professional medical conduct process by recognizing the role of legitimate non-conventional medical treatments in the practice of medicine." Further, the statute "is designed to safeguard patients' rights and guarantee legitimate due process for non-conventional physicians by removing institutional disincentives to the use of sound non-conventional treatments."[54]

Moreover, because the statute "is actually a restatement or affirmation" of the language in the medical practice act defining the practice of medicine, the legislation broadens the concept of medicine, not merely the parameters for the professional discipline.[55] The legislation thus potentially affects not only the breadth of permissible medical practice in New York but also other aspects of health care and health care regulation, such as insurance reimbursement, medical education, and hospital staffing and disciplinary policies. For example, although insurers denying reimbursement claims for complementary and alternative medicine may claim that such treatments are "medically unnecessary" simply because they are not generally accepted by the biomedical community, the statute in fact redefines medicine to include such therapies (see chap. 8).

Finally, the statute places on the state medical board the burden of showing that the physician utilized a treatment lacking in efficacy. The legislation creates "legitimate peer review" for clinical practice that is "foreign, innovative, or has been shown to be effective, but has not yet achieved general acceptance in the United States."[56] Thus, the physician's defense in any medical board hearing can include medical literature from abroad and studies that have not yet been peer reviewed or published in conventional medical journals but that are based on sound science and empirical observation.

Such state medical freedom acts, while controversial, respect the voluntary and knowing choices of the patients who visit complementary and alternative providers, and are consistent with informed consent, the right to refuse treatment, and other legal doctrines protecting the patient's interest in bodily integrity and freedom of choice in health care treatment. The statutes vary from ensuring fairness in disciplinary proceedings to redefining the concept of medicine.[57] These statutes legislatively create a right of patient access to complementary and alternative health care, the right that patients unsuccessfully sought to establish as a constitutional right in *Rutherford, Privitera,* and other litigation.

8

THIRD-PARTY REIMBURSEMENT

Voluntary and Mandated Coverage

Because the biomedical view of what constitutes health care has dominated reimbursement, insurers historically have denied coverage for complementary and alternative health care. Third-party reimbursement has been available for approaches to disease that cure, rather than heal — even if patients remain physically, emotionally, or spiritually fragmented; that focus on biochemical and physiological responses to treatment — even if therapies are toxic, unduly invasive, or potentially lethal; that are based on therapies backed by the results of randomized controlled trials published in generally accepted medical journals — even if such trials fail to account for the consciousness and intention of the researcher; that attack invading agents and perpetuate or enhance biological existence — even if the disease calls for holistic approaches to restoration of function and wholeness. Insurers traditionally have denied claims for therapies focusing on psychosocial or spiritual dimensions of illness or using nutrition, prevention, and self-healing.

The traditional insurance approach — limiting reimbursement to procedures within the biomedical model — is appropriate when health losses are viewed strictly in terms of physical disability or specific technological events. Health insurance in fact grew out of a biomedically oriented system, beginning with employers contracting with physicians to care for employees who had work-related injuries.[1] Only biomedically diagnosable disease was considered an insurable event, and only biomedical treatment was considered a reimbursable event. The system focused on "disease care" rather than "health care." But as notions of health evolve and include preventive choices, holistic healing, and self-care, the notion of reimbursable health "losses" potentially embraces a broader set of deviations from well-being. Lack of proper nutrition, stress, imbalances in vital energy, and even the emotional and spiritual crises underlying disease, such as loneliness, depression, anxiety, and unexpressed frustration and rage, all may, in the future, be viewed as precursors to disease and become appropriate foci for reimbursable health care intervention.

Patients spend significant resources out-of-pocket on alternative health care (see chap. 1). For some, however, access to complementary and alternative therapies, particularly for long-term or chronic conditions, depends on third-party payment. A constitutional or statutory right of access to health care treatments — as embodied in the Access to Medical Treatment Act, in state medical freedom acts, in other legislation, and in cases such as *Andrews v. Ballard,* loses impact if patients cannot afford unreimbursable therapies or if insurance reimbursement schemes skew treatment in favor of risky and potentially debilitating biomedical therapies such as high-dose chemotherapy with autologous bone marrow transplant. Moreover, given the way in which insurance schemes (particularly in managed care) determine the nature and level of medical care the patient receives, including complementary and alternative medicine in insurance reimbursement schemes will facilitate the integration of holistic modalities into the U.S. health care system. Patients seeking to use modalities such as acupuncture and massage to complement biomedical care will require insurance coverage that encompasses both systems of patient care.

Many insurers are experimenting with coverage reimbursing various kinds of holistic care. American Western Life Insurance offers Prevention Plus, an integrated health insurance plan that offers up to twelve annual visits to alternative providers alongside a conventional medical network of over 650 hospitals. Insurers such as Mutual of Omaha Companies cover the Reversal Program, a prevention and behavior modification program to reduce the risk of heart disease through yoga, meditation, diet, and support groups.[2] The Harvard Community Health Plan, in Massachusetts, offers behavioral medicine, including mind-body relaxation, as preventive care. Other plans that do the same include the Oxford Health Plan, in New York; Lovelace Health Systems, in Albuquerque; Kaiser Permanente, in California; and American Medical Security's HealthCareChoice, in Arizona, Wisconsin, Texas, North Carolina, and Colorado. The list of insurers and covered services and providers grows,[3] as insurers contemplate potential cost savings, consumer demand, and a "wellness" approach that is attractive to employers, among others, who will pay for nutritional support, counseling, and lifestyle modifications in exchange for fewer cholesterol screenings and blood pressure checks.[4]

Designing programs to offer holistic therapies in a manner appropriate to insurers, providers, and consumers requires looking to licensing laws and scope-of-practice rules to ensure that providers within insurance networks are properly credentialed and are offering services within their legislative authorization. Providing access to licensed providers will be more palatable than reimbursing visits to unlicensed practitioners. Even among licensed providers, services will range from those more familiar to the biomedical model (such as Swedish massage to relax the body and improve circulation) to the more esoteric (such as movement of human energy fields through noncontact therapeutic touch).[5] Insurers also must familiarize themselves with the professional organizations, ethical codes, standards of care, and malpractice and disciplinary rules relevant to the providers within the holistic health care networks.

Many believe that the insurance industry should stay out of complementary and alternative health care. The argument is that insurance policy coverage and exclusions, utilization review, and other insurance rules and practices already have too much influence over the quantity and quality of medical care delivered. Moreover, the market and economic orientation of the insurance industry may distort the principle of holistic care. For example, such concepts as "prayer" and "managed care" seem incompatible; one may imagine a pastoral counselor visiting a hospitalized patient for an allotted number of minutes to deliver a reimbursable conversation with God.

States have imposed numerous insurance mandates affecting the provision of complementary and alternative medicine. Mandated benefit laws require insurers to cover certain benefits — for example, chiropractic care or acupuncture. Many states (at least forty-six) require insurers to reimburse for chiropractic care; at least six require insurance reimbursement for acupuncture.[6] Mandated provider laws require that insurers cover services offered by various providers — for example, chiropractors and acupuncturists — if the insurer would cover the service when provided by a physician. Some "any willing provider" laws require that insurers offering preferred provider policies establish the terms and conditions governing practitioners' eligibility to be preferred providers; that such terms and conditions may not discriminate against or among health care providers; and that such policies may not exclude any preferred provider willing to meet the terms and conditions set forth. For example, Virginia provides that "no hospital, physician, or type of provider listed . . . willing to meet the terms and conditions offered to it or him shall be excluded."[7] Thus, if a hospital sets contract terms and conditions for providers offering rehabilitative care, and such care is offered by licensed physicians, chiropractors, and physical therapists, each within their authorized scope of practice, then the hospital must make the contract available to any of the three providers and may not discriminate among them.

Some states vary or extend the rule to plans other than preferred provider policies. For instance, Florida provides that "when any health insurance policy, health care services plan, or other contract provides for the payment for medical expense benefits or procedures, such policy, plan or contract shall be construed to include payment to a chiropractic physician who provides the medical service benefits or procedures which are within the scope of a chiropractic physician's license."[8] The insurer may not discriminate against chiropractors who, within their authorized scope of practice, offer the same service or benefit as does a biomedical physician. Similarly, Louisiana provides that whenever an insurance policy provides for reimbursement of any service, and that service may be performed by chiropractors within their scope of practice, the insurer must reimburse for the chiropractic treatment.[9] Likewise, Alaska provides that, with certain exceptions, a person "may not practice or permit unfair discrimination against a person who provides a service covered under a group disability policy that extends coverage on an expense incurred basis, or under a group service or indemnity type contract issued by a nonprofit corporation, if the service is within the scope of the provider's occupational license."[10] The statute defines "provider" to include state-licensed chiropractors, nurse midwives, naturopaths, and certified direct-entry midwives.[11] Florida's statute provides that any policy of individual health insurance that covers acupuncture must cover the services of a certified acupuncturist "under the same conditions that apply to services of a licensed physician."[12]

The state of Washington has enacted a particularly expansive and controversial statute as part of its health care reform effort. The legislation requires that every state health plan permit "every category of health care provider to provide health services or care for conditions included in the basic health plan services to the extent that: (a) The provision of such health services or care is within the health care provider's permitted scope of practice; and (b) The providers agree to abide by standards related to: (i) Provision, utilization review, and cost containment of health services; (ii) Management and administrative procedures; and (iii) Provision of cost-effective and clinically efficacious health services."[13] For example, if coverage for rehabilitation therapy is part of the state's basic health plan, then every Washington insurer must cover a claim for that service, whether the treatment was given by a licensed osteopathic physician, chiropractor, physical therapist, or massage therapist (even if such providers were not originally included in the insurance contract), provided the practitioner is duly licensed, certified, or registered, is providing the treatment within the legislatively authorized scope of practice, and complies with utilization review and other standards indicated in the statute. Similarly, Washington insurers must cover claims for services by acupuncturists (even if acupuncturists were excluded from coverage by the specific health plan) if the condition treated is one covered by the basic health plan and the acupuncturist is providing service within his or her scope of practice.

Some Washington insurers have interpreted the statute narrowly. These insurers have attempted to exclude particular plans or providers, add various hurdles for certain providers, and limit the number of visits or maximum benefit amount depending on the provider. The state insurance commissioner responded in several bulletins to "disturbing reports" that insurers were attempting to evade the statutory requirements. The bulletins clarified, among other things, that carriers may not exclude a category of provider by asserting that the category fails to meet the carrier's standards for provision of "cost-effective and clinically efficacious health services." The bulletins also stated that services within the provider's permitted scope of practice had to be covered "without discrimination on the basis of provider type." The bulletins affirmed the commissioner's willingness "to take all enforcement actions necessary to prevent any other practices that circumvent" the statute.[14] Eight insurers subsequently filed suit, challenging the insurance commissioner's rule making; the litigation is pending.[15]

The possibility of deeper integration of complementary and alternative medicine into health care delivery is offered not only by experimentation with private insurance plans, mandated coverage, and "any willing provider" legislation and other insurance equity laws, but also by managed care. Managed care is driven by the market rather than by statutory mandate and thus permits broad experimentation with varying providers, services, and coverage. Because managed care plans shift the focus to disease prevention and health promotion, and coordinate services "based on patient's total health needs (rather than on isolated responses to specific symptoms),"[16] they can serve as opportunities to explore ways in which biomedical expertise can be integrated with perspectives from other disciplines to determine the optimal course of patients' healing.

Managed care organizations will face issues relating to provider credentialing, scope-of-practice limitations, nutritional therapies and claims, disciplining of providers, and the use of reimbursement policies to facilitate appropriate integration of biomedical and holistic care. As discussed in chapter 5, managed care organizations will need to implement appropriate procedures to minimize direct and vicarious malpractice liability. Finally, managed care organizations will need to monitor consumer satisfaction as well as cost-effectiveness to determine whether managed care truly should be in the business of reimbursing for complementary and alternative therapies.

Selected Exclusions and Coverage Issues
Experimental Treatments

Even when patients are covered by private insurance policies, employee benefit plans subject to the Employee Retirement Income Security Act of 1974 (ERISA), managed care contracts, or other kinds of insurance policies, the acupuncturists, naturopaths, chiropractors, massage therapists, and other complementary and alternative providers who treat such patients sometimes find reimbursement declined, because the insurer views the therapy either as "medically unnecessary" or as falling within the "experimental treatment" exclusion.

Insurers exclude experimental treatments from coverage to avoid paying for expensive medical treatments of unknown efficacy.[17] Although some courts construe experimental treatment broadly to mean treatments that are not generally accepted or supported by satisfactory documentation, experimental treatments also may be defined more narrowly as involving procedures designed to test a hypothesis or contribute to generalized knowledge as part of a defined research protocol. Examples include high-technology organ transplant procedures, high-dose chemotherapy with autologous bone marrow transplant, and the use of a $30-million proton beam accelerator to treat ocular melanoma.[18] Even in these cases, insurers and courts reviewing insurer reimbursement decisions differ as to whether particular procedures can be excluded as experimental.[19]

A therapy is not necessarily experimental simply because it has not found general acceptance within the biomedical community. Complementary and alternative treatments generally are preventive and oriented toward overall health and well-being, since the holistic approach aims to translate psychological, emotional, and spiritual relief into improved physiological functioning. The treatments frequently derive from systems of knowledge that have historically been foreign to conventional scientific research methodologies, are practiced largely by nonphysicians, are individualized and not research-driven, are less expensive than highly technological treatments, and are not subject to proof under "ongoing, recognized and accepted medical research procedures,"[20] although efforts have been made to subject such treatments to scientific study. These factors provide a basis for insurers and for courts reviewing insurance decisions to differentiate complementary and alternative medicine from treatments typically considered excludable as experimental treatments.

Perhaps in recognition of such a distinction, the FDA recently reclassified acupuncture needles as Class II devices, or medical devices for general use, by acupuncture practitioners, rather than as Class III investigational devices limited to research. Under the FDA decision, acupuncture needles must be labeled "For Single Use Only," their sale must be clearly restricted to qualified practitioners of acupuncture, and regulations on "device material biocompatibility" and "device sterility" must be followed.[21] The new FDA policy may prompt insurers to reclassify therapies such as acupuncture as reimbursable, rather than excludable as investigational or experimental.

Many alternative and complementary therapies, such as acupuncture, are supported by research that has not reached a level of general acceptance (such as research published in foreign journals, studies with nontraditional methodologies, and small-scale, private, clinical trials that have not been subject to rigorous peer review). To distinguish between *complementary and alternative* and *experimental* treatment, insurers could look to whether a treatment, such as acupuncture or massage therapy, is supported by research, has been efficacious, or has resulted in a positive outcome for the patient. Courts and insurers should begin expanding the professional community whose judgment on the question matters.

The process of integrating complementary and alternative providers and therapies into legal and professional dialogue concerning the meaning of "experimental treatment" in third-party reimbursement parallels the process of integrating these providers and therapies into decisions regarding malpractice, scope of practice, tort duties relating to referral, misrepresentation, and other legal rules. In the process, insurers and courts may find that notions of what is experimental often are culturally and politically determined and will vary as biomedicine edges toward a health care system that safely integrates previously suspect or marginalized disciplines.

Medically Necessary Treatments

Many health insurance policies, while including a variety of providers and covered services, limit coverage to "medically necessary" treatments, those which are "reasonably intended, in the exercise of good medical practice, for the treatment of illness or injury."[22] A major purpose in limiting coverage to medically necessary treatment is to limit insurers' reimbursement for patients' overconsumption of care. On the whole, chiropractic, homeopathy, acupuncture and massage therapy, vitamins and minerals, and other such treatments—particularly when used on a preventative basis—present less of a financial burden to insurers than biomedical treatments involving hospitalization and surgery.[23]

Insurers argue that complementary and alternative therapies are not medically necessary because they do not enjoy the same level of scientific support as corresponding biomedical treatments. Again, what is medically necessary or experimental frequently depends on the composition of the professional community determining the scope of acceptable treatment. As providers integrate complementary and alternative medicine and biomedicine, notions of medical necessity may evolve to include procedures necessary for balancing chi, for example, and for prevention of disease and maintenance of wholeness as a component of physical health. Homeopathic remedies, nutritional therapies, and spinal manipulation may be considered necessary components of health care, as peer-review panels include complementary and alternative providers to ensure that the services claimed as medically necessary include modalities outside the biomedical model.

Some courts have provided a foundation for this position by accepting treatments such as chiropractic and massage therapy, as well as nonstandard medical treatments, within the notion of medical necessity.[24] In *Day v. Aetna Employees Benefit Division*,[25] an Ohio court upheld the decision of a municipal court that chelation therapy, which the patient decided to undergo in lieu of bypass surgery, was "broadly accepted professionally as essential to the treatment of the disease" and was thus "necessary" treatment, within the meaning of the patient's insurance policy, for reimbursement purposes.[26] In *Dallis v. Aetna*,[27] the Northern District of Georgia held that immunoaugmentative therapy for cancer was not medically unnecessary within the insurance policy. The court relied on the fact that the patient had not responded to conventional cancer treatment, and on the ambiguity inherent in the notion of necessity.

These decisions are consistent with *Taulbee v. The Travelers Company*,[28] in which an Ohio appellate court held that immunoaugmentative therapy was medically necessary because chemotherapy had failed.[29] In *McLaughlin v. Connecticut General Life Insurance Company*,[30] the Northern District of California held that lack of FDA approval of immunoaugmentative therapy did not exclude the treatment from coverage as medically unnecessary. The court observed: "The fact that FDA has not approved a treatment does not automatically mean that a treatment is worthless" (451). *McLaughlin* suggests a departure not only from reliance on the biomedical model for interpretation of medical necessity, but also from insurer dependence on FDA approval to legitimize complementary and alternative therapies.

Such a departure is also reflected in *Harvey v. Travelers Insurance Company*,[31] which centered on an insured patient who had received environmental therapy to treat a brain injury. The court noted that the goals of the treatment had been "to develop [the insured's] ability to actively and productively engage in social intercourse; to treat and attempt to cure her mental and/or emotional deficiencies, and not necessarily to diagnose and care for her physical illnesses" (265).[32]

Similarly, *Tudor v. Metropolitan Life Insurance Company* upheld as medically necessary a treatment based on nutritional deficiencies and food allergies.[33] The court observed that the method of treatment was not so deviant from generally accepted medical practices as to be nonmedical. Finally, in *Shumake v. Travelers Insurance Company*,[34] a Michigan appellate court held that laetrile and nutritional therapies were medically necessary because medicine continually evolves and the patient's physician had recommended these therapies as necessary before laetrile was discredited by the medical community. These decisions suggest some judicial acceptance of reimbursement for therapies outside biomedicine.

Health Care Fraud and Insurance Fraud

Providing fraudulent treatments and/or submitting reimbursement claims to third-party payers for such services can be the basis for sanction under a variety of legal rules, including state medical board disciplinary rules and federal and state criminal and civil fraud laws such as Medicare and Medicaid antifraud rules. These legal rules aim to protect patients from deceitful and dangerous health care practices.

It should be recognized that deviant and dangerous practitioners can exist among holistic as well as biomedical providers.[35] At the same time, the broad reach of antifraud rules must be considered in the context of historical antagonism between medical orthodoxy and its challengers and the effect of this rivalry on the regulatory structure. Because many complementary and alternative treatments are not generally accepted within the biomedical community and/or lack FDA approval, providing such treatments and submitting appropriate claims for reimbursement could be deemed to be fraudulent per se. Drawing the legal boundaries of health care fraud and insurance fraud may be as slippery an exercise as defining scope-of-practice rules for complementary and alternative providers offering nutritional and other treatments, applying medical practice acts to unlicensed holistic practitioners who are not diagnosing and treating biomedically defined disease, and determining the scope of appropriate informed consent where sufficient evidence exists to suggest that holistic modalities provide viable complementary or alternative approaches to disease management.

The difficulty in distinguishing fraud per se from complementary and alternative approaches to health care is suggested in litigation involving controversial cancer treatments, the FDA, and insurance reimbursement. For example, in 1983 the FDA raided Stanislaw Burzynski's offices, seized patients' records and files, and sued the Burzynski Research Institute, alleging violations of the Food, Drug, and Cosmetic Act. The FDA obtained a permanent injunction prohibiting Burzynski from distributing his antineoplaston treatment in interstate commerce but permitting treatment "undertaken strictly and wholly intrastate."[36] Burzynski sued the FDA, alleging wrongful interference with his patients' insurance payments; bad faith in failing to process his Investigational New Drug and Good Manufacturing Practices applications; malicious distribution of false and misleading information regarding antineoplaston to patients and insurers; and malicious and illegal seizure of patients' records.[37] The court denied Burzynski's claims. Quoting *Rutherford,* the trial judge gave little credence to patients' interest in the treatment and to their reports that, while conventional treatment had failed, Burzynski's therapy had been lifesaving. The U.S. Court of Appeals for the Fifth Circuit, affirming, rejected patients' claim that they had a constitutional privacy right entitling them to obtain treatment, stating: "When the subject of investigation is the existence of cancer, the personal testimony of the lay sufferer is entitled to no weight."[38]

Later litigation involved the denial by the Aetna Life Insurance Company of a patient's claim for expenses incurred in connection with Burzynski's antineoplaston treatment. The patient had terminal lung cancer. The cancer had "no known conventional or generally accepted curative treatment."[39] As chemotherapy resulted in no improvement, the patient contacted Burzynski and began antineoplaston treatment as a treatment of last resort. Aetna denied the patient's reimbursement claim as medically unnecessary and experimental. The patient sued Aetna and assigned the claim to Burzynski. Aetna counterclaimed under the Racketeer Influenced and Corrupt Organizations Act (RICO) for mail and wire fraud, alleging that Burzynski had made false representations about the effectiveness of antineoplaston treatment, fraudulently inducing patients to pay for worthless treatments and using fraudulent reimbursement procedures to induce Aetna to pay for these treatments. Aetna thus took the position that the nonconventional care was worthless, and hence not only medically unnecessary but also fraudulent.

Aetna's policy, which excluded charges for services and supplies which are "not necessary for treatment of the disease . . . and which are unreasonable," in fact did not define "necessary" or "unreasonable." Further, the policy made no provision for treatments not generally accepted by the medical profession or lacking FDA approval. The court could have ruled for the insured and for Burzynski on the basis of the ambiguity inherent in the policy, and of the patient's reasonable expectations of coverage.[40] However, the court relied on the conclusion of Aetna's physicians that the treatment had no medical value. The court thus upheld Aetna's denial of coverage, finding that it was not arbitrary or capricious.[41]

In *Trustees of the Northwest Laundry and Dry Cleaners Health and Welfare Trust Fund v. Burzynski,* the fund sued Burzynski for fraud and violations of ERISA and RICO, alleging that it had reimbursed one of its claimants, an Oregon resident with cancer of the esophagus, for illegal treatments.[42] The ERISA plan under which the patient was covered provided for payment for "medically necessary" treatment. Oregon law had two criteria for "medically necessary" treatments: first, the treatments had to be "appropriate and consistent with the diagnosis (in accord with accepted standards of community practice)," and, second, they had to be treatments that "could not be omitted without adversely affecting the covered person's condition or the quality of medical care" (156). The court held that Burzynski's treatments were not "medically necessary" under the plan, and that Burzynski had indeed defrauded the fund by "materially misrepresenting the legality of his antineoplastin *[sic]* treatment."[43] Another Texas court, diverging from this line of cases, upheld a judgment for breach of contract and breach of the duty of good faith and fair dealing rendered in favor of one of Burzynski's patients, against his insurer.[44]

The identification of complementary and alternative health care with treatment that is medical unnecessary, and thus fraudulent, is overly broad. The legal conclusion of fraud must be carefully examined, since *fraud,* like *quackery,* historically has served as an epithet to indict biomedicine's rivals.[45] The legal definition of fraud involves "anything calculated to deceive, including all acts, omissions, and concealments involving a breach of legal or equitable duty, trust, or confidence justly reposed, resulting in damage to another or by which an undue and unconscionable advantage is taken of another."[46] The definition thus includes a mental state, intent to deceive; and an act, deception.[47] The mental state requires knowledge that one's conduct will deceive, as opposed to mere negligence.[48] The applicability of fraud depends on the conduct and mental state. Consider the following examples:

1. The provider promises the patient a complete cure, knowing that the treatment is unsafe and lacks efficacy.
2. The provider promises a cure and honestly believes the promise.
3. The provider, who has no intention of deceiving the patient into expecting a quick cure or forgoing medical treatment, tells the patient, "I am not diagnosing or treating your medical condition. I am diagnosing and treating the vital energy in your field. The risks are as follows, and there is limited scientific evidence of efficacy. The treatment could, in my view, conceivably translate into physiological benefits, but you should consult your medical doctor regarding your disease or condition."

In scenario 1, the provider has intentionally deceived the patient into believing that the treatment is effective — for instance, that drinking watermelon juice will eliminate a cancerous tumor. The elements of fraud are present, resulting in justifiable liability or prosecution.[49]

In scenario 2, the element of intent is missing: the provider honestly believes that the treatment will help the patient. The provider may be liable for civil negligence or criminal negligence, or may be criminally liable under state medical practice acts for holding himself out as a medical doctor, depending on the representation, the conduct, and the statute.[50] However, fraud has not been committed, because the intent to deceive is lacking.

Scenario 3 suggests an appropriate disclaimer and contract with the patient, as well as fulfillment of the duty to refer. As suggested, providers of complementary and alternative medicine who operate within professional practice parameters and ethical guidelines must ensure that their clients understand the limits of holistic health care and receive appropriate biomedical care. The contract or disclosure allows the patient to voluntarily and intelligently assume specific risks, if any. No fraud has been committed, nor has there been misrepresentation or inducement of reliance on non-biomedical care. Appropriate agreement on healing methodology and goals helps to protect the provider in a malpractice claim or a state medical board disciplinary action, each of which may be predicated upon use of an complementary and alternative therapy without appropriate disclosure and informed consent.[51]

The goal of encouraging appropriate integration should underlie future legislative efforts in the area of health care fraud. Although civil fraud and criminal fraud statutes provide means of protecting patients from dangerous health care practices, lawmakers can more fully serve the legitimate public policy goals of preserving and promoting patients' health by disengaging from the historical rhetoric against complementary and alternative providers (see chap. 9). This process, in turn, will strengthen insurers' efforts to meet patients' health care needs by opening responsible reimbursement gateways to alternative and complementary providers.

9

THE EVOLUTION OF
LEGAL AUTHORITY

Professional Licensure and Scope of Practice

In the early twentieth century, chiropractors were imprisoned for practicing spinal manipulation. "Go to jail for chiropractic" was a popular slogan for the profession.[1] The practice of acupuncture was virtually unknown in Western medical circles; there were no licensed acupuncture providers. Massage was outlawed or regulated as prostitution; touch was regarded as invariably connected to prohibited (and sinful) sexual misconduct. Naturopaths, midwives, lay homeopaths, faith healers, and other providers were prosecuted for practicing medicine unlawfully.

Many of these providers now have licensure. Many still risk prosecution under state medical practice acts. Even licensed providers may be viewed as crossing into medical diagnosis and treatment. The line between authorized practice and unauthorized practice is perhaps impossible to draw, particularly where providers are legislatively authorized to engage in their own methods of detecting and managing imbalance and dysfunction — "acupuncture diagnosis," for example, or "chiropractic diagnosis."[2] The legislative authorization embedded in these terms contradicts the narrow interpretation of medical practice acts exemplified in cases such as *People v. Amber* (chap. 3) and *People v. Beno* (chap. 4), which assign all diagnosis and treatment to biomedical doctors.

Scope-of-practice rules reflect the notion that the enterprise of healing can be carved into neatly severable and licensable blocks. Scope of practice, however, is inherently reductionistic and problematic. For example, chiropractors are understood (as in *Beno*) to address only spinal problems, psychologists to address only emotional issues, massage therapists to address only musculoskeletal issues, and physicians to address only physiological and biochemical dysfunction, as if these various aspects of the human organism are disconnected rather than unified. Holistic practice recognizes the interrelatedness of biochemical, environmental, social, nutritional, emotional, and other factors in health care. Professional functions among providers overlap, and "drawing lines between groups of practitioners based on scope of practice definitions that are as broad as the description of a color is futile."[3]

Legislative scope-of-practice language must be specific enough to cover areas of ambiguity (such as nutritional guidance rendered by chiropractors), yet broad enough to support holistic practice. Practice boundaries might better be drawn by specifying what providers may not do: for example, massage therapists may not engage in spinal manipulation, and chiropractors may not prescribe medication.[4] The legal structure should evolve to protect the person's search for wholeness and healing, reflecting the assumption that an intervention, be it spinal manipulation, massage, psychotherapy, nutrition, or spiritual healing, affects the whole being in the healing process, even if the effect does not register under prevailing scientific methodologies in ways wholly satisfactory to the dominant paradigm.

Thus, while continuing to protect patients from truly unscrupulous and dangerous providers, courts can recognize a distinction between healing (a process involving the whole person) and curing (the attempt to create a specific biochemical and physiological outcome).[5] Providers whose practices aim to nourish, balance, and stimulate vital energy, rather than diagnose and treat pathology, should be viewed as outside the purview of state medical practice acts. State medical practice acts should reflect the view that providers other than licensed medical doctors are prohibited only from *biomedical* diagnosis and treatment, or from such specific acts as severing tissues or recommending prescription medication. Narrowing the reach of medical practice acts to redefine medicine in a manner consistent with medical education and training will support independent holistic providers and licensed alternative providers who maintain professional and ethical standards and refer patients to licensed physicians for biomedical treatment of the patients' underlying disease or condition.

Further, because the definitional requirements for criminal liability under medical practice acts rely on overly broad and shifting concepts such as diagnosis and treatment, tort liabilities provide more appropriate tools for sanctioning providers who overstep their professional boundaries. Tort law provides appropriate protection because it serves to compensate an injured party for the harm suffered, whereas in criminal actions there is an implication of "a bad mind [or] immorality."[6] Even if the provider is acting with intent to deceive or with malice, civil liability for malpractice, fraud, and misrepresentation (including, where appropriate, punitive damages) provides appropriate deterrent and punitive functions.

Malpractice and Professional Discipline

Legal authority can more fully and appropriately integrate complementary care if the duty to refer runs both ways: biomedical physicians should have a duty to refer the patient to a chiropractor, massage therapist, acupuncturist, or other provider when the condition is amenable to such treatment. Conventional physicians should be encouraged to stay current with literature on complementary and alternative health care to determine how such treatments as acupuncture and massage therapy can diminish the need for medication, ease suffering, accelerate healing, or otherwise support their patients' recovery.

Expanding the duty to refer in this way achieves mutuality between biomedical and nonbiomedical providers, so that the two paradigms are no longer separate but function integratively in search of knowledge. Such an approach also respects patients' interest in the most complete, comprehensive, balanced, and effective approach to health care, whether within the biomedical or holistic healing paradigm. A two-way duty to refer parallels expansion of the informed consent doctrine (as discussed in chap. 5) to require disclosure of complementary and alternative treatments.

Furthermore, with regard to malpractice, legal rules should acknowledge the goal of facilitating integration between biomedical and complementary and alternative providers and treatments. For example, legal rules such as the respectable minority doctrine and assumption of risk should shield physicians integrating modalities outside present biomedical acceptance.

In the area of professional discipline, legislation should expand not only patients' freedom of access but also physicians' ability to practice medicine autonomously. Medical freedom acts will allow physicians to innovate responsibly in cases in which complementary and alternative treatments provide nondangerous health care options. This goal of expanding patient choice underpins federal legislation proposing to authorize access to treatments that do not fit the conventional scientific mold or may not be verifiable according to contemporary and generally accepted methodologies. Both federal and state legislative reform shift the regulatory paradigm by loosening reliance on biomedical orthodoxy and using disclosure and agreement rather than prohibition as the primary means of patient protection.[7]

Fraud and Health Care Freedom

Legal authority governing complementary and alternative medicine has been dominated by the desire to protect patients from fraud and from their own unwise health care choices. Lawmakers have tended to identify nonbiomedical treatments with fraud or quackery. For example, as noted, in denying terminally ill cancer patients the right to obtain laetrile, the U.S. Supreme Court has emphasized Congress's concern that "individuals with fatal illnesses, such as cancer, should be shielded from fraudulent cures."[8] The same dismissal of patients' interest in their own bodies and health care is reflected in the suggestion of a Louisiana court, to the effect that there are no alternatives to chemotherapy and that a "reasonable patient" would not even consider alternatives.[9] This attitude similarly is reflected in the conclusion of the U.S. Court for Appeals for the Fifth Circuit that the testimony of "the lay sufferer [who has cancer] is entitled to no weight,"[10] and a medical board's decision to exclude patients from a disciplinary hearing involving their physician's license, on the basis of the belief that patients lack competence to make judgments concerning their own medical care.[11]

Such denigration of the right to bodily integrity and autonomy is reflected in the conclusion of a Texas court that "patients are extremely vulnerable. They will pursue any treatment which provides them with even a glimmer of hope. . . . This pursuit of life can at times lead to irrational thoughts, and certain opportunists would not hesitate to prey on their vulnerability. The State of Texas in conjunction with the FDA protects these patients from such exploitation. . . . We will not allow our sympathy for the terminally ill to hinder our duty to uphold the law."[12] The courts and medical boards assume that because individuals are afflicted with serious disease, they lack judgment about their own self-care. The dismissal of patients' perspectives reflects a history of biomedical paternalism, dominance, and monopoly, ostensibly to the benefit of the "lay sufferer."

Many biomedical and legal authorities continue to sweep treatments outside the medical mainstream under the rubric of fraud. For example, recently enacted federal health insurance reform legislation contains a number of provisions of concern to providers using complementary and alternative medicine. The original bill created a new and undefined crime of health care fraud, and also made it fraudulent to submit insurance claims "for a medical or other item or service that a person knows or should know is not medically necessary."[13] After intervention by providers, legislators clarified that "the practice of alternative medicine in itself would not constitute fraud."[14] The bill was revised to allow prosecution for fraud only if the provider "knowingly and wilfully" attempts to defraud a health care benefit program, thus incorporating the requirement of intentionality into the definition of fraud.[15]

Further, the legislative history now notes the "significant concern regarding the impact of the anti-fraud provisions on the practice of complementary or alternative medicine and health care," reaffirms that the practice of "complementary, alternative, innovative, experimental or investigational medical or health care itself would not constitute fraud," and states that the "conferees intend that this proposal not be interpreted as a prohibition of the practice of these types of medical or health care."[16] However, the legislation still contains provisions for special fraud alerts to be issued by the inspector general,[17] and other provisions aimed at increasing governmental ability to prosecute a broadly defined area of health care fraud.[18]

Legal authority should acknowledge the tendency to use words such as *fraud* and *quackery* to discredit nonbiomedical providers. As complementary and alternative medicine increasingly interpenetrates biomedical practice, the antifraud rationale — the desire to protect patients from dangerous health care practices — will be balanced against respect for the patient's right to make informed and voluntary health care choices. The law may recognize in equipoise to the antifraud rationale that healing can take many forms: that touch may be beneficial; that support, communication, and emotional contact facilitate well-being;[19] that hypnotic, intuitive, and trance states, and prayer, potentially stimulate healing; and that personal wholeness, in all its multifaceted richness, is a social good. These perspectives should be included expressly in legislative reform, administrative rule making, and judicial reasoning.

Deeper respect for health care freedom further suggests returning to the regulatory perspective that healing is broader than biomedicine, that nonbiomedical caregivers can nourish the healing process, and that wellness can incorporate not only surgical, pharmaceutical, and biochemical realities, but also the vague and shifting contours of the patient's inner world and social environment. Although these aspects of health may not readily be measurable under prevailing medical standards, legal authority has acknowledged within the regulatory scheme for healing arts the need for providers, such as licensed chiropractors, acupuncturists, naturopaths, midwives, and even hypnotists,[20] who can respond to different needs

within the realm of patient healing.[21] Similarly, as noted, mandated provider laws have created a more level playing field in the area of health care
reimbursement.

Future legislative initiatives could establish insurance policy definitions of medical necessity and experimental treatment so as to support
appropriate reimbursement of complementary and alternative medicine.
Proposed legislation in New York defines medical necessity in insurance
contracts to include "diagnostic, preventive, prophylactic, ameliorative, curative or quality-of-life care which is indicated by the presenting problem,
appropriate examination, history, and tests, and is supported by a thorough
consideration of the treatment options available and a reasonable expectation of efficacy, and is in keeping with consent of the patient, and is not
strictly cosmetic."[22] This definition moves emphasis from clinical trials and
professional consensus to the individual provider's "reasonable expectation
of efficacy," based on professional interaction with the patient. Other currently proposed legislative initiatives loosen requirements for reimbursement of non-FDA-approved treatments under certain circumstances.[23]

At the federal level, health care and insurance reform efforts need to
address the concerns of complementary and alternative providers and patients that complementary and alternative medicine not be viewed in the
same category as medically unnecessary and fraudulent treatments. Relevant
statutes need to be examined in light of concern for access to a fuller range of
health care treatments.[24] Ongoing modifications to federal food and drug
law, including new agency regulations and congressional amendments to
the DSHEA, should reflect greater balance between concern for fraud, and
consumers' need to incorporate nutritional and other complementary and
alternative therapies as part of self-care and preventive health care.

Integral Health Care

The process of integrating biomedical and complementary and alternative approaches to health care ideally will result in integral medicine, a
system attuned to every aspect of well-being.[25] Ultimately, healers from
various disciplines will serve the best interest of the patient by integrating
the knowledge, skills, and wisdom of biomedical and other forms of healing. Biomedical and complementary and alternative health care providers
share the goal of helping human beings who are suffering. Each can recognize the limitations of knowledge, training, and skill in their respective
disciplines; neither biomedicine nor complementary and alternative medi-

cine has a monopoly on healing. Conventional scientific research will, ideally, integrate methodologies appropriate to nonbiomedical therapies that incorporate the healer's intention and consciousness as part of treatment, and utilize an ethic of care consistent with stronger patient autonomy.[26]

Integral health care entrusts the patient with greater responsibility for prevention and self-care. Rather than passively complying with "doctor's orders" and the assumption that "doctor knows best,"[27] the patient should be able to contract for acupuncturists, massage therapists, counselors, and nutritionists within a healing team. The legal framework will protect such freedom by recognizing that the choice of treatment and responsibility for the body ultimately lies with the individual, not the state, and that health care law and policy should minimize governmental intrusion into the private liberty interest in access to treatments. In fact, the "new model for the allocation of authority between doctors and patients" augurs for "the direct creation of an independent interest in medical choice," as opposed to the indirect interest in adequate informed consent.[28]

Integral health care will challenge an existing paradigm that is based on medical paternalism and that involves excessive interference with autonomous choices. The paternalistic approach measures patient well-being solely through the biomedical model. It defines, adjudicates, and resolves legal dilemmas by adopting the opinions of biomedical experts, remote insurance adjusters, judges, and other parties—opinions that are based on purportedly objective criteria such as certain levels of acceptance, forms of documentation, and judgments about medical necessity. The paternalistic approach evaluates patients' choices—ranging from the right to terminate nutrition and hydration to the right to receive insurance reimbursement for nonstandard treatments—through the lens of biomedical orthodoxy. The paternalistic approach assumes that patients are dependent children who cannot be trusted to make appropriate health care choices.[29]

Weak paternalism protects persons against substantially nonvoluntary conduct, such as conduct by an addict, while strong paternalism violates informed, voluntary, and autonomous choice.[30] Strong paternalism is justified only if the following conditions are satisfied: (1) the patient is at risk of a significant preventable harm; (2) the paternalistic action will probably prevent the harm; (3) the projected benefits to the patient of the paternalistic action outweigh its risks to the patient; and (4) the least autonomy-restrictive alternative that will secure the benefits and reduce the risks is selected.[31] With regard to these conditions, many complementary and alternative treatments, such as chiropractic, massage therapy, and highly diluted homeopathic remedies, are generally safe and nontoxic, when provided within appropriate professional parameters, and relative to comparable conventional treatments.[32] Prohibiting or controlling the voluntary, informed choice of patients, particularly terminally ill patients, to access such treatments is a highly restrictive means of protecting patients from therapeutic choices that medical orthodoxy finds objectionable.[33] Clear informed consent forms, disclaimers, mandatory referrals to and consultations with medical doctors, and good communication between providers and patients manage the risks of such treatments in ways that more fully respect patient autonomy.

Deep respect for autonomy may include the anecdotal, the subjective, the emotional, and the interpersonal. This approach may challenge legal and medical structures that are based entirely on scientific measurement, justification, and validation.[34] Further, the patient's perspective on medical necessity may include "ameliorative, curative, or quality-of-life care." It may include nutritional treatment, counseling and emotive therapies, massage or energy healing, and other nonstandard modalities as necessary components of an overall treatment plan.[35]

A regulatory paradigm that balances concern for fraud against health care freedom will not only deepen respect for patient autonomy but also facilitate greater exchange between the field of complementary and alternative medicine and related health care disciplines. Despite the range of bioethical opinions and perspectives represented in bioethical debates, for example, the competing arguments and rules presented in these debates largely reflect the biomedical paradigm. Thus, the American Medical Association opposes physician-assisted suicide as "fundamentally inconsistent with the professional role of physicians as healers."[36] Yet bioethicists have begun to articulate the right to a "peaceful" death, one in which the mind is lucid and clear and the body is free of debilitating pain.[37] This position reflects non-Western teachings such as those found in the *Tibetan Book of the Dead*. Articulation of this right recognizes the patient's interest in lucidity, clarity, and peace, and a transition that is preferable to a perpetuation of biological existence as long as technology makes this possible.[38] Such health care choices "involve profound questions that are not finally referable to professional [biomedical] expertise."[39] Complementary and alternative therapies that address these issues and explore the interconnections between mind, body, emotions, and spirit are particularly appropriate to such debate.

In a similar way, complementary and alternative medicine may affect legal distinctions such as the delineation between "competent" patients and "incompetent" patients (who do not have the right to refuse treatment). Applicable legal rules rest on current biomedical and scientific definitions of competency, yet disciplines such as hypnosis and energy healing assert the possibility of communication and consciousness on subtle levels. For instance, through tiny mind-body movements known as ideomotoric signals, hypnotherapists can communicate with patients who are in deep trance states or under anesthesia.[40] The phenomenon of multiple levels of communication in trance states not fully measurable through conventional scientific epistemologies is well known in shamanic traditions.[41]

Medical familiarity with such traditions, as well as with contemporary tools by which such states may be understood, experienced, and used to help patients, may affect a range of bioethical issues, from multiple fetal pregnancy reduction to genetic engineering and the use of anencephalic infants as organ donors.[42] The legal resolution of each issue frequently turns on biomedical views of life and consciousness; only beings recognized as having "conscious awareness" can have legally cognizable interests; and nonbiomedical views of consciousness therefore can advance the resolution of competing legal interests.[43] The evolution of legal authority in bioethics is particularly relevant if the integration of complementary and alternative medicine and biomedicine leads to deeper contemplation of the relationship between consciousness, scientific validation, and the art of healing.

Conclusion

Existing legal authority purports to protect patients from dangerous or worthless treatments by relying on legal rules governing matters such as licensing, scope of practice, and malpractice to sanction inappropriate provider behavior. Licensing statutes grant nonmedical health care providers limited practice authority, and courts enforce medical practice acts strictly against providers who cross into "diagnosis" and "treatment." Food and drug laws restrict the use of nutritional therapies to treat disease. State medical boards punish deviance from biomedical orthodoxy, and courts grant deference to biomedical authority in cases involving holistic providers.

Although such rules arguably aim to express a sound regulatory concern for preventing overreaching by providers, they also enforce a regulatory paradigm derived from a historical antipathy toward healing modalities outside biomedicine. Enforcement and interpretation of such rules consistent with biomedical authority can result in legislative, regulatory, and judicial ratification of biomedical dominance and biomedicine's attempt to monopolize professional healing. Indeed, efforts to control access to dietary supplements and controversial therapies enjoying widespread support among patients; attacks on practitioners for alleged unlawful manufacture, misbranding, distribution, and sale of such treatments and products; broad statutory antifraud provisions; investigations and prosecutions of independent holistic practitioners or of licensed providers under medical practice acts, based on alleged scope-of-practice violations; aggressive disciplinary actions against physicians using nonstandard approaches; information-sharing between federal and state prosecutorial authorities relating to health fraud; and other regulatory devices and actions have unjustifiably expanded the regulatory presence in consumer's health care choices and have intruded upon the liberty interest in access to nonbiomedical treatments. Particularly when allopathic care fails, patients stymied by regulatory controls find little succor in institutionalized reminders that health care policy aims to protect them from quackery.

Health care law and policy affecting complementary and alternative providers is changing. Many states license numerous such providers, expressly authorize physicians to use complementary and alternative treatments, prohibit unfair and discriminatory medical board discipline of physicians using such practices, respect patients' agreements with independent holistic practitioners, and mandate coverage or insurance equity for a variety of alternative and complementary providers and treatments. Rather than reflecting biomedical orthodoxy or hostility to competing therapies, the legal system is beginning to reflect a paradigm of integral health care, in which biomedical professionals function cooperatively with complementary and alternative professionals, as well as with patients, in a partnership of care and healing.

A new legal authority is arising which seeks to integrate biomedical, holistic, and social models of health care in ways that maximize patients' well-being. While still protecting patients from fraud, legal authority can more fully accommodate holistic therapies' view of the individual as an organic, integrated whole, and respect the patient's interest in choice, self-care, and nutrition. I hope to have outlined the basis for such authority as an organic evolution of existing regulatory schemes.

Legal process ideally respects the patient's search for health as a process at the juncture of social, political, economic, and personal events. The legal view of disease and wellness must embrace a broader understanding of healing than is reflected in biomedical orthodoxy. Legal rules reflect essential social values and culturally accepted models of health care. As these values and models continue to unfold, legal rules, too, will evolve to embrace a more expansive and empowering vision of health care and the healing process.

NOTES

1. The shift also may result from belated recognition that technological healing is not unbounded. On various legal conundrums created by accelerating health technologies, see Daniel Callahan, *What Kind of Life: The Limits of Medical Progress* (Washington, D.C.: Georgetown University Press, 1990), 17–30 (advocating health care rationing); Mary Coutts, "Human Gene Therapy," 4:1 *Kennedy Inst. Ethics J.* 63–83 (1994) (describing human genetic programming); Cruzan v. Director, Missouri Dept. of Health, 497 U.S. 261 (1990) (articulating the limits of technology at death).

2. David Eisenberg et al., "Unconventional Medicine in the United States: Prevalence, Costs, and Patterns of Use," 328:4 *N. Engl. J. Med.* 246 (1993); see also Franklin Hoke, "Alternative Medicine Ideas Widen Horizons in Biomedical Research," 8 *Scientist* 6:1 (Mar. 21, 1994); Bill Moyers, *Healing and the Mind* (New York: Doubleday, 1992) (describing alternative approaches to health maintenance and treatment of disease). A more recent study of family practice patients found that about 50 percent of patients used complementary and alternative medicine, including acupuncture, homeopathy, chiropractic, massage therapy, herbal medicines, and megavitamin therapy. Nancy C. Elder et al., "Use of Alternative Health Care by Family Practice Patients," 6 *Arch. Fam. Med.* 181 (Mar.–Apr. 1997).

3. See 42 *U.S.C.* § 283g(b); see also Charles Marwick, "Alternative Medicine Office Urged to Act Rapidly," 270:12 *JAMA* 1400 (1993). The Office of Complementary and Alternative Medicine supports research training in topics related to alternative medicine, aiming "not to be an advocate [for] any particular alternative medicine treatment, but rather to advocate the fair scientific evaluation of alternative therapies that are found to have potential for improving the health and well-being of a significant number of people." *Alternative Medicine: Expanding Medical Horizons (A Report to the National Institutes of Health on Alternative Medical Systems and Practices in the United States)* (Sept. 14–16, 1992), xlvi (hereinafter cited as *Chantilly Report*). Copies of the *Chantilly Report* can be obtained by contacting the Superintendent of Documents, P.O. Box 371954, Pittsburgh, PA 15250-7954 (202-512-1800).

4. Access to Medical Treatment Act, H.R. 2019, 104th Cong., 1st Sess.; S. 1035, 104th Cong., 1st Sess. (1995). The bill has been reintroduced as H.R. 746,

105th Cong., 1st Sess. (Feb. 13, 1997); and S. 578, 105th Cong., 1st Sess. (Apr. 18, 1997). Another bill, the federal National Center for Integral Medicine Establishment Act, would essentially elevate the Office of Complementary and Alternative Medicine to a center within the National Institutes of Health, with its director reporting directly to the director of the NIH. The center's goals would include promoting "the integration of alternative medical treatment and diagnostic systems and disciplines into the practice of conventional medicine as a complement to such medicine" and evaluating "the extent to which the [complementary and alternative] system or discipline promotes wellness and supports inherent healing processes." The proposed legislation authorizes an appropriation of $198 million for fiscal year 1998. H.R. 1055, 105th Cong., 1st Sess. (Mar. 13, 1997).

A third bill, the National Fund for Health Research Act, focuses on enhancing research into disease prevention and proposes setting aside a certain percentage of premiums from health plans, a portion of which may fund activities of the Office of Complementary and Alternative Medicine and the Office of Dietary Supplements. S. 441, 105th Cong., 1st Sess. (Mar. 13, 1997). See also Federal Acupuncture Coverage Act, H.R. 1038, 105th Cong., 1st Sess. (Mar. 17, 1997).

5. Examples include the Cardiac Complementary Care Center at Columbia Presbyterian Hospital in New York; the Richard and Hinda Rosenthal Center for Complementary/Alternative Medicine at Columbia University; the Department of Holistic and Preventative Medicine at Grant Hospital in Chicago; the Program in Integrative Medicine at the University of Arizona College of Medicine in Tucson; the Mind/Body Medical Institute at Deaconess Hospital, in Boston; and the Center for Alternative Medicine Research at Beth Israel Hospital, in Boston.

6. Timothy Egan, "Seattle Area Giving Natural Medicine a Chance to Come in from the Fringe," *New York Times,* Jan. 3, 1996, A10.

7. See, e.g., Hawaii House Bill 428 (Jan. 17, 1997) (establishing a "health and wellness center pilot project" within the University of Hawaii's John A. Burns School of Medicine, in the department of family practice and community health; the project "integrates complementary healing resources, including native Hawaiian, eastern, western, alternative, and nutritional approaches"); and Minnesota Senate Bill 485 (Feb. 10, 1997) (finding "a need to encourage and support the use of alternative medicine with the ultimate goal of integrating alternative medicine with conventional health care coverage," and requesting a report from the commissioner of health, identifying, among other things, "obstacles that may prevent consumers from receiving alternative medicine therapies" including "issues related to reimbursement and regulation").

8. See, e.g., Gina Kolata, "In Quests outside Mainstream, Medical Projects Rewrite Rules," *New York Times,* June 18, 1996, 1.

9. The findings in the proposed National Center for Integral Medicine Establishment Act include the following:

(1) From 60 to 90 percent of chronic diseases may be largely prevented or treated by addressing lifestyle-related issues and using medical interventions that stimulate and support natural healing processes. . . .

(3) Interventions to address chronic diseases must involve the integration of these behavioral, nutritional, preventive, and alternative medical practices into conventional medical practices, including integration into health care delivery systems. . . .

(6) A center is needed for the support and integration of knowledge across . . . all medical research activities pertaining to wellness and research, rather than further specialization of knowledge based on the division of disease treatment categories. (1997 H.R. 1055, 105th Cong., 1st Sess., § 2.)

CHAPTER 1: BIOMEDICINE AND HOLISTIC HEALING

1. See Thomas Kuhn, *The Structure of Scientific Revolutions* (Chicago: University of Chicago Press, 1970), 10–12, 23, 37, 111–32, 62, 115–16.

2. Ibid., 90.

3. Nathan Spielberg and Bryon D. Anderson, *Seven Ideas That Shook the Universe* (New York: John Wiley & Sons, 1985), 90–92.

4. Gilbert Ryle, *The Concept of Mind* (London: Hutchinson, 1948), 11. Descartes "left as one of his main philosophical legacies a myth which continues to distort" disciplines based on the concept of mind (8). Descartes wrote: "Thought is an attribute that really does belong to me. This alone cannot be detached from me. . . . I am therefore precisely only a thing that thinks." Rene Descartes, *Second Meditation in Discourses or Method and Meditations on First Philosophy,* trans. Donald A. Cress (Indianapolis: Hackett Publishing, 1980), 62–63. Descartes thus "made nature a machine and nothing but a machine; purposes and spiritual significance alike had been banished." John H. Randall Jr., *The Making of the Modern Mind: A Survey of the Intellectual Background of the Modern Age* (New York: Columbia University Press, 1976), 241.

5. See L.F.C. Mees, *Blessed by Illness* (Spring Valley, N.Y: Anthroposophic Press, 1983), 139; Bernie Siegel, *Love, Medicine, and Miracles* (New York: Harper & Row, 1986) (describing deleterious effects of the warfare metaphor); Larry Dossey, *Meaning and Medicine: Lessons from a Doctor's Tales of Breakthrough and Healing* (New York: Bantam Books, 1992), 5–7 (describing physician antipathy to mind-body healing).

6. See R. J. Carlson, "Holism and Reductionism as Perspectives in Medicine and Patient Care," 131 *West. J. Med.* 466–70 (1979).

7. Nine million cannot work, attend school, or maintain a household. *Chantilly Report,* ix.

8. For example, in treatment of Hodgkin disease, "radiation-induced toxicities may include baldness on the back of the head, Lhermette's sign (sudden

electric-like body shocks when the patient's head flexes forward), and deficient thyroid activity. . . . Other long-term potential radiation side-effects include radiation lung fibrosis, pericarditis, premature coronary artery disease and secondary sarcomas, acute and/or chronic radiation injury, especially to the heart, lungs and bone marrow." *Attorneys' Textbook of Medicine,* 3d ed., ed. Roscoe N. Gray and Louise J. Gordy (New York: Matthew Bender, 1996), vol. 3, § 66.51(1), p. 66–32. The complications of combination chemotherapy include "nausea, vomiting, baldness, peripheral nervous system disturbances, bone marrow suppression and effects of corticosteroids" (§ 66.51(2), pp. 66–32 to 66–33).

9. See Council on Scientific Affairs, *Alternative Medicine* (Chicago: American Medical Association, 1996), Report 10-I-96, p. 16 (citing address by Jeremiah Barondess at the 1996 AMA National Leadership Conference, noting that "many physicians may not deal effectively enough with illness . . . [i.e.,] those symptoms, anxieties, and concerns that make people feel sick, as opposed to our emphasis on disease, defined too often in biochemical and molecular terms that are far removed from the person being examined").

10. Jay Katz, *The Silent World of Doctor and Patient* (New York: Free Press, 1994), 209; see also Charles Baron, "Licensure of Health Care Professionals: The Consumer's Case for Abolition," 9:3 *Am. J. Law & Med.* 335, 344 (1983) ("The mastery of medical science and technology which brought allopathic medicine its brilliant success and ascendancy in the late nineteenth and early twentieth centuries has arguably become a monomania which is now producing failure and decline. . . . The new medicine is so scientific, technological, and specialized that the patient as a whole is ignored, and the narrow illness complained of becomes an enemy that must be stamped out at all costs. One result is that the physician becomes responsible for producing an alarming amount of iatrogenic illness in the patients he is trying to cure").

11. Eric J. Cassell, "The Sorcerer's Broom: Medicine's Rampant Technology," 23:6 *Hastings Center Rep.* 32, 34 (1993). Cassell critiques the process in which caregivers get caught up in the technologization of disease, and lose their connection to patients (32–33). See also Ivan Illich, *Medical Nemesis: The Expropriation of Health* (New York: Pantheon Books, 1976); Thomas McKeon, "Determinants of Health," in *The Nation's Health,* ed. Philip R. Lee and Carol L. Estes, 4th ed. (Boston: Jones & Bartlett, 1994), 6 (arguing that the "body as machine" assumption "has led to widespread indifference to the influence of the primary determinants of human health — environment and personal behavior . . . [and] has also resulted in the neglect of sick people whose ailments are not within the scope of the sort of therapy that interests the medical professions").

12. See Denise Niemira, "Life on the Slippery Slope: A Bedside View of Treating Elderly Patients," 23:3 *Hastings Center Rep.* 14 (1993). Niemira asks: "What do I owe patients who cannot speak for themselves and who exist in a state I

consider not worth living? . . . We arrange to feed them when they have forgotten how, clean them when they are unaware of bodily functions, turn them when they can no longer move" (15–17).

13. Daniel Callahan, "Pursuing a Peaceful Death," 23:4 *Hastings Center Rep.* 33, 34 (1993).

14. Callahan notes: "We increase the likelihood of spending our declining years helpless, demented, and incontinent if medicine saves our lives long enough to help us avert all of the lethal diseases that stand in the way of that (not so splendid) final outcome" Ibid., 35.

15. A recent *JAMA* article documented shortcomings in communication, frequency of aggressive treatment, and failure to honor patient preferences not to be resuscitated or receive mechanical ventilation. "A Controlled Trial to Improve Care for Seriously Ill Hospitalized Patients," 274:20 *JAMA* 1634–36 (1995); see also J. M. Teno et al., "Preferences for Cardiopulmonary Resuscitation: Physician-Patient Agreement and Hospital Resource Use," 10:4 *J. Gen. Intern. Med.* 179–86 (1995) (nearly one-third of 2,636 paired physician-patient answers disagreed about preferences for resuscitation; physician misunderstanding of patient preferences to forego CPR could have led to care at odds with patient choices).

16. See Council on Scientific Affairs, *Alternative Medicine,* 16 ("It is clear that in the quest for wellness, the public is seeking new approaches to medical care. Some of the reasons may be understandable, such as the desire to find a healer with time to listen, to receive compassionate care, and to establish a partnership with a provider in seeking health").

17. See generally Stephen Schwartz, "Holistic Health: Seeking a Link between Medicine and Metaphysics," 266:21 *JAMA* 3064 (1991); Ian Coulter, "Alternative Philosophical and Investigatory Paradigms for Chiropractic," 16:6 *J. Manipulative Physiol. Ther.* 419, 420 (1993) (holistic "care would address the physical, mental and spiritual aspects of the patients; it would emphasize personalized, individual care; care would include an understanding and treatment of people in the context of their culture, their family and their community; it should view health as a positive state and not simply the absence of disease; care should emphasize the promotion of health and prevention of disease; emphasize individual responsibility; mobilize the patient's capacity for self healing; be involved in patient education; use a wide variety of diagnostic systems; have physical contact with the patient through touch; should stress nutrition and exercise; appreciate sensuousness and sexuality; view illness as an opportunity for discovery by the patient and doctor; appreciate the quality of life in each of its stages; emphasize the therapeutic value of the setting in which health care occurs; and understand and try to change the social and economic conditions that perpetuate ill health") (citing James S. Gordon, "The Paradigm of Holistic Medicine," in *Health for the Whole Person,* ed. Arthur Hastings et al. (Boulder, Colo.: Westview Press, 1980), 3–35).

18. *Chantilly Report*, xi–xxiii. The report also describes "methods of testing, strategies of validations, proof of efficacy, and the application of these" to complementary and alternative medicine (289).

19. C. Norman Shealy and Caroline Myss, *The Creation of Health: Merging Traditional Medicine with Intuitive Diagnosis* (Walpole, N.H.: Stillpoint Publishing, 1988), 7. The authors observe that "without having to recognize emotional, psychological or spiritual crises, the use of the word 'stress' provides a legitimate and non-threatening term to describe what holistically minded physicians and health care practitioners are comfortable discussing in detail, namely, the human response to the difficulties of life" (7).

20. N.C. Gen. Stat. § 90-143(a). Additional information concerning chiropractic, massage therapy, acupuncture, naturopathy, and other holistic fields can be found in the *Chantilly Report;* in *Alternative Medicine: The Definite Guide,* ed. James Strohecker (Tiburon, Calif.: Future Medicine Publishing, 1994); and in *Textbook of Complementary and Alternative Medicine,* ed. Wayne B. Jonas and Jefrey S. Levin (Baltimore: Williams & Wilkins, 1997).

21. I describe these in "A Fixed Star in Health Care Reform: The Emerging Paradigm of Holistic Healing," 27 *Ariz. State L.J.* 79, 88–95 (1995). See generally Dolores Krieger, *Living the Therapeutic Touch* (New York: Dodd-Mead, 1987); see also Barbara A. Brennan, *Hands of Light* (New York: Bantam Books, 1988).

22. Hans A. Baer, "The Potential Rejuvenation of American Naturopathy as a Consequence of the Holistic Health Movement," 13 *Med. Anthropology* 369, 370 (1992).

23. See, e.g., Stephanie Matthews-Simonton et al., *Getting Well Again: A Step-By-Step, Self-Help Guide to Overcoming Cancer for Patients and Their Families* (New York: St. Martin's Press, 1980) (on the use of visualization and imagery to treat cancer); Ernest Rossi, *The Psychobiology of Mind-Body Healing: New Concepts of Therapeutic Hypnosis* (New York: W. W. Norton, 1986) (on biochemical responses to Ericksonian hypnotherapy); Dean Ornish et al., "Effects of Stress Management Training and Dietary Changes in Treating Ischemic Heart Disease," 249:1 *JAMA* 54 (1983) (demonstrating significant improvement in heart disease patients' duration of exercise and functioning of left heart ventricle, and decrease in cholesterol levels and attacks of angina, as a result of stretching, relaxation, meditation, and visualization).

24. Jan Smuts, *Holism and Evolution* (London: Macmillan, 1926; reprint, Westport, Conn.: Greenwood Press, 1973), 98.

25. See, e.g., Ruth Lloyd, "New Directions in Psychoneuroimmunology: A Critique," 12:1 *Advances: J. Mind-Body Health* 5, 9–10 (1987); Leon R. Kass, "Appreciating *The Phenomenon of Life,* " 25:7 *Hastings Center Rep.* 3–12 (special issue, 1995) (reviewing the work of Hans Jonas).

26. See D. C. Phillips, *Holistic Thought in Social Science* (Stanford: Stanford University Press, 1976).

27. The American Holistic Medical Association, the American Holistic Nursing Association, and the International Alliance of Holistic Lawyers share offices at 4101 Lake Boone Trail, Suite 201, Raleigh, NC 27607. For a description of holistic nursing, see Sara N. Estby et al., "A Delphi Study of the Basic Principles and Corresponding Care Goals of Holistic Nursing Practice," 12:4 *J. Holistic Nurs.* 402 (1994).

28. See, e.g., Norman Gevitz, "Osteopathic Medicine: From Deviance to Difference," in *Other Healers: Unorthodox Medicine in America,* ed. Norman Gevitz (Baltimore: Johns Hopkins University Press, 1988), 123, 156–57.

29. The above data are drawn from Eisenberg et al., "Unconventional Medicine," 246–50.

30. In a recent survey in Quebec, 11 percent of children consulted one or more alternative providers; chiropractic, homeopathy, naturopathy, and acupuncture together accounted for 84 percent of use. Linda Spigelblatt et al., "The Use of Alternative Medicine by Children," 94:6 *Pediatrics* 811 (1994).

31. *Chantilly Report,* xv.

32. The Johns Hopkins University School of Medicine now has an optional rotation for medical students through the Traditional Acupuncture Center and Institute, in Columbia, Maryland.

33. Deborah Daly, "Alternative Medicine Courses Taught at U.S. Medical Schools: An Ongoing Listing," 1:2 *J. Alt. Comp. Ther.* 205 (1995). A database is maintained by the Richard and Hinda Rosenthal Center for Complementary/Alternative Medicine at Columbia University College of Physicians and Surgeons.

34. Daniel L. Blumberg et al., "The Physician and Unconventional Medicine," 1:3 *Alt. Ther. Health Med.* 31 (1995).

35. Recently, the American Medical Association House of Delegates passed a policy that "encourages the Office of Alternative Medicine of the National Institutes of Health to determine by objective scientific evaluation the efficacy and safety of practices and procedures of unconventional medicine; and encourages its members to become better informed regarding the practices and techniques of alternative or unconventional medicine." House of Delegates Policy H-480.973, *Unconventional Medical Care in the United States,* BOT Rep. 15-A-94; Reaffirmed and Modified by Substitute Resolution 514, I-95 (urging the AMA among other things, to encourage its members "to become better informed regarding alternative (complementary) medicine and to participate in appropriate studies of it").

The House of Delegates subsequently referred a resolution to the AMA Board of Trustees, based on a report by the AMA's Council on Scientific Affairs (CSA) on alternative medicine. The CSA report recommended for adoption a policy that "(1) there is little evidence to confirm the safety or efficacy of most alternative therapies, (2) physicians should routinely inquire about the use of alternative or unconventional therapy by patients and educate themselves and their patients about the state of scientific knowledge with regard to alternative therapy,

(3) courses offered by medical schools on alternative medicine should present the scientific view of unconventional theories, treatments and practice, and (4) patients who choose alternative therapies should be educated as to the hazards that might result from postponing or stopping convention[al] medical treatment." See House of Delegates Resolution 507 (Dec. 1996) (citing Council on Scientific Affairs, *Alternative Medicine*).

The CSA report notes that many complementary and alternative therapies "are characterized by a charismatic leader or proponent and are driven by ideology; some spring from folk practices or quasi-religious groups, while others are recognized elements of religions such as those practiced by Native Americans." Council on Scientific Affairs, *Alternative Medicine,* 1. The report does provide considerable detail, however, about various therapies, suggesting continuing reflection by the AMA on its posture toward complementary and alternative providers (3–12).

36. One writes that in medical school, "a 'hands-on' approach involving compassion, laughter and listening was frowned upon by many. We were often discouraged from getting involved with our patients and were taught to focus on their disease and organs rather than seeing them as a whole person with emotional, mental, spiritual and social needs — as well as physical ones." Bambi Ward, "Holistic Medicine," 24:5 *Austr. Fam. Physician* 761, 761 (1995). See also James S. Gordon, *Manifesto for a New Medicine* (Reading, Mass.: Addison-Wesley, 1996), 28–31. Gordon asks first-year medical students to draw two pictures: one of "yourself," the other of "yourself in medical school." In the latter, "facial expressions regularly change from smiles to frowns; hands are missing from the medical school figures; clocks are prominent; faces are turned from the viewer; profanity is scrawled on the page; huge piles of books crowd small figures; prison bars obscure our view of obviously suffering students" (278).

37. D. P. McCann and H. J. Blossom, "The Physician as a Patient Educator: From Theory to Practice," 153 *West. J. Med.* 44–49 (1990).

38. This healthy bond not only comports with medical ethics but also has recognized clinical efficacy because it contributes to the "placebo effect": the patient's trust in the physician accelerates the healing. Many physicians have emphasized the centrality of the relationship in the healing process, while other writers have suggested ways to amplify this goodwill so as to reduce malpractice claims. See, e.g., Jerry Green, "Minimizing Malpractice Risks by Role Clarification: The Confusing Transition from Tort to Contract," 109 *Ann. Intern. Med.* 3: 234 (1988).

39. See Walter Hewer, "The Relationship between the Alternative Practitioner and His Patient: A Review," 40:172 *Psychother. Psychosom.* (1983).

40. Wayne B. Jonas, "Evaluating Unconventional Medical Practices," 5 *J. NIH Res.* 64–67 (1993).

41. Thus: "Wholeness is something more than the sum of its parts. To relate to a person as a doctor, guided by a holistic view of health, means that one must . . .

let oneself be guided by knowledge of symbols and their meaning. The nature of . . . [humanity] is three-dimensional: somatic, psychological and spiritual. One cannot reach the spiritual dimension without being touched or moved." Olle Hellstrom, "The Importance of a Holistic Concept of Health for Health Care: Examples from the Clinic," 14 *Theoretical Med.* 325, 338 (1993).

42. *Chantilly Report*, ix.

43. See, e.g., Hawaii House Bill 428 (Jan. 17, 1997) (since Hawaii emphasizes "the belief that health, which comes from the same root as 'wholeness,' involves the body, mind, and spirit of the whole person," the legislature proposes "to develop a holistic/humanistic model for health care . . . [to facilitate] the healing of the earth and her people," emphasizing: "(1) A whole person approach, which encompasses each person's physical, emotional, and spiritual needs; (2) A collaborative approach, utilizing health care professions from a variety of disciplines, embracing native Hawaiian kahuna, eastern (e.g., acupuncture, Honetsugi, Reiki, Chinese herbal medicine, shiatsu, Ayurvedic and Tibetan medicine), alternative (e.g., massage therapy, Rolfing, art, and music therapy), western (e.g., medical/osteopathic physicians, psychotherapy, pastoral counseling), and nutritional approaches; and (3) A setting distinguished by being home-like and environmentally conscious").

44. See Arnold S. Relman, "Alternative Medicine: A Shot in the Dark," *New York Times*, July 12, 1995, A12; Victor Herbert, review of Douglas Stalker and Clark Glymour, *Examining Holistic Medicine* (Buffalo, N.Y.: Prometheus Books, 1985), 256:9 *JAMA* 1202 (1986) (heralding the book as "dynamite, an absolute smash!" that "lays bare holistic medicine as . . . a melange of banalities, truisms, exaggerations, and falsehoods, overlaid with disparagement not only of scientific conclusions but of logical reason itself"). Herbert urges that "every responsible health professional" not only buy the book but also "send copies to our well-meaning legislators who are suckered by charismatic holistic promoters into supporting the irrational, the unsound, and the dangerous in health care."

45. Willis Harman and Christian de Quincey, *The Scientific Exploration of Consciousness: Toward an Adequate Epistemology* (Sausalito, Calif.: Institute of Noetic Science, 1994), 2. The authors argue that current scientific epistemology mistakenly assumes that consciousness is ultimately biochemical, and the product of objectively observable interactions (25).

46. *Chantilly Report*, xxiii.

47. Ibid., 76–77 (citing studies).

48. Ibid., 81 (citing studies).

49. See S. Bowyer Bigos et al., *Acute Low Back Problems in Adults, Clinical Practice Guideline*, Quick Reference Guide no. 14, AHCPR Pub. No. 95-0643 (Rockville, Md.: U.S. Department of Health and Human Services, Public Health Service, Agency for Health Care Policy and Research, Dec. 1994).

50. *Chantilly Report*, xxiii–xiv.

51. Paradigms from other disciplines, however, such as transpersonal psychology, might be used to integrate spiritual dimensions of holistic healing into the biomedical model. See, e.g., J. F. Hiatt, "Spirituality, Medicine, and Healing," 79 *South. Med. J.* 736-43 (1986).

52. *Chantilly Report*, 293–94.

53. See E. Keller and V. M. Bzdek, "Effects of Therapeutic Touch on Tension Headache Pain," 35 *Nurs. Res.* 101–5 (1986); P. Heidt, "Effects of Therapeutic Touch on Anxiety Level of Hospitalized Patients," 1 *Nurs. Res.* 32–37 (1981).

54. Robert Bradford and Michael Culbert, "The Laetrile Phenomenon: Harbinger of Medical Revolution," *Jurimetrics J.,* winter 1980, 179, 184; see also *In re* Guess, 393 S.E.2d 833 (N.C. 1990) (affirming conviction of a licensed physician for administering homeopathic remedies), *cert. denied,* Guess v. North Carolina Bd. of Medical Examiners, 498 U.S. 1047 (1991), *later proceeding,* Guess v. Board of Medical Examiners, 967 F.2d 998 (4th Cir. 1992).

55. See generally *Psychoneuroimmunology,* ed. Robert Ader (New York: Academic Press, 1981).

56. *Chantilly Report,* 138–39. Methods for cross-cultural research are frequently qualitative, although the Office of Complementary and Alternative Medicine also provides guidance on quantitative studies, including clinical trials, outcomes research, and systematic literature reviews (341–51).

57. See, e.g., David Reilly et al., "Is Evidence for Homeopathy Reproducible?" 344:8937 *Lancet* 1601, 1605–6 (1994).

58. Among other things, the office aims to provide methodological assistance and to link providers with appropriate research institutions. The Office of Complementary and Alternative Medicine also collects existing studies on individual modalities and awards grants for further research. See *Chantilly Report,* 37–43 (collecting studies on mind-body interactions). The office has a Web site at http://www.digiweb.com/iitri/nih.

59. See *Database of Alternative, Complementary AIDS Therapies Should Be Considered by NIAID,* 34(22) F-D-C Rep. 3 (1991); *Chantilly Report,* xxvi; see also *OAM-Funded Exploratory Centers to Support Retrospective Studies and Pilot Projects,* 37(23) F-D-C Rep. 4 (1994) (describing new efforts to collect databases on alternative therapies).

60. The examples are from D. T. Atkinson, *Man, Myth, and Magic* (New York: New World Publishing, 1956), 142, 149–55.

61. *Chantilly Report,* xliv–xlv.

62. Gordon, *Manifesto,* 249. Gordon also predicts: "Massage — desperately needed by people lying lonely and worried in hospital beds and wonderfully effective for improving mood and reducing anxiety — will be universal. Acupuncture . . . will, wherever possible, be used in preference to antinausea and analgesic drugs and sleeping pills. Visual imagery will be taught to patients . . . to help them anticipate and move more easily through the pain and violation of procedures" (253).

63. For a description of a parallel evolution in English law, see Julie Stone and Joan Matthews, *Complementary Medicine and the Law* (New York: Oxford University Press, 1996).

CHAPTER 2: BIOMEDICAL REGULATION IN HISTORICAL CONTEXT

1. See Kuhn, *Scientific Revolutions*, 37.

2. See T. Romeyn Beck, "A Sketch of the Legislative Provision of the Colony and State of New-York, Respecting the Practice of Physic and Surgery," *N.Y. J. Med.* 139 (1822).

3. See Joseph F. Kett, *The Formation of the American Medical Profession: The Role of Institutions, 1780–1860* (New Haven: Yale University Press, 1968), 21.

4. Rosemary Stevens, *American Medicine and the Public Interest* (New Haven: Yale University Press, 1971), 26–27.

5. For a general discussion of the political history of biomedicine, see James G. Burrow, *AMA: Voice of American Medicine* (Baltimore: Johns Hopkins Press, 1963); Harris L. Coulter, *Divided Legacy: The Conflict Between Homeopathy and the American Medical Association* (Berkeley: North Atlantic Books, 1973), 158–95; Kenneth M. Ludmerer, *Learning to Heal: The Development of American Medical Education* (New York: Basic Books, 1985), 167, 180; William G. Rothstein, *American Physicians in the Nineteenth Century: From Sects to Science* (Baltimore: Johns Hopkins University Press, 1972); Richard H. Shryock, *Medical Licensing in America, 1650–1965* (Baltimore: Johns Hopkins Press, 1967); Stevens, *American Medicine;* and Paul Starr, *The Social Transformation of American Medicine* (New York: Basic Books, 1982).

6. Shryock, *Medical Licensing,* 4 (quoting John Stearns, "Presidential Address," 1 *N.Y. State Med. Soc. Trans.* 139 (1818)).

7. Beck, "Sketch," 143 (quoting Smith, *History of New York* (1814), 326).

8. Shryock, *Medical Licensing,* 18.

9. Rothstein, *American Physicians,* 62 (citing Dan King, "The Evils of Quackery, and Its Remedies," *Boston Med. Surg. J.* 40 (1849)).

10. Ibid., 125–27.

11. Ibid., 139 (quoting Samuel Thomson, *New Guide to Health: or, Botanic Family Physician, containing a Complete System of Practice, on a Plan Entirely New; with a Description of the Vegetables made use of, and Directions for Preparing and Administering Them, to Cure Disease, to which is Prefixed, a Narrative of the Life and Medical Discoveries of the Author* (1832), 32).

12. Dana Ullman, "Homeopathic Medicine: A Modern View," 80 *Whole Earth Rev.* 100 (fall 1993).

13. The term *homeopathy* comes from the Greek *homeo* ("same") and *pathos* ("disease, experience, suffering"); *allopathy* derives from the Greek *allo* ("other"). In homeopathy, diseases are treated "by drugs which are capable of producing in healthy persons symptoms like those of the disease to be treated, the drug being administered in minute doses." *The Sloane-Dorland Annotated Medical-Legal Diction-*

ary (St. Paul: West Publishing, 1987), 347. In allopathy, diseases are treated "by producing a condition incompatible with or antagonistic to the condition to be cured or alleviated" (20).

14. See Coulter, *Divided Legacy*, 179–99.

15. Although immunization and allergy treatments are two conventional therapies that stimulate the body's self-healing resources and thus recall the homeopathic law of similars, homeopathy's popular success, together with the lack of scientific explanation for its mechanism, led regular physicians to forcibly remove homeopathy from medical discourse. Coulter argues that homeopathy's wane also resulted from the growing influence of the pharmaceutical industry, which put the economic power of the drug industry behind allopathic medicine. Coulter observes that of the 250 medical journals published at the turn of the century, all except one were supported by advertisements from pharmaceutical companies. Coulter, *Divided Legacy*, 402–3, 415. Internal dissension between purists who strictly followed Hahnemann's teachings (including his extreme dilutions) and "low dilutionists," who deviated from homeopathic orthodoxy, also played a role. See Coulter, *Divided Legacy*, 426–27; Rothstein, *American Physicians*, 239–43.

16. See Ronald Hamowy, "The Early Development of Medical Licensing Laws in the United States, 1875–1900," 3:1 *J. Libertarian Stud.* 73 (1979).

17. Robert G. Richardson, *The Surgeon's Tale: The Story of Modern Surgery* (New York: Charles Scribner's Sons, 1958), 38–46.

18. William G. Rothstein, *American Medical Schools and the Practice of Medicine: A History* (New York: Oxford University Press, 1987), 70.

19. Coulter, *Divided Legacy*, 430 (quoting 36 *JAMA* 515 (1902)).

20. Ibid. (citing 34 *JAMA* 1200 (1902)).

21. The report was published as Abraham Flexner, *Medical Education in the United States and Canada*, Carnegie Foundation for the Advancement of Teaching, Bulletin no. 4 (1910) (hereinafter cited as *Flexner Report*).

22. Ludmerer, *Learning to Heal*, 167, 180.

23. Ibid., 174 (quoting *Flexner Report*, 63).

24. Coulter, *Divided Legacy*, 447 (quoting *Flexner Report*, 156). The *Flexner Report* resulted in a homogenous system of medical education emphasizing the "rule-of-thumb practitioner, who orders unnecessary tests and generates undue expense and discomfort." Ludmerer, *Learning to Heal*, 174.

25. Coulter argues that the AMA classifications, while purporting to be objective, were weighted heavily against homeopaths. The AMA thus "acquired a whip hand over the whole medical educational system." Coulter, *Divided Legacy*, 446–47. See also Council on Scientific Affairs, *Alternative Medicine*, 1 (the *Flexner Report* "led to the acceptance of the biological, disease-oriented models that dominate medicine in the United States today. . . . Many schools that taught practices such as homeopathy were closed, homeopaths and osteopaths were shunned and stigmatized, and

their therapies became the 'alternatives' to the standards that evolved after the Flexner report[']s acceptance").

26. Coulter, *Divided Legacy,* 450 (citing sources).

27. Austin Flint, "Medical Ethics and Etiquette: Commentaries on the National Code of Ethics," 37 *N.Y. Med. J.* 343, 398 (1883) (quoted in Burton J. Bledstein, *The Culture of Professionalism: The Middle Class and the Development of Higher Education in America* (New York: Norton Books, 1976), 192–93).

28. See Norman Gevitz, *The D.O.'s: Osteopathic Medicine in America* (Baltimore: Johns Hopkins University Press, 1982), 110 (citing "Report of the Committee for the Study of Relations between Osteopathy and Medicine," 158 *JAMA* 736–42 (1955)); Walter I. Wardwell, "Chiropractors: Evolution to Acceptance," in Gevitz, *Other Healers,* 157 (noting that chiropractors were labeled "cultists, quacks, and impostors").

29. American Medical Association, *Principles of Medical Ethics* § 3.1 (Chicago: American Medical Association, 1956).

30. Wilk v. American Medical Ass'n, 719 F.2d 207 (7th Cir. 1983), *cert. denied,* 467 U.S. 1210 (1984), *on remand,* 671 F. Supp. 1465 (N.D. Ill. 1987), *aff'd,* 895 F.2d 352 (7th Cir. 1990).

31. Ibid., 895 F.2d at 361, 362.

32. See, e.g., Wengel v. Herfert, 473 N.W.2d 741, 744 (Mich. Ct. App. 1991) (plaintiff's counsel's remarks); Bushman v. State Mutual Life Ass'n Co. of America, 915 F. Supp. 945, 953 (N.D. Ill. 1996) (construing insurance policy in favor of coverage of high dose chemotherapy with autologous bone marrow transplant cancer treatment, stating that "the procedure at issue is not some type of voodoo or alternative medicine prescribed by someone outside the mainstream of medical practice").

See also United States v. LeBeau, 1993 U.S. App. LEXIS 1501, at *5–6 (Jan. 28, 1993) (referring to herbal and homeopathic remedies as "medical chicanery" and stating: "One wonders whether the government would pursue an herbal remedies boutique or a New Age lecturer urging the curative power of crystals as vigourously as it did Lebeau"). Interestingly, the court in *LeBeau* acknowledged changing medical views of such remedies, as well as the establishment of the Office of Alternative Medicine. Cf. Council on Scientific Affairs, *Alternative Medicine,* 17 (attributing "some of the interest in alternative medicine . . . [to] New Age interest in 'channeling' and astrology, modern 'witch trials' concerning Satanic child abuse rituals, and alleged capture by space aliens") (citing C. Krauthammer, "The Return of the Primitive," *Time,* Jan. 20, 1996, 82).

33. Patricia Branca, "Towards a Social History of Medicine," in *The Medicine Show,* ed. Patricia Branca (New York: Science History Publications, 1977), 89.

34. Eric Cassell describes this process as follows: "The first step was reducing the problem of human illness — with all its intricate physical, social, emotional, and

cultural aspects to the biological problem of disease. . . . The second reductive step follows from the scientific investigation of diseases. Here the findings of science become the accepted picture of the disease, further oversimplifying the problem." Eric J. Cassell, "The Sorcerer's Broom: Medicine's Rampant Technology," 23:6 *Hastings Center Rep.* 33 (1986).

35. Smith v. People, 117 P. 612 (Colo. 1911).

36. Ibid. at 615.

37. Ibid.

38. See, e.g., People v. Cantor, 18 Cal. Rptr. 363 (Col. App. Dep't Super. Ct. 1961) (affirming conviction for unlawful practice of medicine where defendant used hypnosis and laid hands to alleviate conditions); State *ex rel.* Bierring v. Robinson, 19 N.W.2d 214 (Iowa 1945) (faith healer's conviction for practicing medicine illegally, upheld); Cowles v. Board of Regents of the Univ. of the State of New York, 44 N.Y.S.2d 911 (App. Div. 1943), *aff'd*, 55 N.E.2d 515 (N.Y. 1944) (suspending license of physician running faith-healing clinic); Sorgen v. Ohio, 172 N.E. 835 (Ohio 1930) (affirming magnetic healer's conviction).

39. See, e.g., Hitchcock v. State, 131 A.2d 714 (Md. 1957).

40. Mark Hall, "Institutional Control of Physician Behavior: Legal Barriers to Health Care Cost Containment," 137 *U. Pa. L. Rev.* 431, 453 n. 80 (1988).

41. Barry Furrow et al., *Health Law* (St. Paul: West Publishing, 1995), § 3-7.a, p. 63.

42. See Donna Peizer, "A Social and Legal Analysis of the Independent Practice of Midwifery: Vicarious Liability of the Collaborating Physician and Judicial Means of Addressing Denial of Hospital Privileges," 2 *Berkeley Women's L.J.* 139, 146 (1986). Peizer argues that biomedicine established male dominance in childbirth by "convinc[ing] the public that childbirth was inherently pathological and unsafe, a dangerous condition that required the attention of the more highly valued male birth attendants" (147). Religious and scientific orthodoxies historically have tended to distrust transcendental or vitalistic approaches to well-being and individuation.

43. United States v. Rutherford, 438 F. Supp. 1287 (W.D. Okla. 1977), *remanded*, 582 F.2d 1234 (10th Cir. 1978), *rev'd*, 442 U.S. 544 (1979), *on remand*, 616 F.2d 455 (10th Cir. 1980), *cert. denied*, 449 U.S. 937 (1980), *later proceeding*, 806 F.2d 1455 (10th Cir. Okla. 1986). The act is codified at 21 *U.S.C.* § 321(p)(1).

44. Ibid., 582 F.2d at 1236.

45. Ibid., 442 U.S. at 555.

46. Ibid., 442 U.S. at 558.

47. See Nancy Ehrenreich, "The Colonization of the Womb," 43 *Duke L.J.* 492, 494–98 (1993) (citing cases, and attributing judicial acceptance of forced medical treatment during pregnancy — particularly Cesarean sections — to a devaluation of motherhood and reproduction).

48. Ehrenreich argues that courts frequently judge physicians' negligence by

the industry custom, allowing the profession of "medicine to be its own judge." Ibid., 565. While use of expert testimony to determine the standard of care arguably allows the medical profession to establish its preferred level of negligence, however, courts in many cases reject industry custom as a defense to medical malpractice. See, e.g., Burton v. Brooklyn Doctors Hospital, 452 N.Y.S.2d 875 (App. Div. 1982).

49. Nancy K. Plant, "The Learned Intermediary Doctrine: Some New Medicine for an Old Ailment," 81:4 *Iowa L. Rev.* 1007, 1057 (1996) (citing cases).

CHAPTER 3: STATE LAW REGULATION OF MEDICINE

1. People v. Amber, 349 N.Y.S.2d 604, 612 (Sup. Ct. 1973); People v. Steinberg, 73 N.Y.S.2d 475 (Mag. Ct. 1947).

2. Dent v. West Virginia, 129 U.S. 114 (1888).

3. Jacobson v. Massachusetts, 197 U.S. 11 (1905).

4. See also Rutherford, 616 F.2d at 455, 457 (see chap. 6).

5. See, e.g., Davis v. Hubbard, 506 F. Supp. 915, 938 (N.D. Ohio 1980); Rogers v. Okin, 478 F. Supp. 1342 (D. Mass. 1979). See also Winters v. Miller, 446 F.2d 65, 69 (2d Cir. 1971) (upholding a damages claim made by a Christian Scientist who was never found mentally incompetent but had been forced to take medication).

6. Washington v. Harper, 494 U.S. 210, 223, 236 (1990).

7. See Reynolds v. McNichols, 488 F.2d 1378, 1382 (10th Cir. 1979) (citing cases).

8. State v. Hinze, 441 N.W.2d 593, 594 (Neb. 1989).

9. Ibid. at 598.

10. See Cohen, "Fixed Star," 79, 155–56 (listing medical practice acts) and 157–59 (listing definitional categories by state) (1995).

11. N.Y. Educ. Law § 6521.

12. Mich. Comp. Laws Ann. § 333.17001(d).

13. Ark. Code Ann. § 17-93-202(2)(B).

14. See Ill. Ann. Stat. ch. 111, para. 4459; Iowa Code Ann. § 148.1; Kan. Stat. Ann. § 65-2869; Neb. Rev. Stat. § 71-1,102; N.C. Gen. Stat. § 90-18; R.I. Gen. Laws § 5-37-1(i); S.C. Code Ann. § 40-47-40; Tenn. Code Ann. § 63-6-204.

15. See Iowa Code Ann. § 148.1; Neb. Rev. Stat. § 71-1,102; Kan. Stat. Ann. § 65-2869; S.D. Codified Laws Ann. § 36-4-9; Tex. Rev. Civ. Stat. Ann. art. 4510a.

16. Haw. Rev. Stat. § 453-2; Minn. Stat. Ann. § 147.081; N.M. Stat. Ann. § 61-6-6; Or. Rev. Stat. § 677.085; Vt. Stat. Ann. tit. 26, § 1311; Wyo. Stat. § 33-26-102(a)(x)(A).

17. Reams v. State, 279 So. 2d 839 (Fla. 1973) (providing that defendant was deemed to be practicing medicine if he held himself out as being able to diagnose disease or physical conditions); People v. Mastromarino, 265 N.Y.S. 864, 864–65 (Sup. Ct. 1933) (holding that one who held himself out as being able to and offered to diagnose, treat, operate, or prescribe for any human disease, practiced medicine

within meaning of § 6521); State v. Nelson, 317 S.E.2d 711, 714 (N.C. Ct. App. 1984) (finding intent of statute to protect public against those who would hold themselves out as medical doctors).

18. Louisiana State Bd. of Medical Examiners v. Craft, 93 So. 2d 298, 300–301 (La. Ct. App. 1957).

19. See State v. Ghadiali, 175 A. 315, 318 (Del. 1933), *cert. dismissed,* 292 U.S. 653 (1934) (holding defendant guilty of practicing medicine where he recommended the use of an appliance to cure an ailment with the intention of receiving, either directly or indirectly, money or some other form of compensation); Nelson, 317 S.E.2d at 714 (declaring the intent of the statute to protect the public against those who would hold themselves out as medical doctors who would expect compensation in return for those services); State v. Greiner, 114 P. 897, 899 (Wash. 1911) (sustaining conviction where defendant diagnosed ailments using vibrator, used manual manipulations, prescribed dietary advice, and collected fee); 10 Op. Att'y Gen. 1003 (Wis. 1921) (finding that one who advised, prescribed methods of treatment, diet and exercise, and charged substantial sums was practicing medicine and should have procured a certificate to do so).

20. Haw. Rev. Stat. § 453-2 ("either gratuitously or for compensation"); La. Rev. Stat. Ann. § 1262 (same); Utah Code Ann. § 58-12-28.

21. Del. Code Ann. tit. 24, § 1703.

22. State v. Buswell, 58 N.W. 728 (Neb. 1894).

23. Ohio Rev. Code § 4731.34; Okla. Stat. Ann. tit. 59, § 492; Or. Rev. Stat. § 677.085 and Vt. Stat. Ann. tit. 26, § 1311.

24. Me. Rev. Stat. Ann. tit. 32, § 3270; Ohio Rev. Code Ann. § 4731.34.

25. State v. Baylor, 439 N.E.2d 461, 462–63 (Ohio Ct. App. 1981).

26. Ind. Code Ann. § 25-22.5-1-1.1(a)(2).

27. Black v. State, 216 S.W. 181 (Tex. Crim. App. 1919).

28. Utah Code Ann. § 58-12-28(4)(a).

29. Commonwealth v. Dragon, 132 N.E. 356, 357 (Mass. 1921).

30. See Ind. Code Ann. § 25-22.5-1-1.1; N.C. Gen. Stat. § 90-18; Utah Code Ann. § 58-12-28.

31. Ind. Code Ann. § 25-22.5-1-1.1. Utah defines "drugs or medicine" using similar terminology in Utah Code Ann. § 58-12-28. Oklahoma also uses a similar definition to define "drugs" in Okla. Stat. Ann. tit. 59, § 353.1, but specifically excludes food from the definition.

32. N.M. Stat. Ann. § 61-6-6. The North Carolina Supreme Court has defined "drug" as "any substance used as a medicine or in the composition of medicines for internal or external use" and has defined "medicine" as "any substance or preparation used in treating disease." State v. Baker, 48 S.E.2d 61, 66 (N.C. 1948) (holding that patent or proprietary remedies that may be purchased without a prescription constitute drugs).

33. Md. Code Ann., Health Occ. § 14-101(k)(2)(ii).

34. Del. Code Ann. tit. 24, § 1703(b)(2); Gross v. Ambach, 71 N.Y.2d 859 (N.Y. 1988) (practice of medicine includes performing an autopsy).

35. Ark. Code Ann. § 17-93-202 ("whether by the use of drugs, surgery, manipulation, electricity, or any physical, mechanical, or other means whatsoever"); Me. Rev. Stat. Ann. tit. 32, § 3270 (manipulation); S.C. Code Ann. § 40-47-40(c) ("manipulation, adjustment or method . . . by any therapeutic agent whatsoever").

36. Haw. Rev. Stat. § 453-1.

37. The AMA "lobbied to . . . have the language of the [medical licensing] statute define the practice of medicine as broadly as possible so as to include all attempts at healing, whether for compensation or not, and whether through the administration of drugs or not, and, finally, to encompass within the purview of the statutory authority of the state boards the power to refuse or revoke licenses for 'dishonorable' or 'unprofessional' conduct." Hamowy, "Medical Licensing Laws," 81. Hamowy quotes the secretary of the Bureau of Medical Legislation as being in favor of "regulating not only the practice of medicine as it is popularly known, but also all those who desire to treat the sick for compensation as a profession. This should include the regulation of midwives and all sects desiring to treat the sick for compensation" (95, quoting Frederick R. Green, "Sixty-six Years of Medical Legislation," 54 *JAMA* 226–27 (June 11, 1910)).

38. See, e.g., Jacobs v. United States, 436 A.2d 1286 (D.C. 1981) (upholding conviction of physician for aiding and abetting a licensed paramedical assistant, employed by him, to engage in the unauthorized practice of medicine; physician permitted assistant to run a medical clinic and examine and treat patients without his consultation and with minimal supervision, and to distribute, without appropriate supervision, drug prescriptions that the physician had pre-signed). Many statutes also make aiding and abetting the unlawful practice of medicine grounds for professional discipline. See, e.g., Ariz. Rev. Stat. § 32-1401(cc) ("maintaining a professional connection with or lending one's name to enhance or continue the activities of an illegal practitioner of medicine"); Colo. Rev. Stat. Ann. § 12-36-117(k) ("aiding or abetting, in the practice of medicine, of any person not licensed to practice medicine").

39. Amber, 349 N.Y.S.2d at 604.

40. Thus, the court denied defendant's motion to dismiss the indictment. Ibid. at 613.

41. Stetina v. State, 513 N.E.2d 1234 (Ind. Ct. App. 1987).

42. See State v. MountJoy et al., 891 P.2d 376, 384 (Kan. 1995) (holding that conviction of midwives for the unauthorized practice of the healing arts does not require proof of criminal intent); State v. Howard, 337 S.E.2d 598 (N.C. Ct. App. 1985) (naturopaths); Sabastier v. State, 504 So. 2d 45 (Fla. Dist. Ct. App. 1987)

(homeopaths); Cantor, 18 Cal. Rptr. at 363 (hypnotherapists); Williams v. State of Alabama *ex rel.* Medical Licensure Comm'n, 453 So. 2d 1051, 1053 (Ala. Civ. App. 1984) (colonic irrigation providers); Stetina, 513 N.E.2d at 1234 (nutritionists; iridologists).

43. Hicks v. Arkansas State Medical Bd., 537 S.W.2d 794, 796 (Ark. 1976) (ear piercing); State v. Brady, 492 N.E.2d 34 (Ind. Ct. App. 1986) (tattooing); People v. Burroughs, 285 Cal. Rptr. 622 (1991) (massage).

44. Mass. Ann. Laws ch. 112, § 7. Most states exempt healers, practicing in a religious context as part of a recognized spiritual tradition and practice. See, e.g., D.C. Code Ann. § 2-3301.4(d)(1).

45. Cf. Sermchief v. Gonzales, 660 S.W.2d 683, 689–90 (Mo. 1983) (reversing conviction of nurses for practicing medicine, citing legislative authorization for the "nursing diagnosis, as opposed to a medical diagnosis," when the nurse "finds or fails to find symptoms described by physicians in standing orders and protocols for the purpose of administering courses of treatment prescribed by the physician in such orders and protocols"); Parma v. Wolff, 635 N.E.2d 76, 78–79 (Ohio Mun. Ct. 1993) (nonlicensed defendant's use of machine to determine imbalances of hips and shoulders did not constitute a chiropractic diagnosis in violation of the chiropractic licensing statute, particularly since defendant told patient: "This is only a preliminary screening, this is not an examination, and . . . any examination must be done by a licensed chiropractor").

46. See Jerry Green, "The Health Care Contract: A Model for Sharing Responsibility," 3 *Somatics* 1 (1982); see also Clark Havighurst, *Health Care Choices: Private Contracts as Instruments of Health Reform* (Washington, D.C.: American Enterprise Institute for Public Policy Research, 1996), 328–29 (arguing that greater "use of private contracts as instruments of privately negotiated health care reforms" can "topple . . . the old paradigm of a centrally regulated health care system supplying an essentially uniform product"); Heidi Rian, "An Alternative Contractual Approach to Holistic Health Care," 44 *Ohio L.J.* 185 (1983) ("When practitioner and client are concerned with maintaining health rather than with treating disease, when the therapy carries a low potential for harm, and when the nature of the agreement and distribution of responsibilities can be made reasonably clear, a contract can protect the interests of both client and practitioners . . . and provide needed flexibility in the developing field of holistic health care").

47. According to one practitioner, "somatics is the study of the body: working with the expression, discovery, and mapping of the body's relation to learning, cognition, and emotional and physical well-being." Jocelyn Oliver, "Conscious Evolution through Somatic Education," *AHP Perspective* (Association for Humanistic Psychology, San Francisco, Calif.), Jan.–Feb. 1996, 8.

48. "Somatic practices enable us to develop a conversation with our body and its systems that results in higher and higher levels of conscious self-regulation. What results is a more conscious body, one which responds easily to positive stimuli and

which is easy to rebalance, one in which conscious attention and intention can be felt to have immediate and dramatic effect on tissue quality and state." Ibid.

49. However, certification in nonlicensed holistic modalities generally has no legal value. See Jack Raso, "Alternative Health Education and Pseudocredentialing," *Skeptical Inquirer,* July–Aug. 1996, 39.

50. This view finds expression in a 1977 settlement involving a criminal case against Dana Ullman, a Berkeley, California, homeopath. Ullman's practice consisted of contracting with clients to provide information concerning homeopathic remedies for particular conditions. Ullman referred his clients to licensed physicians for the diagnosis and treatment of biomedically defined pathology. The municipal court judge, with the district attorney's consent, dismissed the action provided Ullman agreed to not "engag[e] in the diagnosis and treatment of pathology as prescribed by the charging statute." People v. Ullman, No. 98158, *Settled Statement* (Mun. Ct. Ca. 1977). The dismissal implicitly recognized that agreements could define a nonmedical role for holistic providers. Katy Butler, "Pioneer Health Care Accord," *San Francisco Chronicle,* Mar. 30, 1977, 5.

51. Some states have provisions prohibiting discrimination against a particular school or system of medicine. For example, California provides that the medical practice act "shall not be construed so as to discriminate against any particular school of medicine or surgery . . . or any other treatment, nor shall it regulate, prohibit, or apply to any kind of treatment by prayer." Cal. Bus. & Prof. Code § 2063. Similarly, Massachusetts and Rhode Island prohibit construing the medical practice act "to discriminate against any particular school or system of medicine." Mass. Ann. Laws ch. 112, § 7; R.I. Gen. Laws § 5-37-14. These statutes arguably prohibit discrimination against independent holistic providers, who are practicing health care systems not recognized by biomedicine. The statutes above are broader than Indiana's, which prohibits discrimination against "practitioners of any school of medicine holding unlimited licenses to practice medicine recognized in Indiana." Ind. Code Ann. § 16-22-8-39(c). For an interesting interpretation of Texas's constitutional nondiscrimination provision, see *Ex Parte* Halsted, 182 S.W.2d 479 (Tex. Crim. App. 1944) (finding a chiropractic statute unconstitutional because it established lower requirements for chiropractic treatment of human disease than was required in medical licensure).

52. The duty to refer addresses the concern that nonmedical providers will create overreliance on holistic services and induce the patient to forgo adequate medical care (see chap. 5).

53. But see State v. Kellogg, 568 P.2d 514 (Idaho 1977) (statutory language exempting "physician" from the prohibition on dispensing prescription drugs did not include the defendant, who claimed to be a naturopath). Licensed veterinarians in Idaho are permitted the veterinary practice of "acupuncture, chiropractic, magnetic field therapy, holistic medicine, homeopathy, herbology/naturopathy, massage and physical therapy." Idaho Code § 54-2103.

54. Tex. Rev. Civ. Stat. Ann. art. 4495b(e). The provision is similar to exceptions from medical practice acts for the domestic administration of family remedies. See, e.g., Mass. Ann. Laws ch. 112, § 7.

55. Okla. Stat. Ann. tit. 59, § 480.

56. Bledstein, *Culture of Professionalism,* 80–81.

57. Walter Gelhorn, "The Abuse of Occupational Licensing," 44 *U. Chi. L. Rev.* 6 (1976). For additional literature on the critique of occupational licensing, see Baron, "Licensure," 335–48; Sue A. Blevins, *The Medical Monopoly: Protecting Consumers or Limiting Competition?* Policy Analysis No. 246 (Washington, D.C.: Cato Institute, 1995); Daniel B. Hogan, "The Effectiveness of Licensing: History, Evidence and Recommendations," 7:2–3 *L. & Hum. Behav.* 117 (1983); Edwin A. Locke et al., "The Case against Medical Licensing," 3 *Medicolegal News* (Oct. 1980); Michael Pertschuck, "Professional Licensure," 43:12 *Conn. Med.* 793, 793 (1993); Elton Rayack, "Medical Licensure: Social Costs and Social Benefits," 7:2–3 *L. & Hum. Behav.* 147–50 (1983).

58. Citing Ga. Code Ann. § 84-2315.

59. Hogan, "Effectiveness of Licensing," 126.

60. Gelhorn, "Occupational Licensing," 17–18.

61. Rayack, "Medical Licensure," 151.

62. Nev. Rev. Stat. § 644.023(3).

63. Lori Andrews, *Deregulating Doctoring: Do Medical Licensing Laws Meet Today's Health Needs* (Emmaus, Pa.: People's Medical Society, 1983), 26.

64. Botkin v. State Medical Bd., 96 N.E.2d 215, 223 (Ct. Comm. Pleas Ohio 1950).

65. Amber, 349 N.Y.S.2d at 612. Compare *Amber* and *Botkin* with State v. Fite, 159 P. 1183 (Idaho 1916) (holding that the medical practice act does not seek to subject to medical examination persons engaged in other branches of the healing arts).

66. State Medical Soc'y v. Board of Examiners in Podiatry, 546 A.2d 830 (Conn. 1988).

67. It was only in 1961 that the AMA's House of Delegates determined that "it would not be unethical for physicians to voluntarily associate with osteopaths." American Medical Association, *Proceedings of the House of Delegates* (1961), 173–74. Some state licensing boards forbid osteopaths from using the designation *M.D.* See, e.g., Eatough v. Albano, 673 F.2d 671, 678 (3d Cir. 1982) (Weis, J., dissenting) (criticizing the state board's rule for "perpetuat[ing] a distinction between allopathic and osteopathic physicians which the enabling statute does not authorize, and indeed, was intended to eliminate").

68. See Welch v. American Psychoanalytic Assoc., No. 85 Civ. 1651 (JFK), 1986 WL 4537 (S.D.N.Y. Apr. 4, 1986) (antitrust action alleging anticompetitive behavior resulting in exclusion of licensed psychologists from the recognized practice of psychoanalysis); Virginia Academy of Clinical Psychologists v. Blue Shield of Virginia, 624 F.2d 476 (4th Cir. 1980) (antitrust action against insurer and neuro-

psychiatric society based on plans' refusal to pay for services rendered by clinical psychologists unless billed through physicians); California Ass'n of Psychology Providers v. Rank, 793 P.2d 2, 39–40 (Cal. 1990) (holding that "under California law a hospital that admits clinical psychologists to its staff may permit such psychologists to take primary responsibility for the admission, diagnosis, treatment, and discharge of their patients," and that regulations requiring physician supervision are therefore invalid), *reh'g denied*, 1990 Cal. LEXIS 4383 (Sept. 20, 1990).

69. Although some of these providers practice within the biomedical model, the biomedical establishment has opposed either their licensure or their efforts to expand professional scope of practice. See Rayack, "Medical Licensure," 153–54 (on physician assistants); Barbara J. Safriet, "Health Care Dollars and Regulatory Sense: The Role of Advanced Practice Nursing," 9 *Yale J. Reg.* 417 (1992); Peizer, "Midwifery," 157 (describing the organized opposition to midwives by the American College of Obstetrics and Gynecology); *Public Regulation of Health Care Occupations in California* (Sacramento: Public Affairs Research Group, 1981), 15 (citing "growing tension between licensed groups that have 'staked out' an authorized scope of practice and new groups that want 'a piece of the action,'" and describing the scope-of-practice issue as the "most important" issue facing licensing and regulatory agencies).

70. Gelhorn, "Occupational Licensing," 25.

71. Melissa B. Mower, "Certified Touch: The Impact of National Certification," 62 *Massage* 60 (July–Aug. 1996).

72. See People v. Abrams, 576 N.Y.S.2d 338 (App. Div. 1991) (New York statute does not criminalize practice of psychology without a license); Wis. Stat. Ann. § 455.02(1)(a) ("This chapter does not restrict exclusively to licensed psychologists the rendering of services included within the practice of psychology, but only an individual licensed . . . may use the title"). By way of contrast, West Virginia prohibits the unauthorized practice of counseling, finding that individuals without the necessary training and character should not engage in practice. W. Va. Code § 30-31-1.

73. See Barbara B. Mitchell, *Acupuncture and Oriental Medicine Laws* (Washington, D.C.: National Acupuncture Foundation, 1995), 127. The National Commission for the Certification of Acupuncturists (NCCA) examination "represents a broad national consensus on the knowledge and skills necessary for the safe and effective practice of acupuncture." Such exams have included, in addition to theoretical knowledge, a practical component testing location and placement of acupuncture needles (127).

74. Alaska Stat. Ann. § 08.06.101.

75. R.I. Gen. Laws § 23-20.8-3(a); Wash. Rev. Code § 18.108.030(1).

76. Tex. Rev. Civ. Stat. Ann. art. 4512k, § 2.

77. For example, acupuncture schools are accredited by the National Accreditation Commission for Schools and Colleges of Acupuncture and Oriental

Medicine under authority granted by the U.S. Department of Education. The National Commission for the Certification of Acupuncture sets standards of professional competence and certifies diplomates on the basis of the candidate's ability to meet eligibility standards of education and/or experience, pass a written and practical examination, complete an NCCA-approved clean needle technique course, and commit himself or herself to the professional code of ethics. This certification then becomes a basis for licensure in most of the licensing states.

78. Accreditation is "the approval by private organizations of professional training programs such as medical schools and institutional providers such as hospitals." Philip C. Kissam, "Government Policy toward Medical Accreditation and Certification: The Antitrust Laws and Other Procompetitive Strategies," 1983 *Wis. L. Rev.* 1, 2 n. 1. Kissam criticizes the medical profession's ability to influence medical licensure through the accreditation process and suggests a model of limited competition for medical credentialing.

79. However, just as national examinations developed by the American Medical Association and related organizations played a role in developing a biomedical monopoly, efforts at national accreditation by holistic providers can create professional monopolies where groups within the profession (for example, reflexologists and instructors of Alexander technique) either vie for exclusive privileges within the regulatory structure or seek to be permitted to operate outside the licensing framework.

80. Alaska Stat. § 08.06.030(a)(3)-(4).

81. Ibid. § 08.45.0303(2).

82. See, e.g., Ariz. Rev. Stat. §§ 32-1522 through 32-1525 (naturopathic licensure).

83. D.C. Code Ann. § 2-3309.1(f).

84. Mitchell, *Acupuncture Laws,* 132.

CHAPTER 4: SCOPE-OF-PRACTICE LIMITATIONS

1. Walter Wardwell refers to the three groups of professions as the limited medical professions (whose members practice independently of the medical profession with a limited scope of practice), the ancillary professions (whose members function only under the direct supervision of a licensed physician), and the marginal professions (whose members challenge the validity of orthodox conceptions of illness and health and thus constitute a serious threat to biomedicine). Walter J. Wardwell, "Chiropractors: Challengers of Medical Domination," 2 *Research in the Sociology of Health Care* 207, 208 (1981) (hereinafter cited as Wardwell, "Challengers"). Some include midwives within the discussion of complementary and alternative health care providers. See Lori B. Andrews, "The Shadow Health Care System: Regulation of Alternative Health Care Providers," 32 *Hous. L. Rev.* 1273 (1996).

2. Colo. Rev. Stat. § 12-29.5-101.

3. Ariz. Rev. Stat. Ann. tit. 32, ch. 14, art. 1, § 1.

4. N.H. Rev. Stat. Ann. § 328-E:1.

5. Fla. Stat. Ann. § 456.31(1). South Carolina is unique in affirmatively prohibiting the practice of naturopathy. S.C. Code Ann. § 40-31-10. South Carolina also prohibits a physical therapist from practicing homeopathy, naturopathy, and magnetic healing (§ 40-45-220).

6. Cal. Bus. & Prof. Code §§ 1000–1007.

7. Miss. Code Ann. § 73-6-1.

8. Mich. Comp. Laws Ann. § 333.16501.

9. See, e.g., Mont. Code Ann. § 37-26-101 (authorizing a board of naturopathic physicians to adopt rules specifying licensing requirements and scope of practice); 63 Penn. Stat. § 1803(B) (delegating to a board the promulgation of regulations establishing requisite training for acupuncture licensure).

10. See Michael H. Cohen, "Holistic Health Care: Including Alternative and Complementary Medicine in Insurance and Regulatory Schemes," 38:1 *Ariz. L. Rev.* 83, 163–64 (1996) (listing statutory definitions of chiropractic).

11. Del. Code Ann. tit. 24, § 701; see also Ala. Code § 34-24-120(a) ("the science and art of locating and removing . . . any interference with the transmission and expression of nerve energy in the human body"); Ark. Code Ann. § 17-81-102(2)-(3)(A) ("diagnosis and analysis of any interference with normal nerve transmission and expression"); Ind. Code Ann. § 25-10-1-1(1) ("diagnosis and analysis of any interference with normal nerve transmission and expression").

12. Iowa Code Ann. §151.1(2); see also Kan. Stat. Ann. § 65-2871 ("adjust any misplaced tissue of any kind or nature, manipulate or treat the human body by manual, mechanical, electrical or natural methods or by the use of physical means, physiotherapy"); Mo. Ann. Stat. § 331.010(1) ("examination, diagnosis, adjustments, manipulation and treatment of malpositioned articulations and structures of the body"). Many refer to the body's "inherent recuperative capability." See, e.g., Mich. Comp. Laws Ann. § 333.16401(b); Wash. Rev. Code Ann. §18.25.005 (1), (2), (4).

13. N.C. Gen. Stat. § 90-143(a).

14. Cohen, "Holistic Health Care," 161–62.

15. Colo. Rev. Stat. § 12-48.5-103(5).

16. Conn. Gen. Stat. Ann. § 20-206a(d).

17. D.C. Code Ann. § 2-3301.2(6A)(A).

18. Idaho Code § 54-704(1)(c).

19. Utah Code Ann. § 58-47a-2(2).

20. N.M. Stat. Ann. § 61-12C-4(A); Tex. Rev. Civ. Stat. Ann. art. 4512k, § 1(1).

21. See, e.g., W. Va. Code § 7-1-32. To the profession, massage therapy licensure is preferable to local ordinances focusing on sexual rather than therapeutic touch. See Ariz. Rev. Stat. § 11-821.B and D.6 (providing for zoning of "massage

establishments," defined as "an establishment . . . in which a person . . . engages in or permits massage activities, including any method of pressure on, friction against, stroking, kneading, rubbing, tapping, pounding, vibrating or stimulating of external soft parts of the body"). The definition does not apply to physicians, registered nurses, and other designated professionals.

22. See, e.g., Va. Code Ann. § 54.1-3000.

23. Cohen, "Holistic Health Care," 161–62.

24. Alaska Stat. § 08.45.200(3).

25. Conn. Gen. Stat. Ann. § 20-34(a)(2).

26. D.C. Code Ann. § 2-3309.1(b).

27. Haw. Rev. Stat. § 455-1(1).

28. Ibid. at § 455-1(2).

29. N.H. Rev. Stat. Ann. § 328-E:2(IX); Mont. Code Ann. § 37-26-103(7) (Naturopathy's purpose is "to promote or restore health by the support and stimulation of the individual's inherent self-healing processes. This is accomplished through education of the patient by a naturopathic physician and through the use of natural therapies and therapeutic substances").

30. Or. Rev. Stat. § 685.010(5).

31. Wash. Rev. Code Ann. § 18.36A.040; Mont. Code Ann. § 37-26-103(7) ("prevention, diagnosis, and treatment of human health conditions, injury, and disease"); N.H. Rev. Stat. Ann. § 328-E:2(IX) ("prevention, diagnosis, and treatment of human health conditions, injuries, and diseases"); Tenn. Code Ann. § 63-6-205(1) ("prevention, diagnosis and treatment of human injuries, ailments and disease").

32. Ariz. Rev. Stat. § 32-1581A.

33. See Utah Code Ann. § 58-71-102(8)(b).

34. Or. Rev. Stat. § 685.010(4).

35. Or. Rev. Stat. § 685.101(3); Utah Code Ann. § 72 (58-71-201).

36. See, e.g., Utah Code Ann. § 72 (58-71-201) (naturopathic medicine is a "system of primary health care for the prevention, diagnosis, and treatment of human health conditions").

37. Wash. Rev. Code Ann. § 18.36a.020(9).

38. Nev. Rev. Stat. Ann. § 630A.040; Ariz. Rev. Stat. Ann. § 32-2901(4).

39. Ariz. Rev. Stat. Ann. § 32-2901(4).

40. Nev. Rev. Stat. § 630A.240.

41. See, e.g., Alaska Stat. § 08.45.200(3) (naturopathy includes use of homeopathic remedies); Haw. Rev. Stat. § 455-1 (naturopathy includes use of homeopathic medicines); Idaho Code § 54-2103(26) (veterinarians); N.M. Stat. Ann. § 61-4-2(A) (chiropractic includes use of homeopathic remedies); Wash. Rev. Code Ann. § 18.36A.040 (naturopathy includes the prescription, administration, dispensing, and use of homeopathy).

42. Cohen, "Holistic Health Care," 161–62.

43. N.J. Stat. § 45:2C-5.

44. See, e.g., Wash. Rev. Code § 18.06.140.

45. See, e.g., D.C. Code Ann. § 2-3301.2.

46. See, e.g., La. Rev. Stat. § 37:1358.

47. Colo. Rev. Stat. § 12-33-102.

48. See, e.g., Cal. Bus. & Prof. Code § 2191(c) (requiring the Division of Licensing to consider including a course in acupuncture to be taken "by those licensees whose practices may require knowledge in the area of acupuncture"). Section 2191(d) requires the Division of Licensing to encourage every physician and surgeon to take nutrition as part of continuing education. California also requires that medical schools or approved acupuncture schools conducting research into acupuncture report regularly to the legislation on the suitability of acupuncture as a therapeutic technique, and performance standards for persons who perform acupuncture. Cal. Bus. & Prof. Code § 2075.

49. See, e.g., D.C. Code § 2-3309.3(a). In the District of Columbia, such a provider (a "registered acupuncture therapist") must practice "under the direct collaboration" of a person or physician licensed to practice acupuncture.

50. See, e.g., Fla. Stat. Ann. § 457.102(1); Haw. Rev. Stat. § 436E-2; N.M. Stat. Ann. § 61-14a-3(A); R.I. Gen. Laws § 5-37.2-2(1).

51. Md. Code Ann., Health Occ. § 1A-101(b).

52. Nev. Rev. Stat. Ann. § 634A.020(8).

53. Colo. Rev. Stat. § 12-29.5-102(1). See also Cal. Bus. & Prof. Code § 4927(e) ("treatment of certain diseases or dysfunctions of the body"); Fla. Stat. Ann. § 457.102(1) ("diagnostic techniques"). North Carolina refers to "acupuncture diagnosis and treatment." N.C. Gen. Stat. § 90-451(1).

54. 32 Me. Rev. Stat. § 12403.

55. N.M. Stat. Ann. § 61-14A-3(F).

56. See, e.g., Cal. Bus. & Prof. Code § 4937(b) ("drugless substances and herbs"); Nev. Rev. Stat. Ann. § 634A.020(5) ("herbal medicine"). Virginia prohibits the prescribing of herbal preparations. Va. Code Ann. § 54.1-2900.

57. See, e.g., N.M. Stat. Ann. § 61-14A-3(G) ("dietary and nutritional counseling"); Vt. Stat. Ann. tit. 26, § 3401(1) ("nutritional and herbal therapies, therapeutic massage, and lifestyle counseling").

58. Alvarez v. Department of Professional Regulation, 458 So. 2d 808, 808 n. 1 (Fla. Dist. Ct. App. 1984), *aff'd*, 524 So. 2d 700 (Fla. 1988). The statutes also refer to the meridian system. See, e.g., Iowa Code Ann. § 148E.1(1). Acupuncture schools differ with respect to techniques, such as depth and angle of needle insertion, and the way in which a needle is manipulated to stimulate the point. Alvarez, 458 So. 2d at 809. Acupuncture licensure exams include demonstration of knowledge of state rules relating to acupuncture, and acupuncture health and safety requirements; theory and practice of acupuncture; diagnostic techniques and procedures and point/meridian selection; competency in the performance of needle

insertion, manipulation, and removal; and competency in patient care, sanitation, and antiseptic application (808–9).

59. N.Y. Educ. Law § 8216(4).

60. *S.T.O.P.: An Early Drug Intervention and Case Management Program, Aug. 1991–Jan. 1993* (Portland, Ore.: S.T.O.P. Court, Circuit Judge Karl Haas, Multnomah County Courthouse, 1993).

61. See James S. Turner, "Representing Oriental Medicine Providers," in Mitchell, *Acupuncture Laws,* 138. Recently, the National Acupuncture Foundation proposed a model acupuncture statute. Barbara B. Mitchell, *Legislative Handbook for the Practice of Acupuncture and Oriental Medicine* (Washington, D.C.: National Acupuncture Foundation, 1995), 1–24.

62. From time to time, specific providers argue that they are not subject to specific licensing laws — for example, reflexologists have claimed that they do not perform "massage" and are not governed by massage therapy licensing laws. Some states have responded by expressly including or excluding such providers. For example, Arkansas includes reflexology within the definition of "massage therapy." Ark. Code Ann. § 17-86-102(1)(G). Maine exempts from massage therapy registration or certification individuals "who practice other forms of tissue work exclusive of massage therapy, such as rolfing, Trager, reflexology, Shiatsu, Reiki and polarity," if these practitioners do not use the title "massage therapist" or "massage practitioner." 32 Me. Rev. Stat. Ann. § 14307.

63. Feingold v. Commonwealth, State Bd. of Chiropractic, 568 A.2d 1365, 1366 (Pa. Commw. Ct. 1980).

64. See, e.g., Makris v. Bureau of Professional and Occupational Affairs, State Bd. of Psychology, 599 A.2d 279 (Comm. Ct. Pa. 1991). Paradoxically, the problem of unauthorized practice arises because statutes define holistic providers in ways that oppose holism (bracketing "massage," "chiropractic," "counseling," and so forth into separate disciplines with exclusive definitional jurisdictions).

65. Tex. Rev. Civ. Stat. Ann. art. 4512c, § 2(c), § 20.

66. See, e.g., Alaska Stat. § 08.45.200(3) (naturopathy includes use of homeopathic remedies); Haw. Rev. Stat. § 455-1 (naturopathy includes use of homeopathic medicines); N.H. Rev. Stat. Ann. § 328-E:4.I (doctors of naturopathic medicine may use homeopathic preparations).

67. Mont. Code Ann. § 37-26-302. Licensed providers would be required to show that offering homeopathic remedies is within their statutorily authorized scope of practice.

68. Generally, providers cannot practice a healing modality that is subject to separate licensure unless specifically authorized by their licensing statute to do so. For example, chiropractors cannot practice acupuncture or social work and counseling, each of which is separately licensed in many states, unless specifically authorized by the chiropractic licensing statute. Nor can providers practice any modality, licensed or otherwise, by obtaining an ordinary business license from the state.

69. For example, the naturopathic view of illness as "a process or activity initiated by the body in adaptive response to an unnatural environment" challenges the biomedical view of disease as an outside invader. Hans A. Baer, "The Potential Rejuvenation of American Naturopathy as a Consequence of the Holistic Health Movement," 13 *Med. Anthropology* 369, 381 (1992) (quoting J. McKee, *Holistic Health and the Critique of Western Medicine* (1988), 788).

70. Wardwell, "Challengers," 211.

71. Judicial efforts to limit chiropractic use of nutrition arguably suggest an approach to feeding similar to the "medicalization" of birth, death, and procreation. See Branca, "Social History," 89–93; Peizer, "Midwifery," 143–45 (describing the medicalization of birth).

72. Iowa Code Ann. § 151.1.

73. W. Va. Code § 30-16-2(c).

74. La. Rev. Stat. Ann. § 37:2801(3).

75. Mass. Gen. Laws Ann. ch. 112, § 89.

76. Stockwell v. Washington State Chiropractic Disciplinary Bd., 622 P.2d 910 (Wash. Ct. App. 1981).

77. See, e.g., Norville v. Mississippi State Medical Ass'n, 364 So. 2d 1084 (Miss. 1978).

78. Foster v. Board of Chiropractic Examiners, 359 S.E.2d 877 (Ga. 1987).

79. Ibid. at 879 (quoting Ga. Code Ann. § 43-9-1(2)).

80. Ibid. (quoting Ga. Code Ann. §§ 43-9-1(2), 43-0-16(c)).

81. The defendant in *Foster* argued that nutrition is a proper part of chiropractic education and practice, and that the body's inherent recuperative powers cannot be restored without providing the proper vitamins and minerals, which are necessary for "the normal transmission of nerve energy essential to the restoration and maintenance of health." Ibid. (quoting Ga. Code Ann. § 43-9-1(2)).

82. See, e.g., N.H. Rev. Stat. Ann. § 316-A:1 and Wash. Rev. Code Ann. § 18.25.005 (prohibiting); Neb. Rev. Stat. § 71-177 (permitting).

83. D.C. Code Ann. § 2-33-1.2(3)(A).

84. Ohio State Bd. of Chiropractic Examiners v. Fulk, 617 N.E.2d 690 (Ohio Ct. App. 1992).

85. Colonic irrigation is "a cleansing of the colon or bowel with a liquid, normally water, many times under pressure," for hygienic and nutritional purposes. Ibid. at 692.

86. The court did not address whether Ohio requires a license to perform colonic irrigations, which presumably would be relevant to the charge of engaging in unlicensed practice. However, some courts have held that "anyone intending to practice the act of healing can be required to meet the standards set for the medical profession." Reisinger v. State Bd. of Medical Educ. and Licensure, 399 A.2d 1160, 1164 (Comm. Ct. Pa. 1979). Legislatures are not constitutionally required to enact statutes to cover a particular healing modality. Feingold, 568 A.2d at 1365.

87. Fulk, 617 N.E.2d at 692.

88. Ariz. Rev. Stat. Ann. § 32-925; Colo. Rev. Stat. § 12-33-102(1) ("when performed by an appropriately trained chiropractor as determined by the Colorado state board of chiropractic examiners"); La. Rev. Stat. Ann. tit. 37, § 2801(3); Ohio Rev. Code Ann. § 4734.09.

89. Stockwell, 622 P.2d at 910.

90. Acupuncture Soc'y v. Kansas State Bd. of Healing Arts, 602 P.2d 1311 (Kan. 1979).

91. See Kelley v. Raguckas, 270 N.W.2d 665 (Mich. Ct. App. 1978) (holding that acupuncture is a surgical act and requires a license to practice medicine); Ohio v. Rich, 339 N.E.2d 630 (Ohio 1975) (holding that acupuncture constitutes the unlicensed practice of medicine, and that a chiropractor who practices acupuncture has exceeded chiropractic scope of practice).

92. Commonwealth v. Schatzberg, 371 A.2d 544, 544–45 (Pa. Commw. Ct. 1977).

93. Ibid. at 546 (citing the Chiropractic Registration Act of 1951, § 2(b)). An "articulation" is "the structure which unites two bones, usually allowing some movement" (546 n. 3).

94. See also Oregon v. Won, 528 P.2d 594 (Or. Ct. App. 1974) (upholding the conviction of a licensed chiropractor and naturopath who used acupuncture, without physician supervision, for practicing medicine without a license).

95. State v. Beno, 373 N.W.2d 544 (Mich. 1985).

96. Ibid. at 550. The attorney general further argued that a chiropractor was limited to using x-rays to locate spinal subluxations or misaligned spinal vertebrae, and that a chiropractor who wanted to rule out a localized problem had to refer the patient to a physician (550).

97. Ibid. at 551.

98. Ibid. at 552.

99. Ibid. (quoting Mich. Stat. Ann. § 14.15(1111)(2)).

100. Ibid. at 553 and n. 7.

101. Zabrecky v. Conn. Bd. of Chiropractors, No. 0702118, 1991 Conn. Super. Ct. LEXIS 2682, at *7 (Nov. 15, 1991).

102. So long as the patient is not induced to rely on a chiropractic treatment to cure the cancer, the chiropractor should be permitted to complement the patient's biomedical treatment. See Wengel, 473 N.W.2d at 744 (legislative language leaves unclear "whether the practice of chiropractic includes the use of spinal manipulation to ameliorate conditions other than those directly related to the spine").

103. State Bd. of Chiropractic Examiners v. Clark, 713 S.W.2d 621 (Mo. Ct. App. 1986).

104. Ibid. at 626 (quoting Mo. Rev. Stat. § 331.010).

105. Alaska Stat. § 08.20.900(1)(B).

106. See, e.g., Kan. Stat. Ann. § 65-2871; Pa. Stat. Ann. tit. 63, § 602(b); Wyo. Stat. § 33-10-101.

107. See, e.g., Neb. Rev. Stat. § 71-177.

108. See, e.g., Iowa Code Ann. § 151.1. The AMA continues to raise concerns about chiropractic expansion into areas of biomedical responsibility. See Council on Scientific Affairs, *Alternative Medicine*, 7. The report acknowledges that manipulation "has been shown to have some efficacy in ameliorating back pain, headache, and similar musculoskeletal complaints" but adds that some chiropractors "have not renounced the method's original theories, and continue to claim that [chiropractic] treatments cure diseases . . . ranging from infectious diseases to immune therapy, even claiming to prevent future conditions from occurring" (7). The report expresses concern about chiropractors providing "advice in nutrition and other preventive practices" (7).

109. See *In re* Sherman College of Straight Chiropractic, 397 A.2d 362 (N.J. Super. Ct. 1979). The case involved the New Jersey Chiropractic Society's appeal of the New Jersey State Board of Medical Examiners' decision to approve the Sherman College for accreditation, thereby allowing the school's graduates to sit for the state examination and receive state licensing. The society followed the mixing school of chiropractic philosophy. Because of the Sherman College's limited scope, the national Council on Chiropractic Education denied it accreditation.

The society argued that this denial rendered the college's application before the Board of Medical Examiners premature, if not unacceptable. A committee of the Board of Medical Examiners, consisting of a physician and two chiropractors who were of the mixing school, had recommended against accreditation. The full board disagreed. The board found that the college met statutory requirements and taught diagnosis limited to the services a chiropractor may by law provide, and therefore would be approved. The court characterized the dispute as "an attempt by one school of thought to deny entry into the chiropractic ranks to adherents of doctrine disapproved by them." Sherman College, 397 A.2d at 364–65. The court further held that the board's approval of Sherman College was "neither arbitrary nor capricious" and could not be overturned (364–65).

110. See, e.g., Midwestern College of Massotherapy et al. v. Ohio Medical Bd., 656 N.E.2d 963, 969 (Ohio Ct. App. 1995) (noting that Ohio does not require lengthy schooling for licensure in massage therapy, and that the "flip side to the relatively basic educational requirements is that massage therapists must limit their practice to a narrower scope" than some desire).

Chapter 5: Malpractice and Vicarious Liability

1. See Eisenberg et al., "Unconventional Medicine," 246.

2. See Moore v. Baker, 1991 U.S. Dist. LEXIS 14712, at *11 (S.D. Ga., Sept. 5, 1991), *aff'd* 989 F.2d 1129 (11th Cir. 1993).

3. Rogers v. State Bd. of Medical Examiners, 371 So. 2d 1037, 1038 n. 2 (Fla. Dist. Ct. App. 1979), *aff'd*, 387 So. 2d 937 (Fla. 1980).

4. See Moore, 1991 U.S. Dist. LEXIS 14712, at *9.

5. United States v. Evers, 643 F.2d 1043, 1048 (5th Cir. 1981) (quoting 37 *Fed. Reg.* 16503 (1972)).

6. Fifty percent of cancer drug treatment involves off-label use; Medicare and Medicaid patients receive reimbursement for off-label use, if the use is listed in recognized compendia. See U.S. Government Accounting Office, *Off-Label Drugs: Reimbursement Policies Constrain Physicians in Their Choice of Cancer Therapies,* GAO / PEMD-91-14 (1991), 11; Charles G. Moertel, "Off-Label Drug Use for Cancer Therapy and National Health Care Priorities," 266:21 *JAMA* 3031 (1991); Ala. Code § 27-1-10.1(a)(5). Generally, third-party payers have reimbursed off-label uses of approved drugs, unlike experimental or investigational drugs. Drusilla S. Raiford et al., "Determining Appropriate Reimbursement for Prescription Drugs: Off Label Uses and Investigational Strategies," 49 *Food & Drug L.J.* 37 (1994). See also Conn. Gen. Stat. Ann. § 38a-492b(a) and R.I. Gen. Laws § 27-55-2(a) (providing that insurance policies covering certain prescribed, FDA-approved drugs may not exclude coverage for off-label use, under specified conditions).

7. One court has upheld a jury verdict for the defendant physician in a malpractice case, where the plaintiff alleged that seizures were due to chelation treatment, the defendant's expert testified there was no relation between the treatment and the seizures, and there was no evidence that the defendant had used fraud or deception in prescribing the chelation treatment or adversely affected the public interest. Ireland v. Eckerly, 1989 Minn. App. LEXIS 13, at *3 (Minn. Ct. App., Jan. 10, 1989).

8. Ariz. Rev. Stat. § 32-1401(gg)(iii).

9. See, e.g., Chumbler v. McClure, 505 F.2d 489, 491–92 (6th Cir. 1974) (permitting defense where there was "a division in the medical profession" regarding the use of a particular drug for the treatment of cerebral vascular insufficiency, and the minority view was "supported by responsible medical authority," even though only one neurosurgeon in the community followed the minority school); Downer v. Veilleux, 322 A.2d 82, 87 (Me. 1974) (permitting defense when physicians are "merely electing to pursue one of several recognized courses of treatment"); Henderson v. Heyer-Schulte Corp., 600 S.W.2d 844 (Tex. Ct. App. 1980) (permitting defense if a "reasonable and prudent member of the medical profession" would undertake the same mode or treatment under similar circumstances); D'Angelis v. Zakuto, 556 A.2d 431, 432–33 (Pa. Super. Ct. 1989) (allowing defense where physician follows a school of thought having "a reasonable number of followers in the medical community," and which is "reputable and respected by reasonable medical experts," but disallowing defense where the "symptoms of a disease or the effects of an injury are so well known that a reasonably competent and skillful

physician or surgeon ought to be able to diagnose the disease or injury" and physician has failed to make a proper diagnosis).

10. Clark v. Department of Professional Regulation, Bd. of Medical Examiners, 463 So. 2d 328 (Fla. Dist. Ct. App. 1985).

11. See, e.g., Brook v. St. John's Hickey Memorial Hosp., 380 N.E.2d 72 (Ind. 1978).

12. Furrow et al., *Health Law,* § 6-5, p. 252.

13. See Larry Dossey, *Healing Words: The Power of Prayer and the Practice of Medicine* (San Francisco: Harper, 1994).

14. Cf. Oswald v. Legrand, 453 N.W.2d 634 (Iowa 1990) (expert testimony was unnecessary to establish medical malpractice where care provided "fell below the standard of medical professionalism understood by laypersons and expected by them"; further, recovery for emotional distress was allowable without claim of physical injury, due to health care professionals' "extremely rude behavior or crass insensitivity coupled with an unusual vulnerability" on patients' part).

15. Schloendorff v. Soc'y of New York Hosp., 105 N.E. 92, 93 (1914).

16. See 45 *C.F.R.* §§ 46.101-46.117 (1990) (specifying Department of Health and Human Services policy for protection of human research subjects, including requirements for informed consent).

17. See Robert J. Lifton, *The Nazi Doctors: Medical Killing and the Psychology of Genocide* (New York: Basic Books, 1986).

18. See Furrow et al., *Health Law,* § 6-11, pp. 270–79.

19. See, e.g., Thornton v. Annest, 574 P.2d 1199 (Wash. 1978) (malpractice suit for hysterectomy). A minority of states measure the scope of required disclosure by the need of the reasonable patient, rather than by the judgment of a similarly situated, reasonable physician. See, e.g., Dible v. Vagley, 612 A.2d 493 (Pa. Super. Ct. 1992), *appeal denied,* 629 A.2d 1380 (Pa. 1993); Pauscher v. Iowa Methodist Medical Ctr., 408 N.W.2d 355 (Iowa 1987); Wheeldon v. Madison, 374 N.W.2d 367 (S.D. 1985).

20. Lienhard v. State, 431 N.W.2d 861 (Minn. 1988).

21. Plumber v. Dep't of Health and Human Resources, 634 So. 2d 1347, 1351 (La. Ct. App. 1994), *cert. denied,* 637 So. 2d 1056 (La. 1994). Thus, the physician probably is not required to disclose the possibility of a myomectomy, an operation in which a fibroid tumor is removed while the ability to have children is preserved. See Lynn Payer, *Medicine and Culture: Varieties of Treatment in the United States, England, West Germany, and France* (New York: H. Holt, 1988), 22. Payer developed a fibroid tumor while traveling through Europe to research the book. In France, her surgeon insisted on a myomectomy, without even mentioning the possibility of a hysterectomy. Back in the United States, she was placed under "a great deal of pressure" to have a hysterectomy. Payer attributes the difference in therapeutic options to cultural differences in the value placed on child-bearing. Hysterec-

tomy is the second most common operation in the United States; the first is Cesarean section (22, 130).

22. See Marjorie Shultz, "From Informed Consent to Patient Choice: A New Protected Interest," 95 *Yale L.J.* 219, 229–33 (1985).

23. For example, as Shultz notes, in Karlsons v. Guerinot, 394 N.Y.S.2d 933, 938 (App. Div. 1977), the plaintiff's physician failed to perform amniocentesis, which would have identified deformity in the plaintiff's fetus early enough for plaintiff to discontinue the pregnancy. Because there was no touching or body invasion, however, the court found that the plaintiff could not recover on an informed consent theory. The court limited the doctrine to "those situations where the harm suffered arose from some affirmative violation of the patient's physical integrity such as surgical procedures, injections or invasive diagnostic tests" (939).

24. See Shultz, "Informed Consent," 232–41, 253–56.

25. Moore, 1991 U.S. Dist. LEXIS 14712, at *2.

26. Ibid. at *7 (quoting Ga. Code Ann. § 31-9-6.1(a)(5)).

27. On appeal, the Eleventh Circuit, affirming, found that the "evidence overwhelmingly suggests that the mainstream medical community does not recognize or accept EDTA therapy as an alternative to a carotid endarterectomy in treating coronary blockages." Moore, 989 F.2d at 1132. The court relied on the physician's testimony that he never received any instruction in medical school on EDTA therapy as an alternative to a carotid endarterectomy, on an expert's testimony that no one at the Medical College of Georgia teaches about such an alternative or considers it practical, and on evidence that several professional associations oppose such use of EDTA therapy.

28. Gemme v. Goldberg, 626 A.2d 318 (Conn. App. Ct. 1993).

29. Nonphysician providers also may have a duty to obtain informed consent, in some cases as defined by statute. See, e.g., Minn. Stat. § 147B.06.1(b) (requiring disclosure by acupuncturists of side effects and other matters).

30. See Jerry A. Green, "Integrating Conventional Medicine and Alternative Therapies," 2:4 *Alt. Ther. Health Med.* 77 (1996); see also Green, "Health Care Contract"; and Green, "Minimizing Malpractice."

31. Schneider v. Revici, 817 F.2d 987, 992 (2d Cir. 1987).

32. Ibid. at 995 (citing Schloendorff, 105 N.E. at 93); see also Maxwell Mehlman, "Fiduciary Contracting: Limitations on Bargaining between Patients and Health Care Providers," 51 *U. Pitt. L. Rev.* 365 (1990).

33. Schneider, 817 F.2d at 996.

34. Ibid. at 990.

35. Boyle v. Revici, 961 F.2d 1060 (2d Cir. 1992).

36. Shorter v. Drury, 695 P.2d 116 (Wash. 1985).

37. La. Rev. Stat. § 9:2794 (quoted in Piazza v. Behrman Chiropractic Clinic, 601 So. 2d 1378, 1379 (La. 1992)).

38. Nev. Rev. Stat. § 630A.060.

39. These are available from the American Association of Naturopathic Physicians, 2366 Eastlake Avenue East, Suite 322, Seattle, WA 98102.

40. See, e.g., *Oregon Chiropractic Practice and Utilization Guidelines* (Salem: Oregon Board of Chiropractic Examiners, Nov. 1991); see also Practice and Policy Guidelines Panel, National Institutes of Health, Office of Alternative Medicine, "Clinical Practice Guidelines in Complementary and Alternative Medicine: An Analysis of Opportunities and Obstacles," 6 *Arch. Fam. Med.* 149 (Mar.–Apr. 1997).

41. One court declined to include as part of the standard of care the standard within a particular *school* of chiropractic. Kerman v. Hintz, 406 N.W.2d 156, 161 n. 8 (Ct. App. Wisc. 1987).

42. A Virginia study using medical malpractice review panels found that 0.4 percent of claims were made for alleged malpractice in chiropractic, as compared to 11.5 percent of claims for obstetrics and gynecology, 8.9 percent for general surgery, and 8.4 percent for internal medicine. "Medical Malpractice Review Panels: Geographic Breakdown of Claims against Specialties (July 1, 1976–December 31, 1996)," in *Virginia State of the Judiciary Report 1996* (Richmond: Office of the Executive Secretary, Supreme Court of Virginia, 1996). Less than 1 percent of naturopathic physicians nationwide have been sued for malpractice. *Safety, Effectiveness, and Cost Effectiveness in Naturopathic Medicine* (Seattle: American Association of Naturopathic Physicians, 1991), 5 (citing insurance company data).

43. Alan Dumoff, "Including Alternative Providers in Managed Care — Managing the Malpractice Risk: Part 2," *Medical Interface* 127 (June 1995).

44. "Response to Arizona Sunrise Committee," in Mitchell, *Legislative Handbook,* 47, 49.

45. See Susan M. Hobson, "The Standard of Admissibility of a Physician's Expert Testimony in a Chiropractic Malpractice Action," 64 *Ind. L.J.* 737, 741–42 (1989) (citing cases). In addition, even where prohibited from testifying regarding the chiropractic standard of care, a physician may testify as to the *cause* of an injury (for example, a physician may testify that a ruptured disc was caused by chiropractic manipulation). Morgan v. Hill, 663 S.W.2d 232 (Ky. Ct. App. 1984).

46. Wengel, 473 N.W.2d at 744.

47. Cf. Salazar v. Ehmann, 505 P.2d 387, 389 (Colo. Ct. App. 1972) (chiropractor's failure to take x-ray may constitute chiropractic malpractice).

48. See Paul Rosen, "Issues Surrounding Primary Care Status and Incorporation of Western Modalities," in Mitchell, *Acupuncture Laws,* 133. See also Or. Rev. Stat. § 677.757(1)(b)(A) (authorizing acupuncturists to engage in "traditional and modern techniques of diagnosis") and § 677.762(3) (providing that legislation does not prohibit dispensing of vitamins or minerals or dietary advice).

49. Rosen, "Issues," 134.

50. Kerman v. Hintz, 418 N.W.2d 795, 802–3 (Wis. 1988).

51. See, e.g., Mostrom v. Pettibon, 607 P.2d 864 (Wash. Ct. App. 1980).

52. Tschirhart v. Pethtel, 233 N.W.2d 93, 94 (Mich. Ct. App. 1975).

53. Salazar, 505 P.2d at 389.

54. See, e.g., Minn. Stat. § 147B.06.1(a) (before treating a patient, the acupuncturist must ask whether the patient has been examined by a licensed physician and must review the diagnosis); Wash. Rev. Code § 18.060.140 (requiring every licensed acupuncturist to develop a written plan for consultation, emergency transfer, and referral to other providers).

55. Wengel, 473 N.W.2d at 744.

56. Managed care organizations range from health maintenance organizations (HMOs), to preferred provider organizations (PPOs), to a variety of hybrid health and insurance vehicles. HMOs combine the delivery and financing of health care and provide basic health services to voluntarily enrolled subscribers for a fixed prepaid fee. PPOs limit patients to a preapproved list of providers and require a financial penalty for access to providers outside the pool. See generally Diana Bearden and Bryan Maedgen, "Emerging Theories of Liability in the Managed Health Care Industry," 47 *Baylor L. Rev.* 285 (1995).

57. Darling v. Charlston Community Memorial Hosp., 211 N.E.2d 253 (1965), *cert. denied,* 383 U.S. 946 (1966).

58. The court noted that the jury could have reasonably concluded that the nurses did not test for circulation in the patient's leg as frequently as necessary; that the nurses failed to inform the attending physician or, if he failed to act, the hospital authorities; and that the hospital failed to review the negligent physician's work or require a consultation. Ibid., 257.

59. Thompson v. The Nason Hospital, 591 A.2d 703 (Pa. 1991).

60. The court added that a hospital could only be liable if it had "actual or constructive knowledge of the defect or procedures which created the harm," and that the hospital's negligence "must have been a substantial factor in bringing about the harm the injured party." Ibid., 707–8.

The court found that there was a sufficient question of material fact, sufficient to defeat summary judgment, as to whether the hospital was negligent in supervising the quality of medical care the plaintiff had received, where plaintiff allegedly developed an intracerebral hematoma, resulting in permanent disability, from negligent care during administration of an anticoagulant therapy (703). See also Hamby v. University of Kentucky Medical Ctr., 844 S.W.2d 431, 434–35 (Ky. Ct. App. 1992) (violation of duty to enforce published policies and regulations results in imposition of direct liability if a hospital has knowledge that policies are being broken but fails to enforce the policies).

61. See Furrow et al., *Health Law,* § 7-4, p. 304 (citing cases).

62. See Wickline v. State of California, 239 Cal. Rptr. 810 (Cal. Ct. App. 1986), *review dismissed, cause remanded,* 741 P.2d 613 (Cal. 1987) (state could be liable where plaintiff's leg was allegedly amputated due to complications following premature discharge from hospital following discontinuance of Medi-Cal eligi-

bility). The *Wickline* court stated that the patient who is injured by negligent care should recover from "all those responsible for the deprivation of such care, including, when appropriate, health care payors. Third party payors of health care services can be held legally accountable when medically inappropriate decisions result from defects in the design or implementation of cost-containment mechanisms as, for example, when appeals made on a patient's behalf for medical or hospital care are arbitrarily ignored or unreasonably disregarded or overridden" (818–19).

In Wilson v. Blue Cross of Southern California, 271 Cal. Rptr. 876 (Cal. Ct. App. 1990), *review denied,* 1990 Cal. LEXIS 4574 (Cal., Oct. 11, 1990), the court narrowed aspects of *Wickline*. The court, however, held that a triable issue existed as to whether the conduct of the decedent's insurance company and certain related entities was a substantial factor in causing the decedent's death. The court relied in part on testimony by the decedent's treating physician that had the decedent completed his planned hospitalization, there was a reasonable medical probability that he would not have committed suicide. Ibid., 883.

63. See Boyd v. Albert Einstein Medical Ctr., 547 A.2d 1229 (Pa. Super. Ct. 1988) (vicarious liability applied to HMOs); McClellan v. Health Maintenance Org. of Pennsylvania, 604 A.2d 1053 (Pa. Super. Ct. 1992); but see Harrell v. Total Health Care, 781 S.W.2d 58 (Mo. 1989) (rejecting, on the basis of statutory immunity from malpractice liability granted to health services corporations, the application of vicarious liability to an HMO).

Some courts require that the patient prove reasonable reliance on representations of the health care institution that the physician was its employee or agent. See, e.g., Porter v. St. Mary, 756 F.2d 669, 672 (8th Cir. 1985) (finding evidence insufficient to support apparent authority, where plaintiff may have considered physician to be an employee of the hospital because of "occasional similarity of hospital personnel dress, the occasional use of name tags by personnel and the medical staff and the statement made that 'He's our (hospital's) best man'").

64. See, e.g., Weldon v. Seminole Municipal Hospital, 709 P.2d 1058 (Okla. 1985) (independent contractor defense upheld where there was a pre-existing doctor-patient relationship with the treating physician, the patient merely viewed the hospital as the place of treatment, and the patient had no basis for believing that the physician was acting in the emergency room on behalf of the hospital).

65. See Bing v. Thing, 163 N.Y.2d 656 (N.Y 1957); Sloan v. Metropolitan Health Council of Indianapolis, 516 N.E.2d 1104 (Ind. Ct. App. 1987) (finding HMO vicariously liable for the physician's negligent failure to diagnose, on the basis of the HMO's control of staff physicians through a medical director, who set policy for health care services); Smith v. St. Francis Hosp., 676 P.2d 279, 281 (Okla. Ct. App. 1983) (rejecting independent contractor defense, noting that contract between hospital and physician "reveals merely an attempt by Hospital to disclaim responsibility for emergency care services in its facility, while maintaining substantially the

same or, arguably, greater control as exercised over all staff physicians admitted to practice at Hospital"; among other things, the hospital controlled billing and provided clerical and medical support personnel, instruments, and supplies).

66. Different rules may apply for services provided to patients under an employee benefit plan, where state law rules are preempted by the federal Employee Retirement Income Security Act (ERISA) of 1974, Pub. L. No. 93-46, 88 *Stat.* 829, 28 *U.S.C.* §§ 1001-1461. See Katherine Benesch, "Emerging Theories of Liability for Negligent Credentialing in HMO's, Integrated Delivery and Managed Care Systems," 9:1 *Health Lawyer* 14, 17–19 (1996).

Chapter 6: Access to Treatments

1. See generally George M. Burditt, "The History of Food Law," 50 *Food & Drug L.J.* 197 (1995); Peter B. Hutt, "Government Regulation of the Integrity of the Food Supply," 4 *Ann. Rev. Nutrition* 1 (1984).

2. Pure Food and Drug Act, ch. 3915, 34 *Stat.* 768 (1906).

3. Ibid. §§ 7 and 2, 34 *Stat.* at 769–770.

4. Food, Drug, and Cosmetic Act, Pub. L. No. 75-717, 52 *Stat.* 2040 (1938), as amended, 21 *U.S.C.* §§ 301 et seq.

5. Drug Amendments of 1962 (Kefauver-Harris Amendments), Pub. L. No. 87-781, 76 *Stat.* 780 (1962), codified at 21 *U.S.C.* § 355.

6. 21 *U.S.C.* § 355(d).

7. 21 *C.F.R.* § 312.23.

8. See 21 *C.F.R.* § 314.126(b) (defining "adequate and well-controlled").

9. Michael Evers, *Unconventional Cancer Treatments: Legal Constraints on the Availability of Unorthodox Cancer Treatments* (Washington, D.C.: Office of Technology Assessment, GPO, 1990). See also *The Food and Drug Administration's Process for Approving New Drugs,* Report of the Subcommittee on Science, Research, and Technology of the House Committee on Science and Technology, 96th Cong., 2d Sess. (Washington, D.C.: GPO, 1988).

10. The Treatment IND is generally a bridge for distribution of the drug during FDA review following Phase III and may be granted if no comparable or satisfactory drug or therapy is available to treat the patient, a clinical investigation has been completed or the drug is currently subject to investigation under a clinical IND, and the drug's sponsor is, with due diligence, seeking marketing approval of the drug. 21 *C.F.R.* § 312.34(a)–(b).

11. See "Expanded Availability of Investigational New Drugs through a Parallel Track Mechanism for People with AIDS and Other HIV-Related Diseases," 57 *Fed. Reg.* 13250 (Apr. 15, 1992). Among other things, the drug must be shipped directly to the physician, and the physician must monitor the treatment and its effect. Because drug toxicities have not been established, the patient signs an appropriate informed consent form acknowledging awareness of relevant risks.

12. 21 *C.F.R.* § 312.80.

13. 21 *C.F.R.* § 314.500. In expedited approval, the sponsor reaches agreement with the FDA on the design of Phase II controlled clinical trials, to ensure that such testing is adequate to provide data on safety and effectiveness sufficient to support approval without Phase III studies (§ 312.82(b)). In accelerated approval, instead of relying on a clinical endpoints (e.g., survival) to show efficacy, the drug sponsor can rely on a surrogate endpoint "that is reasonably likely, based on epidemiologic, therapeutic, pathophysiologic, or other evidence, to predict clinical benefit" (§ 314.510).

14. *Hearing of the Oversight and Investigations Subcommittee of the House Commerce Committee on Access to Medical Treatment* (Feb. 29, 1996) (available on LEXIS, LEGIS library, CNGTST file).

15. See Thomas D. Elias, "Doctor's Lifesaving Effort Could Land Him in Prison: FDA Ignores Cancer Drug's Success," *Washington Times,* Dec. 5, 1996, A1. The article goes on to note that "these occur so rarely in brain tumors that the American Cancer Society doesn't even bother keeping statistics on them."

16. 21 *U.S.C.* § 321(g)(1)(B) and (C). New food additives are subject to prior premarket approval requirements. 21 *U.S.C.* § 348.

17. Health claims are claims that characterize the relationship of nutrients to a disease or health-related condition (see next subsection). 21 *U.S.C.* § 101.14(a)(1).

18. See, e.g., LeBeau, 1993 U.S. App. LEXIS at 1501 (affirming summary judgment against manufacturer, where literature accompanying products such as Licorice Root Tea showed that products were intended to be used as treatments for cancer, AIDS, and other diseases). In addition to federal food and drug law, providers and manufacturers must familiarize themselves with state food and drug legislation. See, e.g., Cal. Health & Safety Code § 109325 (establishing criteria for use of investigational drugs). States also address dietary supplements in their licensing and scope-of-practice rules. For example, registered dieticians and licensed nutritionists may prescribe dietary supplements. See, e.g., Ky. Rev. Stat. Ann. § 310.070 (Baldwin 1994); N.M. Stat. Ann. § 61-7A-4. As noted in the discussion of *Stetina* in chap. 3, while unlicensed providers may provide educational services concerning nutrition, they may not make a diagnosis or treatment related to nutrition. As noted in chap. 4, some states authorize chiropractors to provide nutritional guidance and recommend or dispense dietary supplements, while other states authorize acupuncturists to prescribe nutritional supplements in the form of herbal remedies. See, e.g., Cal. Bus. & Prof. Code § 4937.

19. See Evers, 643 F.2d at 1053 n. 16 ("public advocacy of medical opinions not shared by the FDA," including promoting unapproved drugs to other physicians, is not misbranding since it does not constitute holding the drug for sale under 21 *U.S.C.* § 331(k); further, the FDA may not regulate the practice of medicine, which falls under the police power).

20. See Comments of Senator Tom Harkin, in *Hearing of the Senate Labor and Human Resources Committee on the Access to Medical Treatment Act* (July 30,

1996) (available on LEXIS, NEWS library, CURNWS file) ("[In] the case of Dr. Wright . . . what happened with people in the FDA, carrying guns, breaking into the office, taking his files — this throws a lot of fear throughout the United States for people to conduct investigations like that . . . fear out there that if people try different things, even if their patients want that, and even though they have not been proven harmful to others, the FDA will come in and take punitive actions"). Ultimately, the charges against Jonathan Wright were dismissed. Danny Westneat, "Government Drops Case against Nationally Known Vitamin Doctor," *Houston Chronicle,* Oct. 1, 1995, A12.

21. Access to Medical Treatment Act, H.R. 746, § 3(a) (Feb. 19, 1997); S. 578, 105th Cong., 1st Sess. (Apr. 18, 1997).

22. Ibid., § 3(B). "Danger" is defined as "any negative reaction" that causes serious harm, occurs as a result of the treatment, would not have otherwise occurred, and "is more serious than reactions experienced with routinely used medical treatments for the same medical condition" (§ 2(2)). "Advertising claims" means "any representations made or suggested by statement, word, design, device, sound, or any combination thereof with respect to a medical treatment" (§ 2(1)). The act (§ 3(c)) exempts from the prohibition on "advertising claims" the following: "(1) an accurate and truthful reporting by a health care practitioner of the results of the practitioner's administration of a medical treatment in recognized journals or at seminars, conventions, or similar meetings or to others," so long as the reporting practitioner as has no financial conflict of interest; (2) statements by a practitioner to an individual patient about the treatment; (3) statements or claims relating to dietary supplements, permitted pursuant to 21 *U.S.C.* § 343-2 and 343(r)(6).

23. Ibid., § 4. The practitioner must report to the Office of Complementary and Alternative Medicine positive effects of treatments that are significantly greater than those of corresponding conventional medical treatments (§ 5). The act further permits persons to produce, or introduce or deliver into interstate commerce, a food, drug, device, or any other equipment not approved by the FDA, solely for use in accordance with the act provided no advertising claims have been made by the manufacturer, distributor, or seller (§ 6). The act provides that a health care practitioner who "knowingly" violates its provisions receives no protection under the act and is subject to all other applicable laws and regulations (§ 8).

24. See C. Frederick Beckner III, "The FDA's War on Drugs," 82 *Geo. L.J.* 529, 529–62 (1993).

25. *Report of the Senate Committee on Labor and Human Resources on the Dietary Supplement Health and Education Act of 1994,* Report 103-410, 103d Cong., 2d Sess. (Oct. 8, 1994) (hereinafter cited as *DSHEA Report*) (citing A. F. Subar and G. Block, "Use of Vitamin and Mineral Supplements: Demographics and Amounts of Nutrients Consumed," 132 *Am. J. Epidemiol.* 1091 (1990)).

26. Nutrition Labeling and Education Act, Pub. L. No. 101-535, 104 *Stat.* 2353 (1990).

27. *DSHEA Report,* 23, 24.

28. *U.S.C.* § 343(r)(5)(D).

29. See, e.g., Dietary Supplement Act, Pub. L. No. 102-571, 106 *Stat.* 4491 (1992); United States v. Two Plastic Drums, More or Less of an Article, Labeled in part: Viponte Ltd. Black Currant Oil, 984 F.2d 814, 817 (7th Cir. 1993) (holding that encapsulated black currant oil, a dietary supplement, was not a "food additive"; that the FDA's regulatory "interpretation would defy logic and common sense"; and that the "only justification for this Alice in Wonderland approach is to allow the FDA to make an end run around the statutory scheme"); United States v. 29 Cartons of *** An Article of Food, Etc., 987 F.2d 33, 38 (1st Cir. 1993) ("The proposition that placing a single-ingredient food product [black currant oil] into an inert capsule as a convenient method of ingestion converts that food into a food additive perverts the statutory text, undermines legislative intent, and defenestrates common sense"). A third court, however, found that related FDA regulations were supported by a substantial government interest: "preventing the spread of unsubstantiated health claims on labels so that consumers may not be deceived and follow unsound health practices." Nutritional Health Alliance v. Shalala, 95 Civ. 4950, 1997 WL 51872 (S.D.N.Y., slip op. 7, Jan. 31, 1997). This court, however, ultimately found that the FDA regulations were not narrowly tailored to advance the governmental interest.

30. Dietary Supplement Health and Education Act of 1994, Pub. L. No. 103-417, 108 *Stat.* 4325, 21 *U.S.C.* §§ 301 et seq. (1994). Senator Tom Harkin observed that changing health care financing without opening of consumer access to nutritional supplementation would be "just rearranging the deck chairs on the Titanic." 10 *Cong. Rec.* S14780-81 (Oct. 7, 1994).

31. *Congressional Findings Related to Dietary Supplements Health and Education Act of 1994,* Pub. L. No. 103-417, § 2, 15(A), 108 *Stat.* 4325, 4326 (Oct. 25, 1994).

32. *DSHEA Report,* 14. Among other activities, between 1966 and 1973 the FDA issued proposed regulations to classify vitamins as over-the-counter drugs if the product exceeded 150 percent of the Recommended Daily Allowance. In the 1970s, the FDA attempted to regulate vitamins by claiming that they were toxic. The history is further summarized in *DSHEA Report,* 15. See also Peter B. Hutt and Richard A. Merrill, *Food and Drug Law,* 2d ed. (Westbury, N.Y.: Foundation Press, 1991), 204-28 (citing cases).

33. DSHEA, 21 *U.S.C.* § 321(ff). This assumes that the dietary supplements are not intended for use in diagnosis, cure, mitigation, treatment, or prevention of disease or to affect the structure or any function of the body of man or other animals, and that no disease-oriented claims are made. See the last sentence of 21 *U.S.C.* § 321(ff), referring back to § 321(g)(1) and § 343(r)(6).

34. Ibid. at § 321(ff)(1)(A)-(F).

35. Ibid. at § 321(ff)(2)(A)-(B).

36. Ibid. at § 321(ff)(2)(C).

37. Ibid. at § 343-2(a)(1)-(5).

38. Ibid. at § 343-2(b)-(c).

39. Ibid. at § 343(r)(6). A manufacturer making such a structure/function claim must notify the FDA within thirty days of first using the statement.

40. Ibid. The NLEA standard for FDA approval of health claims, "significant scientific agreement," remains in effect for dietary supplements during a study by the Dietary Supplement Commission established under the DSHEA.

41. 21 *U.S.C.* § 343(s).

42. Ibid. at § 342(g)(2).

43. See, e.g., Food and Drug Administration, "Food Labeling: Timeframe for Final Rules Authorizing Use of Health Claims," 62 *Fed. Reg.* 12579 (Mar. 17, 1997) (describing public comments concerning standard for health claims regarding dietary supplements, and FDA response to such comments).

44. The AMA has expressed concern that the DSHEA "will make it easier for nutrition to be misused by hucksters, and will hamper the FDA's ability to effectively monitor safety and efficacy of the growing number of herbal and nutritional remedies offered to the public." Council on Scientific Affairs, *Alternative Medicine*, 5.

45. Griswold v. Connecticut, 381 U.S. 479 (1965); Eisenstadt v. Baird, 405 U.S. 438 (1972).

46. Roe v. Wade, 410 U.S. 113 (1973); Planned Parenthood of Southeastern Pennsylvania v. Casey, 505 U.S. 833 (1992).

47. *In re* Quinlan, 355 A.2d 647 (1976), *cert. denied,* 429 U.S. 922 (1977); Rasmussen v. Fleming, 741 P.2d 674 (Ariz. 1987).

48. Cruzan, 497 U.S. at 277–78.

49. Many states, such as Virginia, recognize this right by authorizing competent adults to make a written advance directive "authorizing the providing, withholding or withdrawal of life-prolonging procedures." Va. Code Ann. § 54.1-2983.

50. Rutherford, 442 U.S. at 544.

51. Ibid., 616 F.2d at 457.

52. People v. Privitera, 591 P.2d 919 (Cal. 1979).

53. Compare Justice Bird's view with Howard, 337 S.E.2d at 598 ("Neither the United States Supreme Court nor any North Carolina court has recognized a fundamental right of the terminally ill to choose unorthodox medical treatment, let alone recognize protection extending to anyone willing to provide it").

54. See, e.g., Okla. Stat. Ann. tit. 76, § 20.2.

55. Mass. Gen. Laws Ann. ch. 111, § 70E. But see Cohn v. Wilkes Regional Medical Ctr., 437 S.E.2d 889 (N.C. 1994) (holding that hospitals were not required to give chiropractors staff privileges, under statute prohibiting health service from denying patients the freedom to choose the services of licensed chiropractors).

56. Andrews v. Ballard, 498 F. Supp. 1038 (S.D. Tex. 1980).

57. Ibid. at 1045 (quoting Superintendent of Belchertown State Sch. v. Saikewicz, 370 N.E.2d 417, 426 (Mass. 1977)).

58. Ibid. (citing Carey v. Population Servs. Int'l, 431 U.S. 678, 685 (1977)).

59. Ibid. at 1047 (quoting Roe, 410 U.S. at 152–53).

60. Ibid.

61. Ibid. The court also emphasized the safety and efficacy of acupuncture, as demonstrated by the evidence at trial, as compared to Western techniques such as drugs or surgery.

62. Ibid. (quoting Lindsey v. Normet, 405 U.S. 56, 74 (1972); and Roe, 410 U.S. at 727–28).

63. One plaintiff testified that he could not find a single licensed physician in Texas who was skilled in acupuncture. Other witnesses corroborated this testimony. Ibid.

64. Ibid. at 1053 (quoting Tex. St. Bd. of Med. Exam. Rule 386.01.12-001(c)).

65. Ibid. at 1056 (quoting Williamson v. Lee Optical Sch. of Oklahoma, 348 U.S. 483, 488 (1955)). According to the court in LeBeau, 1993 U.S. App. LEXIS 1501 at *4, the district court's decision in *Andrews* was "implicitly rejected" by the Fifth Circuit's decision in United States v. Burzynski Cancer Research Institute, et al., 819 F.2d 1301, 1313 (5th Cir. 1987) (rejecting, based on *Rutherford,* patients' claim of a constitutional right to obtain a specific cancer treatment) (see chap. 8), *reh'g denied en banc,* 829 F.2d 1124 (5th Cir. 1987), *cert. denied,* 484 U.S. 1065 (1988).

66. Suenram v. Soc'y of the Valley Hosp., 383 A.2d 143 (N.J. Super. Ct. 1977).

67. New York State Ophthalmological Soc'y v. Bowen, 854 F.2d 1379 (D.C. Cir. 1988).

68. The court noted that some decisions might have dramatic and immediate consequences, while others might be motivated largely by personal taste, convenience, or finances. Ibid. at 1390.

69. Ibid. at 1395. See also Carnohan v. United States, 616 F.2d 1120 (9th Cir. 1980) (no constitutional right of privacy or personal liberty to obtain laetrile free from lawful exercise of government power).

70. Compassion in Dying v. Washington, 79 F.3d 790 (9th Cir. 1996), *amended,* 96 Daily Journal D.A.R. 6139 (9th Cir. 1996), *stay granted,* Washington v. Glucksberg, 116 S. Ct. 2494 (1996), *and amended, reh'g, en banc, denied,* 85 F.3d 1440 (9th Cir. 1996), *cert. granted sub nom.,* Washington v. Glucksberg, 117 S. Ct. 37 (1996), *rev'd,* 117 S. Ct. 2258 (1997).

71. Ibid. at 834 (quoting Casey, 505 U.S. at 852). The court held that the provision of a Washington statute banning assisted suicide, "as applied to competent, terminally ill adults who wish to hasten their deaths by obtaining medication prescribed by their doctors," violated the Due Process clause (793).

72. Quill v. Vacco, 80 F.3d 716 (1996), *cert. granted,* 117 S. Ct. 36 (1996), *rev'd,* 117 S. Ct. 2293 (1997). The court rejected plaintiffs' argument that they had a fundamental constitutional liberty interest in assisted suicide under the Due Process

Clause of the Fourteenth Amendment (723). The court held, however, that in prohibiting a physician from "prescribing medications to be self-administered by a mentally competent, terminally-ill person in the final stages of his terminal illness," the New York statutes violated the Equal Protection clause because they were not rationally related to any legitimate state interest (731). See also Kevorkian v. Thompson, 947 F. Supp. 1152, 1166-70 (E.D. Mich. 1997) (declining to find a constitutionally protected liberty interest in physician-assisted suicide).

Chapter 7: Discipline and Sanction

1. See, e.g., N.Y. Educ. Law § 6503.

2. See, e.g., N.Y. Educ. Law § 6509. Arizona defines unprofessional conduct for homeopaths as "any conduct or practice contrary to recognized standards of ethics of the homeopathic medical profession, any conduct or practice which does or might constitute a danger to health, welfare or safety of the patient or the public, or any conduct, practice or condition which does or might impair the ability to practice homeopathic medicine safely and skillfully." Ariz. Rev. Stat. § 32-2933(8).

3. Guess, 393 S.E.2d at 835 (quoting N.C. Gen. Stat. § 90-14(a)(6)).

4. See, e.g., N.Y. Educ. Law § 6510. Similar statutes exist for other professions. See, e.g., Cal. Bus. & Prof. Code § 1000-10 (chiropractic). Some include unusual examples of unprofessional conduct, such as advertising that the practitioner will treat "any person afflicted with any sexual disease, or lost manhood, sexual weakness or sexual disorder or any disease of the sexual organs" (§ 1000-10(b)).

5. See, e.g., N.Y. Educ. Law § 6510.4.c.

6. See, e.g., ibid. § 6511.

7. Keigan v. Board of Registration in Medicine, 506 N.E.2d 866, 869 (Mass. Ct. App. 1987) (quoting Levy v. Board of Registration & Discipline in Medicine, 392 N.E.2d 1036 (Mass. 1979)).

8. See, e.g., N.Y. Educ. Law § 6510.1.a.

9. Alter v. New York State Dep't of Health, State Bd. for Professional Medical Misconduct, 546 N.Y.S.2d 746 (Sup. Ct. 1989).

10. See, e.g., Sletten v. Briggs, 448 N.W.2d 607, 608 (N.D. 1989), *cert. denied,* 493 U.S. 1080 (physician agreed to cease prescribing chelation therapy for patients with arteriosclerosis, heavy metal poisoning, and strokes, and agreed that such chelation therapy departs from acceptable and prevailing medical standards).

11. See, e.g., Doe v. Minnesota State Bd. of Medical Examiners, 435 N.W.2d 45 (Minn. 1989) (dismissed complaints against physician are not part of the board's decision and not public documents) (citing Minn. Stat. Ann. §§ 13.41, 13.03).

12. See, e.g., Colorado State Bd. of Medical Examiners v. Reiner, 786 P.2d 499, 500 (Colo. Ct. App. 1989) (board's determination should be upheld "unless it bears no relation to the conduct, is a gross abuse of discretion, or is manifestly excessive in relation to the needs of the public"); Kessler v. Department of Educ.,

440 N.Y.S.2d 87 (App. Div. 1981), *appeal denied,* 54 N.Y.2d 604 (Sup. Ct. 1981); Gold v. Nyquist, 376 N.Y.S.2d 670 (Sup. Ct. 1975).

13. According to proponents of chelation therapy, a typical bypass surgery costs the patient more than $30,000, while an average course of chelation therapy treatments costs $5,000. *Position Paper,* 5 (Laguna Hills, Calif.: American College for Advancement in Medicine, 1995).

14. Guess, 393 S.E.2d at 833.

15. Ibid. at 835 (quoting N.C. Gen. Stat. § 90-14(a)(6)).

16. Ibid. (quoting the Superior Court's order).

17. Ibid. The court of appeals initially dismissed for lack of jurisdiction, but the decision was reversed and remanded by the North Carolina Supreme Court.

18. Ibid. (quoting 382 S.E.2d 459, 461 (N.C. Ct. App. 1989)).

19. Ibid. at 836. The court upheld the statute as a valid exercise of the state's police power, bearing a reasonable relationship to the protection of public health. Guess would presumably have been protected under North Carolina's amended statute, which is quoted later in this chapter.

20. See also Guess, 967 F.2d at 998 (declining on jurisdictional grounds to review North Carolina Supreme Court's decision that Guess's license was properly revoked, as well as related claims by patients based on right to homeopathic care); Majebe v. North Carolina Bd. of Medical Examiners, 416 S.E.2d 404, 407 (N.C. Ct. App. 1992) (citing *Guess,* holding that "there exists no protected privacy right to practice unorthodox medical treatment, here acupuncture"), *appeal dismissed, review denied,* 421 S.E.2d 355 (N.C. 1992).

21. Cf. Bryce v. Board of Medical Quality Assurance, 229 Cal. Rptr. 483 (Ct. App. 1986) (citing Cal. Bus. & Prof. Code §§ 2227-29) (severity of the discipline that may be imposed on physician does not depend on whether patients have been injured by illegal medical practices); Morfesis v. Sobol, 567 N.Y.S.2d 954 (App. Div. 1991), *appeal denied,* 574 N.Y.S.2d 937 (App. Div. 1991).

22. Guess, 393 S.E.2d at 833 (Frye, J., dissenting).

23. Rogers, 371 So. 2d at 1037.

24. Ibid.

25. Ibid. at 1041.

26. The court further stated: "Orthodoxy in medicine is like orthodoxy in any other professional field. It starts as a theory or tentative belief in some particular course of action . . . [and] begins to be held as a passionate belief in the absolute rightness of that particular view. Right or wrong, a dissenting view is regarded as a criminal subversion of the truth and the holder is frequently exposed to slander and abuse by his orthodox colleagues. . . . It was the dead hand of orthodoxy that delayed the advance of knowledge through the Middle Ages. Even today, these same oppressive forces may shackle the advancement of medicine. . . . It is only on the edges of the stream of medicine in which advancement can take place." Ibid. at

1041–42 (quoting Harold Harper and Gary Gordon, *Reprints of Medical Literature on Chelation Therapy*).

27. State Bd. of Medical Examiners v. Rogers, 387 So. 2d 937 (Fla. 1980).

28. Ibid. at 938 n. 4 (quoting Fla. Stat. Ann. § 458.1201(1)(m) (West 1975)).

29. Ibid. at 939–40. The decision departs from United States v. Dent, 129 U.S. 114 (1888).

30. Atkins v. Guest, 601 N.Y.S.2d 234 (Sup. Ct. 1993), *aff'd*, 607 N.Y.S.2d 655 (App. Div. 1994).

31. The hyperbaric chamber is used to treat scuba divers suffering from the "bends," or nitrogen in the bloodstream. Ibid. at 236.

32. Ibid. at 237.

33. Ibid. at 237–38 (quoting *In re* Levin v. Murawski, 449 N.E.2d 730, 730 (N.Y. 1983)).

34. Atkins, 601 N.Y.S.2d at 238–39 (citing N.Y. Pub. Health Law § 230(10)(l)). The appellate court upheld the decision, citing the "important public interest in investigating misconduct by licensed physicians." Atkins, 607 N.Y.S.2d at 657.

35. Atkins, 601 N.Y.S.2d at 239 (citing N.Y. Pub. Health Law § 230(11)(a)).

36. See Chip Brown, "The Experiments of Dr. Oz," *New York Times Magazine,* July 30, 1995, 21, 23.

37. See generally Shealy and Myss, *Creation of Health*. Shealy, a conventionally trained neurosurgeon, reported that in his collaboration with Myss, the healer, Myss was 93 percent accurate in her intuitive diagnoses of patients (74–78).

38. Environmental medicine attributes disease to "biologic dysfunctions triggered by environmental stressors in susceptible patients"; these stressors include "dusts, molds, pollens, danders, venoms, food . . . radiation, and electro-magnetic fields." See Gary R. Oberg, *An Overview of the Philosophy of the American Academy of Environmental Medicine* (Denver: American Academy of Environmental Medicine, 1992), 6, 9.

39. A related phenomenon is the "tomato effect in medicine," which occurs "when an efficacious treatment for a certain disease is ignored or rejected because it does not 'make sense' in the light of accepted theories of disease mechanism and drug action." James S. Goodwin and Jean M. Goodwin, "The Tomato Effect: Rejection of Highly Efficacious Therapies," 251:18 *JAMA* 2387 (1984); see also E. Olszewer and J. Carter, "EDTA Chelation Therapy in Chronic Degenerative Disease," 27:1 *Med. Hypotheses* 41 (1988) (suggesting that EDTA chelation therapy "resulted in 'marked' improvement in 76.89% and 'good' improvement in 16.56% of patients with ischemic heart disease"; "The possibility of a 'tomato effect,' i.e., a drug which works, but the majority of physicians believe that it doesn't work, needs to be ruled out"); R. Podell, "The 'Tomato Effect' in Clinical Nutrition: New Treatments Languishing on the Vine?" 76:8 *Postgrad. Med.* 49 (1984).

40. Furrow et al., *Health Law*, § 3-18, pp. 73–74.

41. See, e.g., Ariz. Rev. Stat. Ann. §§ 32-1401.25(gg), 32-1854.42; Okla. Stat. Ann. tit. 76, § 20.2; S.D. Codified Laws Ann. § 36-4-29.

42. The Ad Hoc Committee on Health Care Fraud of the Federation of State Medical Boards has taken the position that such legislation endangers patients' welfare and that the federation should monitor, oppose or modify such legislative initiatives. William H. Fleming III, "Fraudulent Medical Practices — Watch and Be Wary!" 1996 annual meeting, Federation of State Medical Boards, Chicago, Illinois.

43. A number of bills are being introduced in various state legislatures. These can be accessed through LEXIS or through Internet sites such as http:/www.healthy.net and http:/www.naturalhealthvillage.com. Legislative developments also can be found on LEXIS in the LEGIS library, STTEXT file. For example, the Colorado General Assembly recently enacted a bill providing that the state medical board may not take disciplinary action against a physician solely on the grounds that the physician practices alternative medicine. Alternative medicine is defined as "those healthcare methods of diagnosis, treatment, or healing that are not generally used but that provide a reasonable potential for therapeutic gain in a patient's medical condition that is not outweighed by the risk of such methods." A physician who practices alternative medicine must inform each patient in writing of the physician's education, experience, and credentials relating to the alternative medical practice. Colorado House Bill 1183 (Apr. 16, 1997), amending Col. Rev. Stat. § 12-36-117.

44. Alaska Stat. § 08.64.326.

45. "Demonstrably physical harm" is significant because, as noted, holistic care often results in a temporary aggravation of symptoms (the so-called healing crisis) as healing begins. See also Gordon, *Manifesto*, 42, 44, 157 (defining a healing crisis as "a chronic illness becoming acute prior to an improvement").

46. Wash. Rev. Code Ann. § 18.130.180(4).

47. N.C. Gen. Stat. § 90-14(a)(6).

48. Okla. Stat. Ann. tit. 59, § 509.1(d).

49. Or. Rev. Stat. § 677.190(1)(b).

50. Ibid. at § 677.190(1)(b)(A).

51. N.Y. Educ. Law § 6527(4)(e).

52. N.Y. Pub. Health Law § 230.

53. Letter of July 20, 1994, from Senator Joseph R. Holland to Elizabeth D. Moore, Counsel to the Governor, regarding Legislative Sponsor's Memorandum in Support of S. 3636C, July 20, 1994, p. 1 (hereinafter cited as *Holland Letter*).

54. N.Y. State Assembly Memorandum in Support of Legislation, Bill No. 5411-C (Assembly), 3636-C (Senate) (1994) (hereinafter cited as *Assembly Memorandum*).

In Gonzalez v. New York State Dep't of Health, 648 N.Y.S.2d 827 (App. Div. 1996), the court reviewed a professional misconduct charge involving a physician who treated six incurable cancer patients who had either exhausted conventional treatment or rejected the only conventional options remaining. The court, interpreting New York's medical freedom legislation, confirmed the determination of misconduct. The court held that the legislation did not guarantee that a nonconventional physician would be on any particular hearing committee. The court further rejected the physician's claim that the charges against him reflected a bias against complementary and alternative medicine, agreed with the State Board of Professional Medical Conduct that the physician's conduct should be measured against the standard of care applicable to all New York physicians, held that patients' consent did not relieve the physician from the obligation to follow this standard of care, and rejected the physician's assertion that the board's direction that he undergo further educational training in oncology was "harassing and wasteful."

55. *Holland Letter.*

56. *Assembly Memorandum.*

57. Abuse of prosecutorial or disciplinary authority also could be shown by one or more of the following factors: (1) the therapy is controversial or disfavored by biomedical orthodoxy or this particular medical board and has triggered investigation by the state medical board in the past (e.g., chelation therapy, ozone therapy, or homeopathy); (2) the complaint is anonymous and appears motivated by personal animus or professional jealousy; (3) the penalty imposed by the medical board is disproportionate to the alleged infraction (for example, loss of licensure for prescribing a homeopathic remedy); and (4) the sanction is disproportionate when compared to sanctions for similarly situated physicians using conventional treatment.

CHAPTER 8: THIRD-PARTY REIMBURSEMENT

1. Congressional Research Service, *Health Insurance and the Uninsured: Background Data and Analysis* (Washington, D.C.: GPO, House Committee on Education and Labor, 1988).

2. The Reversal Program costs $4,000 per individual (whereas bypass surgery on average costs $43,000 and angioplasty, $18,000). "Insurers Unlikely to Embrace Alternative Therapies in Policies," 1 *Health Care Pol'y Rep.* 16 (1993).

3. See Margaret A. Colgate, "Gaining Insurance Coverage for Alternative Therapies," 15:1 *J. Health Care Mktg.* 24, 27 (1995) (suggesting that alternative therapies gain reimbursement when they can fit into the existing diagnosis-based system, can be viewed as complementary rather than competing, follow the "generally accepted biomedical model of professionalism" by providing education standards, accreditation, licensure, and clinical practice guidelines, and are supported by "adequate and appropriate" research); David Weber, "The Mainstreaming of Alternative Medicine," 6:39 *Healthcare Forum J.* 6 (Nov.–Dec. 1996) (describing plans).

4. Presentation by Hassan Rifaat, Manager, Alternative Medicine Department, Oxford Health Plans, "Integrating Alternative Medicine and Managed Care" (San Francisco, Calif., Sept. 9–10, 1996). Oxford's plan permits access to core

providers (acupuncture providers, chiropractors, and naturopathic physicians) and supplemental providers (yoga teachers, massage therapists, nutritional counselors, and others).

5. At the conference cited in n. 4, one insurance company executive referred to this as "reimbursing for the 'woo-woo' factor."

6. See Furrow et al., *Health Law*, § 11-4b, p. 510 n. 7, and accompanying text; Mitchell, *Acupuncture Laws*, 141. Although the provisions of ERISA generally pre-empt state laws relating to employee benefit plans, some courts have held that certain state laws mandating coverage constitute insurance regulation that is saved from ERISA preemption. See Furrow et al., *Health Law*, § 11-8, p. 519 n. 35 and accompanying text (citing cases).

7. Va. Code Ann. § 38.2-3407.B.

8. Fla. Stat. § 627.419(4) (cited in Weldon v. All Am. Life Ins. Co., 605 So. 2d 911, 912 (Fla. Dist. Ct. App. 1992)).

9. In fact, terminology "in such policy or contract deemed discriminatory against any such person or method of practice" is considered void. La. Rev. Stat. Ann. § 22:668 (quoted in Chiropractic Ass'n of Louisiana v. State, 595 So. 2d 316, 317 (La. Ct. App. 1991)).

10. Alaska Stat. § 21.36.090(d).

11. Ibid. Acupuncturists are not included within the definition.

12. Fla. Stat. § 627.6403. See also Mont. Code Ann. § 33-22-111(1) (providing that the insured "has full freedom of choice in the selection" of any licensed physician, chiropractor, acupuncturist, or other provider).

13. Wash. Rev. Code 48.43.045 (1996).

14. Deborah Senn, *Insurance Commissioner, Every Category of Provider,* Washington Office of Insurance Commissioner Bull. No. 95-9 (Dec. 19, 1995).

15. Blue Cross v. Senn, No. 96-2-00137-3 (filed in the superior court for the state of Washington). See Mike Maharry, "Insurers Sue over Coverage of Alternative Health Care," *News Tribune*, Jan. 9, 1996, A1; Diane West, "Court Blocks Enforcement of Wash. 'Alternative' Statute," 100:40 *National Underwriter, Life/Health/ Financial Services Edition* 2 (Sept. 30, 1996).

16. Wendy K. Mariner, "Business vs. Medical Ethics: Conflicting Standards for Managed Care," 23 *J. L., Med., & Ethics* 236 (1995).

17. See James S. Cline and Keith A. Rosten, "The Effect of Policy Language on the Containment of Health Care Cost," 21 *Tort & Ins. L.J.* 120 (1985).

18. Gary Stix, "Beam of Hope: A Proton Accelerator Is the Most Costly Yet," *Scientific American*, Dec. 1990, 24.

19. See, e.g., Dahl-Eimers v. Mutual of Omaha Life Ins. Co., 986 F.2d 1379, 1382–84 (11th Cir. 1993) (relevant medical specialists do not consider high-dose chemotherapy with autologous bone marrow transplantation experimental; moreover, the policy term *experimental* is ambiguous); Pirozzi v. Blue Cross–Blue Shield, 741 F. Supp. 586 (E.D. Va. 1990) (accepting testimony of insured's expert that

high-dose chemotherapy with autologous bone marrow transplantation was no longer experimental).

20. Fuja v. Benefit Trust Life Ins. Co., 18 F.3d 1405, 1410 (7th Cir. 1994) (referring to high-dose chemotherapy and autologous bone marrow transplantation treatment under policy).

21. See "Medical Devices: Reclassification of Acupuncture Needles for the Practice of Acupuncture," 61 *Fed. Reg.* 64616 (Dec. 6, 1996) (FDA believes "there is sufficient information to establish that special controls will provide reasonable assurance of the safety and effectiveness of acupuncture needles"); 21 *C.F.R.* § 880.5580.

22. Sarchett v. Blue Shield, 729 P.2d 267, 270 (Cal. 1987).

23. Some observers have expressed doubt that greater reimbursement of complementary and alternative therapies will reduce patient and insurer costs. See, e.g., Weber, "Mainstreaming" (comments of physicians and industry analysts). Patients may be just as likely to engage in overconsumption of vitamins or of treatments such as massage therapy. Such overconsumption arguably creates an ex post facto moral hazard, creating incentives for insureds to seek excessive treatment. Whereas many conventional treatments carry nonmonetary costs (such as time and postoperative pain in recovery from surgery), treatments, such as massage therapy, that "feel good" will not in themselves inhibit overconsumption. See generally Tom Baker, "On the Geneology of Moral Hazard," 75 *Tex. L. Rev.* 237 (1996).

24. See, e.g., Scalia v. Liberty Mut. Ins. Co., No. 9308, 1995 WL 296772, at *3 (Mass. App. Div., May 10, 1995) (chiropractic); Wait v. Metropolitan Life Ins. Co., 564 N.Y.S.2d 535 (App. Div. 1990).

25. Day v. Aetna Employees Benefit Div., No. 88CA004463, 1989 Ohio App. LEXIS 2458 (Ohio Ct. App. June 21, 1989).

26. The parties had submitted conflicting articles in medical journals as to the acceptance of chelation therapy. In reviewing these materials, the trial judge had placed great weight on an article from the *Journal of Holistic Medicine,* which suggested that chelation therapy had been used extensively over twenty years and had resulted in fewer deaths than bypass surgery. On appeal, the appellate court found that this reliance was not "erroneous or arbitrary, unreasonable, or unconscionable." The opposite result was reached in Westover v. Metropolitan Life Ins. Co., 771 F. Supp. 1172 (M.D. Fla. 1991) (dismissing an insured's claim for coverage of chelation therapy for arteriosclerosis, and finding that although procedure may have been widely used, not harmful, and performed by a licensed physician with patient consent, the therapy failed to conform to generally acceptable medical standards).

27. Dallis v. Aetna, 574 F. Supp. 547 (N.D. Ga. 1983), *aff'd,* 768 F.2d 1303 (11th Cir. 1985). Immunoaugmentative therapy involves supplementing immune serum protein fractions through intramuscular injections to fight cancer.

28. Taulbee v. Travelers Co., 537 N.E.2d 670 (Ohio Ct. App. 1987).

29. Compare *Taulbee* with Jacob v. Blue Cross & Blue Shield, 758 P.2d 382

(Or. Ct. App. 1988) (immunoaugmentative therapy was found not to be "medically necessary" because it deviated from generally accepted medical standards, and fell within the "experimental" or "investigational" treatment exclusion).

30. McLaughlin v. Connecticut Gen. Life Ins. Co., 565 F. Supp. 434 (N.D. Cal. 1983).

31. Harvey v. Travelers Ins. Co., 339 F. Supp. 262 (N.D. Ga. 1971).

32. See also Washington v. Fireman's Fund Ins. Cos., 708 P.2d 129, 138 (Haw. 1985) (holding that chiropractic and massage both constitute "therapy" and were "reasonable expense[s] incurred as a result of the accident," within the meaning of no-fault insurance statutes, although such therapy would not be covered for claimants receiving public assistance at no cost).

33. Tudor v. Metropolitan Life Ins. Co., 539 N.Y.S.2d 690 (Dist. Ct. 1989).

34. Shumake v. Travelers Ins. Co., 383 N.W.2d 259 (Mich. App. 1985), *appeal denied*, 425 Mich. 859 (1986). But see Zuckerberg v. Blue Cross & Blue Shield, 490 N.E.2d 839 (N.Y. 1986) (holding that insured had failed to present significant evidence to controvert the conclusion of insurer's expert, and the medical literature on which his opinion was based, that a nutritionally based treatment known as Gerson therapy was not a generally accepted cancer treatment and hence was properly excludable from coverage as experimental or unnecessary treatment).

35. For example, in People v. Andrews, 260 Cal. Rptr. 113 (Ct. App. 1989), a religious organization's minister purported to have special knowledge of body symptoms and needs, diagnosed ailments, and prescribed treatments, including dangerous fasts. The court, noting that the purpose of the fasts and other treatments was therapeutic and not religious, found the minister to have practiced medicine unlawfully.

36. See United States v. Burzynski Cancer Research Inst., No. H-83-2069 (S.D. Tex., May 24, 1983) (order granting permanent injunction); Trustees of the Northwest Laundry and Dry Cleaners Health and Welfare Fund v. Burzynski, 27 F.3d 153–55 (5th Cir. 1994), *reh'g, en banc, denied*, 38 F.3d 571 (5th Cir. 1994), *cert. denied*, 115 S. Ct. 1110 (1995). The FDA actions also triggered a state medical board investigation and suspension of licensure, to be stayed under certain conditions. Burzynski unsuccessfully challenged the medical board action in Texas State Bd. of Medical Examiners v. Burzynski, 917 S.W.2d 365 (Tex. Ct. App. 1996), *writ of error filed* (May 30, 1996).

37. Burzynski, C.A. No. H-83-2069 (slip op., S.D. Tex., Jan. 21, 1986).

38. Burzynski, 819 F.2d at 1313–14 (quoting United States v. Hoxsey Cancer Clinic, 198 F.2d 273, 280 (5th Cir. 1952), *cert. denied*, 346 U.S. 897 (1953)).

39. Burzynski v. Aetna Life Ins. Co., Inc., No. H-89-3976, 1992 U.S. Dist. LEXIS 21300 (S.D. Tex., Mar. 31, 1992). See also Burzynski v. Aetna Life Ins. Co., 967 F.2d 1063 (5th Cir. 1992), *remanded*, 989 F.2d 733 (5th Cir. 1993).

40. See, e.g., Shumake, 383 N.W.2d at 262–63.

41. The court, however, denied Aetna's counterclaim, finding that Aetna knew that the antineoplaston was experimental and thus did not detrimentally rely on any alleged misrepresentation by Burzynski.

42. Trustees, 27 F.3d at 153.

43. According to the court, treating a nonresident patient violated the 1984 injunction against Burzynski and thus was illegal; Burzynski had a duty to disclose to the fund the illegality of his treatment. The court further rejected Burzynski's argument that intrastate antineoplaston treatment was authorized under the Texas Medical Practices Act, which allowed a licensed physician to provide "any drugs, remedies, or clinical supplies as are necessary to meet the patient's immediate needs." Ibid. (quoting Tex. Rev. Civ. Stat. Ann. art. 4495b (1994)).

44. Prudential Ins. Co. of Am. v. Brown, No. B14-89-00695-CV (Tex. Ct. App. 1990). The court noted that Brown had been diagnosed with bladder cancer, that chemotherapy had proved ineffective, that Brown had undergone radiation treatment in preparation for surgery to remove his bladder and prostate gland, that without the surgery, the probability that Brown would die within five years was 85 percent, and that prior to the surgery, Brown had contacted Burzynski for antineoplaston treatment. "Within six weeks of beginning Dr. Burzynski's treatment, Brown was diagnosed by his urologist as being free from all bladder cancer. Over ten years later he has had no recurrence of bladder cancer" (*1–*2).

45. The AMA continues to use such terms, urging, for instance, that complementary and alternative therapies can be understood through a definitional "continuum": *proven, experimental, untested, folklore,* and *quackery.* Council on Scientific Affairs, *Alternative Medicine,* 3–4.

46. Stuart Speiser et al., *The American Law of Torts* (New York: Clark Boardman Gallagher, 1992), vol. 9, § 32.1, at 212 (citing cases).

47. See ibid., 213 ("It is a deception deliberately practiced with a view to gaining an unlawful or unfair advantage").

48. See ibid., 213, 290 (citing Shaffer v. Wolbe, 148 S.E. 2d 437 (Ga. Ct. App. 1966) ("not prompted by an honest mistake, but prompted by some sinister motive")). Fraud vitiates contracts, and subjects a party to liability for the wrong. Speiser et al., *Law of Torts,* 221.

49. See, e.g., Richard Thompson, "The Sad Allure of Cancer Quackery," 19 *Food & Drug Admin.* 36 (1985). Under certain circumstances, mail and wire fraud statutes also may be applicable. See 21 *U.S.C.* §§ 1341, 1343.

50. The medical practice acts serve as a consumer protection statute to prevent false, misleading, and deceptive practices in the purchase of health services. Cf. 15 *U.S.C.* §§ 45, 52 (defining what constitutes "false advertising" of food products or cosmetics within §§ 5 and 12 of the Federal Trade Commission Act).

51. As noted, for disciplinary purposes fraud is within the definition of "unprofessional conduct" in many states.

CHAPTER 9: THE EVOLUTION OF LEGAL AUTHORITY

1. Wardwell, "Chiropractors," 165. Patients' support was critical in leading legislators to pardon jailed chiropractors and enact licensing laws. For example, when Melvin Turner opened his chiropractic office in Oregon in 1901, he was jailed for practicing medicine unlawfully each time he treated a patient; his patients paid the one-dollar bail each time to free him. Eventually, Turner, his son, and his grandson were licensed. *Chiropractic Practice Guidelines*, 4.

2. See, e.g., Alaska Stat. § 08.20.900 ("'chiropractic diagnosis' means a diagnosis made by a person licensed under this chapter based on a chiropractic examination").

3. Sandra H. Johnson, "Regulatory Theory and Prospective Risk Assessment in the Limitation of Scope of Practice," 4:4 *J. Legal Med.* 447, 449 (1983); cf. Milton Friedman, *Capitalism and Freedom* (Chicago: University of Chicago Press, 1962), 158 (arguing that licensure "should be eliminated as a requirement for the practice of medicine").

4. See, e.g., Ariz. Rev. Stat. § 32-925 (a chiropractor "shall not prescribe or administer medicine or drugs, perform surgery or practice obstetrics").

5. The distinction is suggested by the definition of "drug" in the Food, Drug and Cosmetic Act ("articles intended for use in the diagnosis, cure, mitigation, treatment, or prevention of disease"). 21 *U.S.C.* § 321(g)(1)(B).

6. Wayne R. LaFave and Austin W. Scott Jr., *Criminal Law*, 2d ed. (St. Paul: West Publishing, 1986), § 1.3(b), p. 13.

7. Cf. Haw. Rev. Stat. § 453-1, which permits "giving or furnishing any remedial agent or measure" by any person, when requested by or on behalf of a patient, but only when a licensed physician provides a written certificate pronouncing the patient "hopeless and beyond recovery."

8. Rutherford, 442 U.S. at 555.

9. Plumber, 634 So. 2d at 1351.

10. Burzynski, 819 F.2d at 1313–14.

11. Rogers, 371 So. 2d at 1041 n. 3. This attitude echoes a statement by the AMA's Council on Scientific Affairs attributing interest in complementary and alternative medicine in part to "an outbreak of irrationalism" and noting that books and tapes on the subject "are gobbled up by an uncritical public that does not understand how to sort quack theories from what might be reasonable." Council on Scientific Affairs, *Alternative Medicine*, 17.

12. Burzynski, 917 S.W.2d at 365.

13. Health Coverage Availability and Affordability Act, S. 1028 and H. 3103, 104th Cong., 1st Sess. (Oct. 12, 1995). The problematic language was in the House version of the bill.

14. Colloquy between Senators William Cohen and Orrin Hatch, 142:50 *Cong. Rec.* S3569 (Apr. 18, 1996).

15. Pub. L. No. 104-191 (Aug. 21, 1996), 110 *Stat.* 2016, § 242(a)(1), creating 18 *U.S.C.* § 1347: "Whoever knowingly and willfully executes, or attempts to execute, a scheme or artifice — (1) to defraud any health care benefit program; or (2) to obtain, by means of false or fraudulent pretenses, representations, or promises, any of the money or property owned by, or under the custody or control of, any health care benefit program, in connection with the delivery of or payment for health care benefits, items, or services, shall be fined under this title or imprisoned not more than 10 years, or both."

The other provision now criminalizes submitting Medicare or Medicaid claims for "a pattern of medical or other items or services that a person knows or should know are not medically necessary." 42 *U.S.C.* § 1320a-7a(a)(1)(E). The term *should know* means that "a person, with respect to information — (A) acts in deliberate ignorance of the truth or falsity of the information; or (B) acts in reckless disregard of the truth or falsity of the information, and no proof of specific intent to defraud is required." 42 *U.S.C.* § 1320a-7a(i)(7).

16. "Report on H.R. 3103, Health Insurance Portability and Accountability Act of 1996," 142:115 *Cong. Rec.* H9537-38 (July 31, 1996).

17. See 42 *U.S.C.* § 1320a-7d(c).

18. These include a program to coordinate federal, state, and local law enforcement programs to control fraud and abuse with respect to health plans, and a health care fraud and abuse control account (to which significant sums are appropriated, and to which gifts and bequests may be made). 42 *U.S.C.* § 1320a-7c; 42 *U.S.C.* § 1395i(k). A licensed physician who successfully integrates nutritional support with conventional cancer therapy could find, for example, that a complaint from an ill-motivated professional colleague results in coordinated federal and state investigations aimed at curbing health care fraud, followed by loss of licensure, criminal prosecution, significant fines, and jail.

19. See, e.g., David Spiegel et al., "Effect of Psychosocial Treatment on Survival of Patients with Metastatic Breast Cancer," 2:8668 *Lancet* 888 (1989); W. E. Ruberman et al., "Psychosocial Influences on Mortality after Myocardial Infarction," 311:9 *N. Engl. J. Med.* 552 (1984).

20. See Fla. Stat. Ann. § 456.31(1).

21. See, e.g., Southwest Office Supply and Global Indem. Co. v. Smith, 1994 WL 410869 (Va. Ct. App. 1994) (acupuncture treatment was reasonable and necessary and resulted in patient relief); Gabai v. Grinker, 560 N.Y.S.2d 384 (Sup. Ct. 1990) (denial of a claim for reimbursement of acupuncture, to treat disabling chronic pain, was an unsupported and unreasonable interpretation of applicable Medicaid regulations).

22. New York Assembly Bill 2049 (Jan. 21, 1997).

23. See, e.g., Health Care Consumer Protection Act of 1996, 1995 New York Assembly Bill 6800 (Jan. 3, 1996); 1997 New York Assembly Bill 1020 (Jan. 10, 1997).

24. See Paul J. Molino, "Reimbursement Disputes Involving Experimental Medical Treatment," 24:11 *J. Health & Hosp. L.* 329 (1991) (describing potential challenges under ERISA when an insurer, as fiduciary, denies reimbursement under an employee benefit plan for alleged experimental treatments).

25. *Integrated* means formed, coordinated, or blended into a functioning whole; *integral* means essential to completeness, formed as a unit with another part, or composed of parts that make up a whole. *Merriam-Webster Dictionary* (Springfield: Merriam-Webster, 1995).

26. See Cohen, "Fixed Star," 141–43 (describing an ethic of care within complementary and alternative medicine) (citing sources).

27. In response to the question, "What kind of human beings are patients?" senior medical students responded: "Patients are children who must be taken by the hand and guided to make the decisions we think best for them." Katz, *Silent World*, 101. Katz suggests that patients' fear and helplessness result in part from the "regressive manifestations" of unconscious infantilization by physicians. He advocates "uprooting the prevailing authoritarian value and belief systems and replacing them with more egalitarian ones" by challenging the presumption that doctors should make health care decisions for their patients (28).

28. Shultz, "Informed Consent," 276. Shultz notes: "Protection of patient autonomy remains derivative rather than direct, episodic rather than systematic. As a result, significant harms to patients' interest in choice go unredressed" (299).

29. I present three examples in "Toward a Bioethics of Compassion," 28 *Ind. L. Rev.* 667, 667–74 (1995).

30. A nineteenth-century professor of midwifery and medical jurisprudence argued: "The very first principle of our government is that man is capable of governing himself, and requires no protection from his own acts; if he chooses to employ a Thomsonian or botanic or Indian doctor (as they term themselves), he has a perfect right to do so, and to prevent him is to interfere with the *inalienable rights* of man, and is not to be tolerated." Charles Coventry, "History of Medical Legislation in the State of New York," *N.Y. J. Med.* 152, 156 (1845).

31. Tom L. Beauchamp and James F. Childress, *Principles of Biomedical Ethics,* 4th ed. (New York: Oxford University Press, 1994), 277, 283. The authors advocate adding a fifth condition: that autonomy not be substantially restricted. The suggested example is that of a Jehovah's Witness who refuses a blood transfusion because of religious beliefs (283).

Susan Sherwin cites three traditional arguments used by physicians to support medicine's paternalism: that illness and the debilitating fear of illness compromise patients' reasoning abilities; that only those who possess technical scientific knowledge can make adequate medical decisions; and that patients benefit from their belief in the physician's wisdom and power. Sherwin argued that alluding to patients' "reasoning" is in itself a tool to perpetuate physician dominance; that many personal decisions have been "medicalized" and involve neither illness nor fear; that medicine overly relies on laboratory reports and dismisses patients' subjective experience of their own diseases; that "the use of mystifying, exclusionary language in science helps to defend its hierarchical structures and discourages challenge"; and that patients who actively participate in their own health care heal more thoroughly than those "who are kept as passive recipients of authoritative treatment." Susan Sherwin, *No Longer Patient: Feminist Ethics and Health Care* (Philadelphia: Temple University Press, 1992), 139–51.

32. The development of an adverse effects registry for complementary and alternative modalities, perhaps by the Office of Complementary and Alternative Medicine, will facilitate more accurate weighing of risks against benefits of specific procedures for particular conditions, although this again brings holistic modalities further into the biomedical model.

33. See Plant, "Learned Intermediary," 1036 (arguing for legal rules respecting the fact that patients "are extremely well-educated about the [AIDS] disease and applicable therapies . . . [and in general] increasingly interested in and receptive to information about their diseases and possible modes of treatment") (citing sources).

34. See Michael R. Flick, "The Due Process of Dying," 79 *Cal. L. Rev.* 1121, 1165 (1992) (arguing that the "impersonal norms of the legal system are not appropriate for an enterprise of care," and urging courts to encourage physician-patient communication, rather than "take a person's dying from him" through excessive procedural rule making).

35. See, e.g., Southwest Office Supply, 1994 WL 410869; Gabai, 560 N.Y.S.2d at 384.

36. See American Medical Association, *Code of Medical Ethics: Reports,* Rep. 59 (July 1994).

37. Callahan, "Peaceful Death," 34.

38. James Gordon argues: "Instead of acting out of a blind instinct to preserve life, any kind of life, at all costs, we ought, as many hospices are currently doing, to devote our time, energies, and resources to spending time with dying people and their families; to helping them accept death; and to holding and talking to them as they make the transition out of this life." Gordon, *Manifesto,* 255.

39. Shultz, "Informed Consent," 222.

40. See David Cheek, "Communication with the Critically Ill," 12:2 *Am. J. Hypnosis* 75 (1969); Michael D. Yapko, *Trancework: An Introduction to the Practice of Clinical Hypnosis,* 2d ed. (New York: Brunner/Mazel, 1990), 294–95.

41. See, e.g., Michael Harner, *The Way of the Shaman* (San Francisco: Harper & Row, 1990), xii–xix; Mircea Eliade, *Birth and Rebirth,* trans. William R. Trask (New York: Harper & Row, 1958).

42. See Cohen, "Bioethics of Compassion," 679–80. Multiple fetal pregnancy reduction is a reproductive technology that involves increasing the potential number of fertilized eggs, then selectively "reducing" the number of embryos, typically

by injecting potassium chloride into their hearts with a needle passed through the mother. Ethicists deem selective termination appropriate to protect the mother's health when four embryos or more result, or in multiple pregnancies where more than one anomalous fetus results (679–80, citing sources).

43. Bonnie Steinboch, *Life before Birth: The Moral and Legal Status of Embryos* (New York: Oxford University Press, 1992), 14. Some argue, for example, that anencephalic infants should be harvested for organ donation, because they "experience no pain or suffering, and therefore, can never be aware of what happens to them" (33, quoting Ronald Cranford and John Roberts, "Use of Anencephalic Infants as Organ Donors: Crossing the Threshold," in *Pediatric Brain Death and Organ Tissue Retrieval: Medical, Ethical, and Legal Aspects,* ed. Howard M. Kaufman (New York: Plenum, 1989), 193).

INDEX

Access to Medical Treatment Act, 78–79, 97, 158 nn. 22–23

Acupuncture, xii, 4, 6; access to, 82–84; clean needle technique, 66; controlled studies of, 10; and legislative intent, 39; licensure, 37, 43–45, 145 n. 58; malpractice, 59, 65–67; third-party reimbursement for, 97–100, 102; as unlicensed medical practice, 29–31; use of, 8–9, 121 n. 2; —, by chiropractors, 43, 50–51

Agency for Health Care Policy and Research, 10

Alexander technique, 5, 32, 33, 142 n. 79

American Association of Naturopathic Physicians, 65

American Massage Therapy Association, 38

American Medical Association (AMA), 124 n. 9; and chiropractic, 20–21, 149 n. 108; and complementary and alternative medicine, 127 n. 35, 133 n. 32; and dietary supplements, 160 n. 44; rise and influence of, 19–20, 137 n. 37; and role of physician, 116

Andrews v. Ballard, 82–84, 97, 161 n. 65

Assumption of risk, 62–64, 111

Ayurvedic therapies (Ayurvedic medicine), 4–5, 65, 129 n. 43; studies of, 10

Bioethics, 116–17

Biofeedback, 8–9, 11, 45

Biofield therapeutics, 5, 11

Body-oriented psychotherapy, 5

Catholic Church, 22

Chantilly Report, 4–5, 13, 92, 121 n. 3

Chiropractic, xii, 5; Agency for Health Care Policy and Research endorsement of, 10–11; and AMA, 20–21, 149 n. 108; licensure, 41; malpractice, 64–70; and medical practice, 39, 109; scope of practice of, 46–55; third-party reimbursment for, 98–100; unlicensed practice of, 45; use of, 8–9, 121 n. 2

Christian Science, 27, 32, 135 n. 5

Colonic irrigation (colonic hydrotherapy), 6, 30–31, 40, 49, 54, 55

Compassion in Dying v. Washington, 85–86, 161 nn. 70–71

Complementary and Alternative Medicine, Office of, xi, 12, 94, 121 n. 3, 122 n. 4, 127 n. 35, 130 nn. 56 and 58, 158 n. 23, 174 n. 32

Consolidated Omnibus Budget Reconciliation Act of 1985, 85

Corporate negligence, 70

Cruzan v. Director, Missouri Department of Health, 82

Darling v. Charlston Community Memorial Hospital, 70

Diet, 9, 63, 97. See also Food and drug law; Nutritional treatments

Dietary Supplement and Health Education Act, 80–81, 114

Dietary supplements. See Food and drug law; Nutritional treatments

Dietary Supplements, Office of, 122 n. 4

Drugs, 26, 28, 78

Due process, 25, 90–91, 95, 162 n. 72

EDTA chelation therapy, 5, 13; and malpractice, 56–59, 61–62, 150 n. 7; and professional discipline, 57, 82, 93; and third-party reimbursement, 103

Emotional distress, 59

Employee Retirement Income Security Act of 1974, 101, 106, 156 n. 66, 167 n. 6, 173 n. 24

Energy healing, 8, 9, 31, 32, 35, 116, 117. *See also* Biofield therapeutics; Faith healing; Prayer; Therapeutic touch
"Experimental treatment," 23, 101–2

Faith healing (laying on hands), 22, 109, 138 n. 138
Family remedies, 140 n. 54
Federal Acupuncture Coverage Act, 122 n. 4
Federation of State Medical Boards, 165 n. 42
Feldenkrais method, 5, 33
Flexner Report, 19–20
Food and Drug Administration, 63, 73, 86, 112; and dietary supplements, 80–81; and health claims, 79–80; and litigation, 81–82, 105–6; and new drug approval, 74–76; and off-label use, 57; and unapproved therapies, xii, 94, 77–79, 102, 104, 114; —, patient response to, 76–77. *See also* Food and drug law; Nutritional treatments
Food and drug law: history of, 73–74; legal definition of *drugs,* 78; regulation of dietary supplements, 79–81. *See also* Food and Drug Administration; Nutritional treatments
Food, Drug, and Cosmetic Act, 74, 105
Fraud (fraudulent treatments), 9, 73, 118; and federal legislation, 112–13; legal definition of, 107–8; and litigation, 23; and third-party reimbursement, 104–7

Health and Human Services, U.S. Department of, 11, 78–79, 151 n. 16
Health Coverage Availability and Affordability Act, 171 n. 13.
Herbal remedies (herbal therapies, herbal medicine), 5, 6, 9, 28, 44, 121 n. 2; and malpractice, 56, 59; and professional discipline, 94
Holistic health care: critique of, 10; definition of, xiii, 3–4, 6–8, 125 n. 17; methodological issues in, 13; use of, 8–9
Homeopathy (homeopathic medicine), xii, 13; authorized use by nonmedical providers, 46; definition of, 42–43, 131 n. 13; history of, 18–19; and malpractice, 59, 65; and professional discipline, 88–90; as unlicensed medical practice, 31–33, 109; use of, 121 n. 2

Hypnosis (hypnotism, hypnotherapy), xii, 4, 39, 92, 113, 117; as unlicensed medical practice, 22, 29, 31, 32; as unlicensed practice of psychology, 45–46; use of, 8–9

Imagery, 4, 8–9, 11
Informed consent, 23, 60–62, 79, 93, 95, 105, 108, 111, 115, 152 n. 23, 156 n. 11
In re Guess, 88–90, 91, 93, 163 n. 20
Insurance. *See* Third-party reimbursement

King County Department of Health, xii

Laetrile: and disciplinary action, 58; litigation concerning, 23, 82, 84, 112; third-party reimbursement for, 104
Legislation. *See* Access to Medical Treatment Act; Consolidated Omnibus Budget Reconciliation Act of 1985; Dietary Supplement and Health Education Act; Employee Retirement Income Security Act of 1974; Federal Acupuncture Coverage Act; Food, Drug, and Cosmetic Act; Health Coverage Availability and Affordability Act; National Center for Integral Medicine Establishment Act; National Fund for Health Research Act; Nutrition Labeling and Education Act; Pure Food and Drug Act
Licensure: in acupuncture, 36–37, 43–45; in chiropractic, 40–41; in homeopathy, 42–43; in massage therapy, 35–37, 41; in naturopathy, 37, 41–42; and professional discipline, 11, 87; purpose and critique of, 24, 33–35; types of, 35–38. *See also* Medical licensure

Malpractice: assumption of risk as defense against, 62–64, 111; and chelation therapy, 56–59, 61–62, 150 n. 7; clinical innovation defense against, 58, 61; by complementary and alternative providers, 64–70; failure to refer as basis for, 68–69; by health care institutions, 70–72; lack of informed consent as basis for, 60–62, 108; legal definition of, 56; respectable minority defense against, 58, 61, 111
Managed care: and malpractice, 70–72; and third-party reimbursement, 97–98, 100–101

Massage (massage therapy), xii, 5; licensing, 35–38, 41; malpractice, 59, 64–70; as unlicensed medical practice, 8, 22, 29, 31; use of, 8–9, 121 n. 2
Medical boards. *See* Professional discipline
Medical licensure: critique of, 34–35; history of, 15–20
"Medically necessary" services, 23, 103–4, 106
Medical schools, xi; and acupuncture, 145 n. 48; courses on complementary and alternative medicine, 8, 127–28 nn. 34–35; and licensure, 15–20, 94
Medicare (and Medicaid), 85, 104, 150 n. 6, 172 n. 15
Medicine: critique of, 2–3; legal definitions of, 26–29; liability for unauthorized practice of, 29–33
Meditation, 9, 11, 97
Megavitamin therapy, 5, 9, 121 n. 2. *See also* Nutritional treatments; Vitamins
Midwifery (midwives), 22, 31, 35, 113
Misrepresentation, 69–70, 111
Moore v. Baker, 61–62, 152 n. 27

National Center for Integral Medicine Establishment Act, 122 n. 4, 122–23, n. 9
National Commission for the Certification of Acupuncturists, 37–38, 66, 141 n. 73, 142 n. 77
National Fund for Health Research Act, 122 n. 4
Native American medicine, xii, 4, 11, 18, 128 n. 35
Naturopathy (naturopathic medicine), 4, 6, 14, 39; licensing, 41–42; malpractice, 65; as unlicensed medical practice, 22, 29, 31–32
New England Journal of Medicine, xi, 10
Nuremberg Code, 60
Nutritional advice: and chiropractic, 47–49; as unlicensed medical practice, 22, 30–31
Nutritional treatments, xiii, 4–5, 97; and continuing medical education, 145 n. 48; and informed consent, 60; third-party reimbursement for use of, 104; as unlicensed medical practice, 30–33. *See also* Food and drug law
Nutrition Labeling and Education Act, 79–80

Office of. *See other part of name*
Off-label use, 57, 150 n. 6
Osteopathy, 5, 20, 27, 35, 43, 100, 132 n. 25, 140 n. 67

Paternalism, 73, 115–16
People v. Privitera, 82, 95
Placebo effect, 128 n. 38
Police power, 24–26
Prayer, 4, 59, 98, 113, 139 n. 51
Privacy, right to, 23, 25, 81–86, 105, 161 n. 69, 163 n. 20
Professional discipline: and chelation therapy, 5–7, 57, 88, 90–91, 93; and homeopathy, 88–90; and lack of informed consent, 108; legal definitions of, 87; legislation concerning, 92–95, 111; and ozone therapy, 88, 91–92; procedural matters, 87–88
Psychology (psychotherapy), 4; licensure, 35–36, 45; unauthorized practice of, 24, 45–46
Psychoneuroimmunology, 11
Pure Food and Drug Act, 74

Quacks (quackery), 9, 17, 112, 113, 170 n. 45, 171 n. 11; and malpractice, 59; and professional discipline, 91
Quill v. Vacco, 86, 161 n. 72

Reflexology, 33, 142 n. 79, 146 n. 62
Rolfing, 9

Schneider v. Revici, 63
Shorter v. Drury, 64

Therapeutic touch, xii, 5–6, 92; and insurance coverage, 98; as unlicensed medical practice, 29, 32. *See also* Biofield therapeutics; Energy healing
Third-party reimbursement: "any willing provider," 98–99; "every category of health provider," 99–100; "experimental treatment" exclusion, 101–2; mandated coverage, 98; "medically necessary" coverage, 103–4, 106–7; private coverage, 97–98
Thomsonism, 17–18

United States v. Rutherford, 23, 82, 83, 89, 95, 105, 161 n. 65

Unprofessional conduct. *See* Professional discipline

U.S. Constitution: First Amendment, 25; Fourteenth Amendment, 162 n. 72

U.S. Court of Appeals for the District of Columbia, 85

U.S. Court of Appeals for the Second Circuit, 63, 86

U.S. Court of Appeals for the Fifth Circuit, 105, 112, 161 n. 65

U.S. Court of Appeals for the Ninth Circuit, 85

U.S. Court of Appeals for the Tenth Circuit, 23, 82, 83

U.S. Court of Appeals for the Eleventh Circuit, 152 n. 27

U.S. Department of. *See other part of name*

U.S. Supreme Court, 23, 24–25, 82, 83, 86, 112, 160 n. 53

Veterinarians, 139 n. 53, 144 n. 41

Vicarious liability, 70–72

Vitamins, 5, 48, 52, 54, 103. *See also* Food and drug law; Megavitamin therapy; Nutritional treatments

Wilk v. American Medical Association, 21

Yoga, 4, 33, 97

Library of Congress Cataloging-in-Publication Data

Cohen, Michael H.
    Complementary and alternative medicine : legal boundaries and
regulatory perspectives / Michael H. Cohen.
        p.   cm.
    Includes bibliographical references and index.
    ISBN 0-8018-5687-6 (alk. paper). — ISBN 0-8018-5689-2 (pbk.: alk. paper)
    1. Alternative medicine — Law and legislation — United States.   I. Title.
KF3821.C64   1998
344.73'041 — dc21   97-21874
                                                                      CIP